These Live Tomorrow

Twenty Unitarian Universalist Lives

Clinton Lee Scott

Second Edition

SKINNER HOUSE BOOKS: Boston

Photography credits

Susan B. Anthony used by permission of the Schlesinger Library, Radcliffe College.

Benjamin Rush courtesy of the Free Library of Philadelphia, Pennsylvania.

Abner Kneeland courtesy of the Unitarian Universalist Church of the Restoration, Philadelphia, Pennsylvania.

Because of the time in which George de Benneville lived, no photograph or portrait of him is available.

Note: The Unitarian Universalist Association is committed to using gender-inclusive language in all of its publications. This edition has been completely revised with the cooperation of the author's son, the Rev. Peter Lee Scott, to conform to the gender-inclusive usage.

Library of Congress Cataloging-in-Publication Data

Scott, Clinton Lee, 1887–1985
    These live tomorrow.

    1. Unitarians—Biography. 2. Univeralists—Biography. I. Title.
BX9867.S3 1987 288'.32'0922 [B]   87-16321
ISBN 0-933840-32-2

Contents

Foreword

William F. Schulz
President, Unitarian Universalist Association

"We seldom stop to observe," remarked Lytton Strachey, "that it is perhaps as difficult to write a good biography as it is to live a good life!" A silly claim, that. And yet it is true that good biographies are almost as scarce as truly well-lived lives. Put the two together and the combination can be powerful.

That is exactly what Clinton Lee Scott and his twenty "collaborators" have provided us here: a feast of twenty well-lived lives now well-written.

Clint's own life was worthy of remark. The tenth of twelve children, he was raised in the Free Will Baptist Church, but early on grew disillusioned with orthodoxy, having, among other things, watched wide-eyed as his brother Walter took an axe to a Bible without being struck down immediately by God. Frequently outspoken, he was the only Universalist to sign the 1933 Humanist Manifesto and so received a good deal of criticism from his more conservative colleagues. But Clint was held in respect, even by those who disagreed with him, and that respect took on institutional form when in 1977 he received the Award for Distinguished Service to the Cause of Liberal Religion from the Unitarian Universalist Association.

Always a witty man, Clint was heard to remark shortly before his death at almost one hundred years of age, "If I'd known I was going to live this long, I'd have taken better care of my health."

Part of the caretaking of health is the cultivation of memory. It has been said that God gives us memory that we—or at least those of us who live in frigid climes—might have roses in December.

And yet, perhaps because Unitarian Universalism is not premised upon some mythic tale nor inspired by the adventures of one heroic founder, we religious liberals are sometimes tempted by a fatal notion: that the past has no claim upon us; that our religion (unlike that of our fuddy-duddy neighbors) is unhampered by the prejudices of precedent or the trappings of tradition.

Kaiser Wilhelm once visited the observatory in Bonn and asked the resident astronomer a friendly question, "Well, my dear Arlander," he said. "What's new in the starry sky?" "Ah," the astronomer replied, "But does your Majesty already know the old?"

What history offers us is a grounding for our values; a sense of right tradition; a focus for our faith. To be deprived of an historical tradition or to disregard it is to be shorn of our identity.

When someone asks, "But what *is* a Unitarian Universalist ?"—as, fortunately enough, they persist in doing—part of our appeal for an answer is to the examples set by those of our faith who have gone before. Where a more orthodox religion might appeal to revelation or hierarchical judgment or the final authority of Scripture, we rely on individual experience, *but* individual experience, *tempered by tradition* and tested against the insights and conviction of the gathered community. This is our way of discovering religious truth. The twenty people whose stories are collected here embody that tradition.

Except for one thing! Only three of the twenty are woman. In that respect this book, originally prepared in 1964, is woefully deficient. It is not, of course, that the lives of the seventeen men depicted here are not important. (That they are is exactly why we have reprinted the book.) But where are Dorothea Dix and Olympia Brown, Aurelia Henry Reinhardt and Frances Ellen Watkins Harper? Their stories too "live tomorrow" but we must tell them also if we are to forge a tradition that can truly speak to us all.*

*Fortunately we are beginning to repair these age-old oversights, and not just with regard to women's "herstory" but with regard to our black pioneers as well. See, for example, Catherine F. Hutchings, *Universalist and Unitarian Women Ministers* (Boston: Unitarian Universalist Historical Society, 2nd ed. 1985); Mark D. Morrison-Reed, *Black Pioneers in a White Denomination* (Boston: Beacon Press, 1984); and "A Wider Horizon: UU Women with a Vision"; ed. Pamela I. Pierson and Linda C. Schreiber (UUA Pamphlet, 1985).

That neglect apart, this book is designed to help us reclaim our heritage and our heroes, as if for the first time. In one respect or another all twenty of these men and women are models of Unitarian Universalist virtues. "Virtue" is an ancient but valuable concept. If we cannot name our intended virtues—like self-respect and respect for others; fidelity; open-mindedness; courage and deep, deep care— we give up what makes us most fully human, namely, the capacity to imagine ourselves better than we are.

This is what the Apostle Paul had in mind when he told the church at Corinth, "You are not your own. You were bought with a price." The twenty whose well-lived lives are well-told here paid that price for us. Our obligation now and tomorrow is to deserve it.

September, 1987

Introduction

The persons whose brief biographies are in this book were pioneer Universalists and Unitarians. Their lives, together with many others that could be named, contributed to the development of liberal religion and to world-wide intellectual and moral enlightenment.

They were, of course, related to the times in which they lived. We of today have outgrown some of their ideas, but they were "ahead of their time," and in some ways they are ahead of our time. If we have advanced beyond their thinking it is because they helped us to grow.

Unitarianism and Universalism have roots that reach far back into the history of human guesses about the nature of God, of the world, and of our human kind. If we think of Unitarianism only as the belief that God exists in one Person in contrast to the doctrine of the Trinity, and of Universalism only as the belief in universal salvation, many witnesses to these views can be found in Christian history. Yet the proper history of the two movements began only with the Reformation of the sixteenth century. This period of upheaval gave rise to independent thinking, and to the open declaration of theological ideas that were contrary to the doctrines of both Catholics and Protestants.

Michael Servetus, a Spanish theologian reared in the Catholic faith, lived during the stormy days of the Reformation. In his study of the Bible he came to unitarian convictions about God and Jesus. He declared that "God is one and indivisible." In 1531 Servetus wrote a book, *On the Errors of the Trinity*, which was widely circulated before it was banned by Catholic and Protestant officials. He was imprisoned, tried for heresy, and burned at the stake.

In the middle of the sixteenth century a band of anti-trinitarians influenced by the writings of Servetus were driven out of Catholic Italy. They settled in Poland and were later joined by a young Italian scholar named Faustus Socinus. He became their leader and his followers were called Socinians. In spite of resistance and persecution, churches were built and schools established. Books and tracts were printed and distributed throughout the kingdom of Poland, and sent abroad to Holland, France, and England. For a hundred years the Socinian movement in Poland prospered. It was destroyed by Catholic and Calvinist political influence.

Soon after the beginning of Socinianism in Poland, Unitarian ideas took form in Transylvania. (Transylvania, formerly a province of Hungary, is now a region of Romania.) The movement here is dated from 1568, the year King John Sigismund, who held unitarian views, issued a decree on religious freedom "in order that each might hold the faith which he wished." In the same year, Francis David, in a prolonged debate with Calvinists, won a decisive victory for the unitarian cause. These two events ushered in the golden age of Unitarianism in Hungary. The movement survived later under severe conditions of opposition and persecution. Today there are about a hundred Transylvanian Unitarian churches, representing the longest record of continued existence of organized Unitarianism in the world.

In England, Theophilus Lindsey left the Church of England and in 1774 founded in London the first church in Great Britain to take the Unitarian name. Prior to this time there had been several sporadic movements of a unitarian nature in England. Socinian influences from Poland had invaded the Church of England, and there were isolated individuals who taught and wrote their unitarian views under the name Arianism. John Biddle, sometimes called the Father of English Unitarianism, was one of those who helped blaze the trail for later organized movements. He published a catechism based on the writings of Socinus. There were no organized societies, however, until Lindsey gathered a congregation and with the help of Joseph Priestley established the first of the Unitarian churches in England. During Lindsey's life a score of churches in England of Episcopal and Presbyterian origin adopted the unitarian views.

Theological writings supporting belief in the final salvation of all people are found in the works of the finest scholars throughout the Christian centuries. With the Reformation, the doctrine became a major subject of controversy wherever independent thinking punctured the hard shell of Christian orthodoxy. Radical religious reformers, unhappy over the halfway measures of the Reformation, rejected both Catholic and Protestant views and ceremonies and split into a number of independent movements. Several of them, the Mystics, the many varieties of Anabaptists, and others, embraced the doctrine of a final salvation of all humanity.

Universalist ideas became so widespread that Protestant forces found them a threat to their security and took steps to check the heresy. The English Parliament in 1552 in its forty-two Articles of Religion condemned Universalism as heretical and fixed the death penalty for anyone found guilty of teaching it. In 1648, the Presbyterians passed laws against opinions at variance with their orthodoxy, one of them aimed at the doctrine "that all men shall be saved."

While at this time no churches were created bearing the name Universalist, the influence of some of the radical reformers can be traced to the later organized Universalist movements.

In 1700 George Klein-Nicolai, a German minister who was turned out of the Lutheran Church because he preached Universalism, wrote a book under the name of Paul Siegvolck, *The Everlasting Gospel*. This work, setting forth the principles of Universalism, passed through five editions in Germany and became a best seller in other countries. It reached America in the middle of the eighteenth century. It was translated into English, printed by Christopher Sower, a Universalist Quaker, and extensively circulated by him in the eastern and southern colonies. More than any book, except the Bible, *The Everlasting Gospel* provided for the early Universalists of America a sure theological foundation for their convictions.

In 1720, George de Benneville, at the age of seventeen, began preaching Universalism in France. Frequently imprisoned and hounded from place to place, he nevertheless continued his mission in Germany and Holland where he met and exchanged Universalist views with leaders among the Spiritual Reformers. Some of them later came to America, where they added strength to the Universalist and other liberal groups. De Benneville translated into the German language French and English theological works favoring his own faith, and placed them in the libraries of German schools and universities. In 1741, he joined the William Penn Colony and became the first preacher of Universalism in America. His missionary journeys in Pennsylvania and New Jersey were an inspiration to the small bands of Universalists that in his fifty years in the Colony grew into churches.

In 1750, James Relly brought together a group of anti-Calvinists in London and there planted the first Universalist Church in England. John Murray, a former Methodist, attended Relly's meeting and was converted to the Universalist faith. After suffering several forms of persecution for his convictions he fled in 1770 to the American Colonies, where he was instrumental in laying the foundations for the organized Universalist denomination in America.

James Relly's *Union*, a work on Universalist theology, was published in London in 1759. In 1770, a copy of this book reached Gloucester, Massachusetts. It was read in this community by a small group of Calvinists who were persuaded by it to leave the Congregational Church and to form the first Universalist Society of continued existence in America.

The Universalist and Unitarian denominations had quite different beginnings in America. Both, however, organized their first churches in Pennsylvania and both had their largest early growth in Massachusetts. When in 1790 a Convention of Universalists was held in Philadelphia, ten societies in Pennsylvania and New Jersey were represented.

In 1796, two years after coming to Pennsylvania, Joseph Priestley founded the first religious society in America to take the Unitarian name, the First Unitarian Church in Philadelphia.

Universalists and Unitarians, while different in origin, were only slightly different in their religious emphases. Universalists gave weight to the doctrine of Divine Love as the promise of the final harmony of all souls with God. Unitarians stressed the unity of Divine Nature and freedom of inquiry. Many Universalists held Unitarian views, however, and Unitarians shared Universalist convictions.

The experience of the years of separate existence brought them closer together in aim and purpose until in 1961 their pathways were joined. They were consolidated in an organized whole, even as they had long been one in spirit.

CHAPTER ONE

George de Benneville
1703-1793

It was a morning in the year 1722. In the old stone prison of the seaport city of Dieppe in northern France two young men awaited their execution. Their crime was preaching Universalism. Outside the prison a great crowd gathered. Executions were no novelty at that time in France or in other countries: the death penalty was fixed for a variety of crimes, from chicken stealing to murder. Executions were public affairs, providing entertainment for people with few other forms of amusement.

One of the most serious crimes was preaching or teaching heresy (religious opinions unlike those approved by the church and state). It was for this crime that the two young men had been arrested with others while preaching to a large gathering in an open field. Some of their number had been hanged already; others had been whipped in public, branded with hot irons, or sent to sea as galley slaves. The two now to be put to death were leaders of the outlawed company. Together they were led to the place of execution. One of them, George M. Durant, a twenty-four-year-old minister, had been sentenced to be hanged. While the holiday crowd looked on with wild excitement, Durant climbed the ladder, sang a psalm and joyfully died, as one who preferred death to life without religious liberty.

The other prisoner was George de Benneville. Because he was of noble parentage he was to be beheaded, a privilege denied those of common birth. The guards led him to the scaffold and tied his hands

1

together. They tried to blindfold him but he preferred to face death with open eyes. He knelt, with his head on the block, and the executioner stood ready with the axe. At this moment, while the people waited for the death stroke, a man on horseback tore through their midst—a messenger bringing a reprieve from King Louis XV! The prisoner was returned to his cell, and was finally set free through the influence of Queen Marie of France.

George de Benneville is honored today, especially by religious liberals, as a pioneer who preached and practiced Universalism in Europe and in America. At the time of his near execution he was only nineteen, but his few years had been filled with exciting and important experiences. He was born in London in 1703. His father, a French nobleman, had been driven from France because of his activity among the Huguenots (a small Protestant sect opposed to certain forms of religious and political tyranny). He had taken refuge under the protection of the British king and had been given a position of trust at the royal court.

George was the youngest of nine children. His mother had given birth to twins four times in four years, then died when George was born. Queen Anne of Great Britain, with whom Mrs. de Benneville had had a close friendship, took the young child under her care and gave him the advantages that wealth and social position provided. He was given an education equal to the best of that time.

But living with the royal family had disadvantages too. The boy was pampered and, according to his own admission, thought he belonged to a different class from humanity in general. He considered himself above most other persons. This feeling of superiority was to receive a jolt when first he came in contact with a non-Christian, dark-skinned people—the Moors of Africa. At the age of thirteen he was sent to sea to learn navigation and was taken on a warship belonging to the Royal Navy bound for the Barbary Coast. When the ship arrived at Algiers, some Moors came aboard to sell their wares to the sailors. One of them fell, injuring his leg. The man's companions laid him on the deck, treated the wounds with great care and then, turning toward the rising sun, cried out in language strange to de Benneville. George, in anger, thinking that they were sun worshippers, comanded his servant to bring the men before him. Upon being asked the reason for their strange actions, they answered that they turned to the rising sun to ask the Creator of the sun to have pity on their unfortunate brother and to heal him. De Benneville was so deeply moved by the goodwill, kindness, and religious sincerity of these non-Christians that he declared, "Are these men Heathens? No, I confess before God that they are Christians, and I myself am a Heathen." This broad meaning of the term Christian, including all who practiced love, thus learned, became a principle which he maintained throughout life.

A sailor's lot was not for de Benneville. The routine and rigid discipline aboard ship were in sharp contrast to the freedom enjoyed at the royal court. Back in London, he passed through the soul-searching that is not uncommon with other generations of youth. On the one hand, he was tempted into the gay life of the city, and, on the other, suffered periods of guilt because of his lack of serious purpose. Then, too, he was torn between a need for some sort of religion and an inability to accept the teachings of the church. He was tall and good-looking, danced well, possessed social graces and had plenty of money. London night life offered many attractions to youth with such qualifications, and George took full advantage of them. Yet, in all the reckless merrymaking, he could not forget the moral influence of his godmother, the Queen, or his spiritual experience at Algiers.

One night, after returning home from a dancehall, he fell into a faint and had a vision of himself as a firebrand burning in hell. He was ill for fifteen months, suffering the agonies of mental conflict. During this time, resident French clergy visited him and tried to help him out of his despondency. They made light of his sins, however, saying that they were no greater than usual for a young person of his station—a view that brought no comfort to the sufferer. They gave him up as a lost soul, and left him to his own devices. Now he fell into a state of dark melancholy, feeling that there was no hope for his salvation. He longed for death.

Finally light broke upoon his tortured mind. Out of the depth of misery came the discovery of two truths that never left him during a long and useful life: first, that good and evil have their beginnings in one's inner life; and second, that God in "his holy love for all creatures will save all the human species." This was Universalism, although perhaps de Benneville up to that time had never heard the word. In that day those who believed in universal salvation were called Restorationists.

The Protestant clergy, always on the lookout for heretics, were disturbed when they heard about de Benneville's religious views. The common belief was that all persons were born in sin that could be

3

removed only through the sacrificial death of Christ. It was also believed that it was God's will that only a few persons should go to heaven when they died, and that almost everybody would end up in hell. Any ideas that denied these notions were heresy. French ministers in England called de Benneville for trial, questioned him at length and, upon his confession of belief that all humanity would be saved, put him out of the church.

De Benneville felt moved to go to France to make his newfound faith known. For a time he resisted this urge, fearing how it would be received and anxious for his own safety. Again he was thrown into a state of inner conflict, torn between the intense desire to share his religion and fear of the rough treatment that awaited anyone who dared oppose the popular doctrines of the churches. The decision was a difficult one, but his newfound ardor prevailed, and at once he recovered his health and usual good spirits. Now seventeen years old, he gave up his life of luxury and gaiety, and pledged himself to make known to a world unfriendly to new ideas the glad tidings of the unlimited love of God and the free spirit of humanity.

As soon as he landed at Calais, he began preaching in the market place. He was arrested, taken before a magistrate, locked up in jail for eight days, and, when released, ordered to get out of the city. This experience, far from discouraging him, served to add strength to his courage. Moreover, to his great joy, he found, as he went from town to town, a number of persons who held religious views like his own. They too were outcasts from the church. Groups gathered wherever preaching was to be heard—in fields, in forests, sometimes in borrowed halls, and in private homes. Often they came into conflict with authorities of the law and of the church, and often they found themselves in prison. It was after many such experiences that de Benneville came to the group meeting in the field, was surrounded by soldiers, and was led to the prison from which Durant was hanged and where he came so near to death himself.

After the harrowing ordeal at Dieppe and release from prison, de Benneville went to Germany and Holland, where he continued to preach for about eighteen years. During this period he learned the languages of these countries. Although he found German speech difficult, he mastered it well enough to use it later in translating several English theological works into that language. He also found time to study the natural sciences, especially medicine, preparing himself as a practicing physician.

4

Zeal for learning and greater zeal for missionary activities led de Benneville to overtax his strength. He became seriously ill with a fever. For days friends rallied to his aid, praying for his recovery, but he grew weaker and weaker and they despaired of his life. Finally he appeared to have died and was prepared for burial. His body was placed in a coffin and people came for the funeral. Suddenly, to the amazement of friends, de Benneville sat up and began to speak! Consciousness had returned. Joyfully they helped him get out of the coffin, and shed his grave clothes. In a few days he was able to resume his work. Ever after, he felt certain that during this crisis his spirit had left his body, wandered in far places beyond this world, and had seen and heard many strange things.

Both in Holland and in Germany, de Benneville came in contact with various minority religious sects. They were known by names more or less descriptive of the faith and practices to which they were devoted—Anabaptists, Mystics, Spirituals, Seekers of the Light, Philadelphians, Humanists, Enthusiasts, Pietists, and others. They were free-thinking people who would not be told what they had to believe, whose religious needs neither the Catholic nor the Protestant churches could satisfy. Some of their ideas were crude, and even dangerous, while othere were centuries ahead of the times. De Benneville rejected the more extreme views such as the most literal interpretation of the scriptures, belief in the return of Jesus to the earth, and objection to the institution of marriage. There were other opinions, however, that were in accord with his own principles—complete separation of church and state, refusal to bear arms, opposition to capital punishment, and full freedom of belief in religion. Universal salvation was a belief held by persons in a number of these sects.

The chief differences that separated these groups from other Christians were their objection to church ceremonies, which they thought were substitutes for religious experience; their solid conviction that religion was a way of living with God and humanity; and their emphasis upon the inner life as the source from which came good and evil. The term now generally used to describe such views is the Spiritual Reformers.

In every country in Europe, at one time or another, these people and others whose teachings were contrary to those of the regular churches were persecuted. Anabaptists were outlawed everywhere except in Holland. In Germany it was lawful to kill them without trial. Thousands met a martyr's death.

For years people persecuted in Europe had come to the New World to find safety. Several of the Spiritual Reformers settled in Eastern Pennsylvania and New Jersey because there was more religious tolerance at the colony founded by Willian Penn than anywhere else in America. Friends whom de Benneville had known in Europe, who had found freedom in the Pennsylvania colony, urged him to join them. He came in 1741, in his thirty-eighth year.

He was taken into the family of Christopher Sower in Germantown, now a part of the city of Philadelphia. Sower was a universalist Quaker, a printer and publisher and a leading cititzen. De Benneville was sick from the long sea voyage and weakened by the frequent periods spent in prison, but in the Sower home he regained his health and was soon taking an active part in the life of the community.

Sower was working on the publication of a German-language Bible and was glad to have de Benneville's help. All passages of the scriptures supporting universalist beliefs were set in boldface type. Together the two men also printed and circulated an English translation of *The Everlasting Gospel* by Paul Siegvolck. This book, written in German, first appeared in Europe in 1700 and was one of the earliest to give support to Universalist ideas. Several of the effective leaders in liberal religious movements in America were introduced to their faith by reading this book.

At the time de Benneville arrived in Germantown, there was exteme privation and suffering in the colony. That year had seen one of the frequently recurring yellow fever epidemics; there had been a severe winter; fires in Philadelphia had destroyed homes; and the people, especially the poor, were in deep distress. Immigrants brought into port without money and unable to find work were sold into slavery by the ship's agents. These conditions were brought vividly to Dr. de Benneville's attention by an advertisement in a Philadelphia newspaper of "several likely tradesman, husbandmen and servants, mostly young, to be sold reasonably." He used his money to buy freedom for some and he contributed his medical skill freely for their relief.

After a brief residence in Germantown he moved to the Oley Valley, about forty miles northwest of Philadelphia. Here he taught a country school, preached, and practiced medicine. He accepted no pay for his preaching and only very modest fees for his ministry to the sick.

De Benneville built a large stone farmhouse on land he had purchased in Oley Valley, with an upper room for religious meetings and community gatherings. To this home he brought his bride Esther, the daughter of Jean and Susanna Bertolet, a Huguenot family who had come from Germany. They were married February 24, 1745. Esther was twenty-five and he was forty-one.

He found life in the valley interesting and quickly made friends among his school children and their parents. As well as the native Indians, there were settlers of many national backgrounds—German, French, Dutch, English, and Welsh. And many religions were represented—Quakers, Dunkards, Lutherans, Catholics, Huguenots, and others from the Spiritual Reformer sects. There were those by whom his Universalist preaching was gladly received and others whose views were opposed to his own; but there was a good deal of tolerance in the area, and invitations to speak to congregations of various faiths were frequently offered and accepted.

His preaching was not limited to the boundaries of the neighborhood. Twice each year, until he was an old man, he went on journeys to spread his faith. These visits took him to western Pennsylvania, Virginia, and Maryland. From some of the places where he preached, converts carried the Universalist gospel to Ohio, Indiana, and points further north and west.

His friendly ministry of teaching and healing was carried on also among the nearby Indian tribes. To some persons "the only good Indian was a dead Indian," but to de Benneville they were as truly members of the human family as any other people. He learned their language and put together a dictionary of Indian words and phrases with their English and German meanings, in order to encourage communication and understanding between them and other members of the community. He took their healers into the woods to show them plants and herbs valuable for healing, and learned from them the medicinal use of plants that he had not known.

On one of his missionary journeys to the western part of the state, he visited an Indian village in the grip of some sort of epidemic. Dr. de Benneville stayed until the crisis was over, treating the sick and comforting the bereaved. Years afterwards members of the village came to visit their physician friend, and set up their tents in the field back of his house.

At another time he learned that the people in a frontier settlement were greatly alarmed because of a threatened attack by a hostile Indian band. Alone and unarmed he went to investigate. He ap-

7

proached the Indian's camping place with words and gestures of peace, and not only went unmolested, but was invited into their council circle. The dreaded attack was averted.

In 1757 the de Bennevilles moved to Philadelphia. There were now five children and the parents had plans for a better education for them than the country schools afforded. Two of the sons, David and George Jr., became noted physicians. In Philadelphia, de Benneville and his wife entered in the intellectual life of the city; old friendhips were renewed and new ones formed. Benjamin Franklin was a neighbor and a close friend. Dr. de Benneville continued his preaching and his medical practice, and opened an apothecary shop.

His skill as a physician, in a period when medical science was quite limited, evidently was considerable. His writing on medical subjects filled a half dozen volumes, one of them now preserved in the library of the College of Physicians in Philadelphia.

The de Benneville family was actively involved in the American Revolution. The sons served in the Continental Army. The father, although in his seventy-fifth year, was in the midst of the combat at the Battle of Germantown ministering to the wounded and the dying of both the American and the British armies, another example of his belief in the worth of all persons.

In the latter years of his life he was invited by Louis XVI to return to France as royal advisor to the king, but he declined; he had breathed the free air of America too long to be happy in the stifling atmosphere of the royal court.

Until his death in 1793, this good man lived and labored among all sorts of people, making known to them the larger faith in God and humanity, not by preaching alone, but more by the example of a well-lived life. He built no church, he founded no denomination, but Universalists of today trace their religion in America to the influence of Dr. George de Benneville and his comrades of the free spirit.

When we speak of religion as an inner experience of light and understanding rather than as assent to a creed, when we proclaim that we are all of one family, we are asserting principles expressed in faith and practice by de Benneville and his fellow Spiritual Reformers. The ideal of the supreme worth of persons, perhaps the deepest note in our present-day religion, was a conviction central to the Spiritual Reformers. No one gave it a more certain sound than did George de Benneville.

CHAPTER TWO

Joseph Priestley
1733-1804

The world best remembers Joseph Priestley as the discoverer of oxygen. Religious liberals think of him not only as a great scientist, but also as a famous preacher of Unitarianism in England and America.

He was born in 1733 near the city of Leeds, England, the son of a cloth maker. Orphaned at six, he was brought up by his aunt. A frail child, he was not strong enough to go to school or to take part in outdoor games with children in the neighborhood. He turned this handicap to good account, however, for while they played he read books and studied under the direction of his aunt. At the age of fourteen he had already learned to read Latin, Greek, and Hebrew. He also became interested in the sciences, and made some investigations into the lives of spiders.

His aunt was a strict Calvinist, a member of the Independent (Congregational) Church, and she hoped that her nephew would become a minister. She instructed him in the teachings of her faith, and pointed out the passages in the Bible that supported the Calvinistic beliefs: the sinfulness of all people inherited from "the first man, Adam"; the "election," or God's choice of a few to go to heaven while the rest of humanity burned in hell; and the sacrifice of Jesus on the cross to cancel the sins of the saved. But young Joseph had been doing some thinking of his own along with reading and studying. He found in the scriptures some passages that denied the Calvinist teachings. At eighteen, when examined for membership in the church, he

11

was rejected because of his unwillingness to accept its doctrines. It was impossible for him to believe everything for which his aunt and her church stood. Yet he wanted to be a minister, to find out what was true, and spend his life in preaching it.

The frail child became a strong young man. With better health, and with his chosen life mission before him, he entered an academy at Daventry and spent the next four years preparing for the ministry. This school, unlike others in England at that time, did not require of students the acceptance of a church creed. Free discussion was allowed, and independent thinking was encouraged. These privileges Priestley used to full advantage, liking nothing better than open discussions and freedom to express personal opinions.

He came out of school with some definitely unorthodox ideas. One was Arianism, the teachings of Arius, condemned by the Council of Nicea in 325 A.D. The belief that Jesus, while superior to all human beings, was less than God, was opposed to the view of most Christians that Jesus was one of the Trinity--God the Father, God the Son, and God the Holy Ghost, making Jesus equal with God. This belief was one step toward Unitarianism and is important in liberal church history.

There were as yet no Unitarian churches in England. Priestley took the first church available, a small struggling Presbyterian parish in Suffolk. The salary was only thirty pounds a year (about $146), although it could have been a little more had he been willing to accept the creed of the church. He also secured a teaching position, but the pay was small. The two salaries hardly covered the barest necessities. He often went hungry in order to buy books, wore patched clothing, and lived in the cheapest quarters to be found.

Increasingly there was trouble with the church people. The new minister's delivery was poor. Ideas came faster than words; he stammered, and this annoyed the congregation. Soon they were even more disturbed by the ideas. For the more he studied and the more he thought, the more liberal he became. Members complained that the minister was not preaching the true gospel, that his sermons were too radical. Some witheld financial support, and others left the church to go where the preaching was acceptable to them. The salary was reduced and Priestley nearly starved. He endured this situation for three years. Then a call came from a church in Nantwich, which he joyfully accepted.

Here the congregation was less orthodox than in Suffolk, but the

12

salary, although somewhat larger, was still meager. Priestley continued to teach, but the demands upon his time and strength were less than in the former parish. There was some opportunity to continue the study of theology and also to read all the available scientific works. In his desire to find truth, he turned increasingly to the unexplored world of science. Somehow he managed to save money enough to buy books and some equipment for experiments in science.

During six of the nine years at Nantwich, Priestley taught in a liberal academy at Warrington, the first school in England to offer courses in science. Here he found other liberal-minded persons among the teachers and in the town. In addition to lecturing on science and history he began writing, an interest he continued throughout life. He also found time to court and marry an intelligent girl. Now with a wife, life looked much brighter.

These years at Nantwich and Warrington were a creative period in the life of the young scientist and minister. He wrote a book on theology, one on English grammar, and other works on natural science. In both religious and scientific circles he was becoming well known. In recognition of his scholarship, the University of Edinburgh gave him the honorary degree of Doctor of Laws.

In the autumn of 1764 Priestley was excited to learn that Benjamin Franklin was to be in London for a short time before returning to America. Franklin was acclaimed in the scientific world as one of its leaders. Famous for his experiments with electricity, he was looked upon by the public as one with magical powers who could bring the lightning from the heavens. Priestley wanted nothing so much as to meet this world-famous scientist, philosopher, and diplomat, now in England to plead the cause of the American Colonies. He borrowed money, bought some new clothes, and journeyed to London. Whatever doubts he may have had regarding his reception disappeared when he was ushered into the presence of the noted man. Franklin, then in his fifty-sixth year, greeted the visitor of thirty-one with genuine friendliness. They talked about science and religion. Franklin was impressed with this tall, slender young man with delicate features, and more impressed with his honest mind, keen wit, and liberal ideas. Afterwards, in talking about the meeting, Franklin said that for a preacher Priestley held some extremely free opinions, and was rather elegantly dressed.

During the London visit Franklin had remarked that the history of electricity ought to be written, and suggested that Priestley might be the one to do it. Thus encouraged, Priestley went to work, writing to everybody known to have carried on experiments in this field, checking the results of their labors, and noting the various theories in the new science of electrical forces. A year later he completed *The History and Present State of Electricity*. It not only covered all the important discoveries in electrical sciences, but also contained an account of the author's own experiments, which had led to the use of carbon as a conductor of electric currents. The book was received with widespread interest by the scientific world. In recognition of this service he was elected to the Royal Society, one of the oldest scientific societies in Europe. Each year two persons who were considered to have made the most valuable contribution to science were chosen as members.

The honors that came to Dr. Priestley because of his work in science never drew him away from his chief interest in the ministry. In 1767, he became minister of Mill Hill Chapel at Leeds. This was the largest dissenting congregation in northern England. Dissenters were congregations outside of the Church of England, and their houses of worhip were called Chapels since they were not allowed to use the word Church. Priestley was in Leeds for six years. He threw himself into the work with great energy, preaching twice on Sundays, once on a week night, teaching the young people, organizing the parish into educational and social action groups, and meeting successfully the competition of the new Methodist movement that was winning many people through its emotional appeal.

He continued studying theology and wrote several books on the subject. These were widely read throughout Europe and were making him as well known in the field of religion as in science. He had advanced beyond his previous Arian views, and had become an out-and-out Unitarian, believing in the simple humanity of Jesus, a doctrine held by few in England in his day.

In Leeds, the Priestleys lived next door to a brewery. The fumes of the beer-making bothered Mrs. Priestley, but they only awakened curiosity in her husband. At this time in Europe many experiments were being carried on to discover the chemical nature of the physical world. His investigations led to important studies in the nature of air and later to the discovery of oxygen, which made him one of the founders of modern chemistry. He also invented carbonated water, now used in the manufacture of all sorts of "soda pop." Many have grown rich from this invention; Priestley's reward was a medal from the Royal Society.

His next project brought deep disappointment. The Royal Navy had been persuaded by Captain James Cook, navigator and astronomer, to send a ship to the south Pacific to observe an eclipse of the moon. Priestley was invited, along with other scientists of the first rank. He made great preparations and was appointed chaplain of the crew. At the last minute the invitation was cancelled; the clergy had warned the captain that Priestley, with his Unitarianism, would be a bad influence on the sailors!

Soon afterwards he accepted a position as literary companion to Lord Shelburne, a wealthy patron of the arts and sciences. This meant opportunity for travel as well as time for study and writing. Priestley was glad to see some of the world beyond England. He was taken to the Continent, and in Paris was received with high honors by scientists. When the American Revolution broke out, however, Priestley, always on the side of freedom, openly championed the cause of the Colonies and for this stand was forced by his employer to resign.

Priestley's name is closely linked with that of Theophilus Lindsey, founder of the first church in England to take the name Unitarian. Lindsey had been pastor of a Church of England congregation in Yorkshire, where he had devoted himself especially to young people and had established one of the early Sunday Schools in England. He had thought his way into Unitarianism, had given up his pastorate in Yorkshire, and had come to London. Here at the age of fifty Lindsey began gathering people who were seeking a more liberal religion than was found in other churches.

The Essex Street Chapel opened on April 17, 1774. This first meeting place was an old tumbledown auction house. The upper hall was made to look as much like a chapel as possible. A crude stand served for a pulpit, and roughhewn benches for pews. People in growing numbers climbed the rickety stairs to listen to the quiet scholarly man who led them into a reasonable religion. The venture was a small beginning, but it grew under Lindsey's ministry of twenty years and is still going. While in Lord Shelburne's employ, Priestley frequently visited London and attended the Essex Street meetings. A lasting friendship developed between the two ministers. Priestley and Lindsey are recognized today as the two founders of the Unitarian Church in England.

Soon after resigning his position as literary companion, Priestley was called as one of the ministers of the large dissenting church in

Birmingham. Here began his happiest and most fruitful years, though they led to tragedy in the end. Priestley was to serve the church only on Sundays, preaching and teaching youth classes, and be free on all other days for literary and scientific work. He enjoyed the fellowship of distinguished men in Birmingham, several of whom were in his church, and was invited to join the Lunar Society of scholars and scientists. The name was derived from the Latin word luna, the moon. The society met in houses of the members on the Monday nearest the full moon, so that after the evening's program they could find their way home more easily through the unlighted streets.

Priestley published two books, *History of the Corruptions of Christianity* and *History of Early Opinions Concerning Jesus Christ*. Both caused a great furor. These works showed that the earliest beliefs about Jesus were Unitarian, and that the later theories came from non-Christian influences. He attacked the Trinitarian theories of Father, Son, and Holy Ghost as superstitions, and held that Christians should follow the teachings of the man Jesus instead of worshipping him as God. These writings brought down upon his head a great storm of abuse. The clergy were especially bitter, attacking him from their pulpits, writing vicious pamphlets calling the author bad names, and sending letters of protest to the newspapers. When the books reached Holland they were given the honor of a public burning. Priestley defended his position, every year sending forth a new volume on the *Defenses of Unitarianism*, and boldly hammering away at the foundations of orthodoxy. His stand against Trinitarianism made many converts to Unitarianism, and his church grew rapidly.

When he began working for the separation of church and state, he met with opposition, the most vicious from the clergy of the Church of England. There were laws in England passed more than hundred years earlier that gave special privileges to the Church of England and denied full freedom to all other religious groups. Priestley led a campaign of the liberal Dissenters to have the laws abolished. This of course stirred up bitter resentment among the favored clergy. They were determined to destroy him and they nearly succeeded. Taking advantage of his known sympathy with the political revolutions both in America and in France, they accused him of disloyalty and of plotting to overthrow the government of Great Britain. For several weeks word was spread by leaflets, posters, and in various meetings that the Unitarian leader was an enemy of the people. Joseph Priestley became a marked man.

The blow came on a date decided upon by his enemies, July 14, 1791. This was Bastille Day, the second anniversary of the triumph of the French Revolution. Dr. Priestley had invited a few of his friends to his home to celebrate the occasion. For several days prior to the gathering, pamphlets were distributed throughout the neighborhood accusing those who planned to attend the dinner of plotting treason, and suggesting lynching them. As a result, while the family and guests were still at the dinner table, a mob descended upon the house. Before the mob came, they escaped. The unruly crowd smashed the windows and doors, set the house on fire, destroyed his laboratory and all its valuable equipment, and threw his books and papers into the street and burned them.

The family and guests barely escaped with their lives. For three days and three nights destruction went on in the city. The local authorities made no attempt to restore order. More than one hundred houses and a dozen churches of the liberal dissenters were torn down or burned. The minister who had done the most to stir up the riot was soon afterwards made a bishop, and only four of the several hundred hoodlums were convicted and sent to jail. On that first night of terror the Priestley family fled from the burning house and found refuge at the home of a friend. The mob had intended to destroy not only the house but also the family. The next night the Priestleys made their escape from the city. By taking back roads and travelling only under cover of darkness, they finally reached London, a hundred miles away.

Dr. Priestley never dared return to Birmingham. For a while he preached in a small church on the outskirts of London and did some teaching. Letters of sympathy and gifts of money came from many persons in England, France, and America, but in London the Priestleys were outcasts. Former friends, fearing the stigma of guilt by association, avoided meeting them on the streets. Priestley was even shunned by members of the Royal Society. His sons, unable to find work, went to America. After nearly three painful years, their parents joined them.

In New York, Priestley received a warm welcome. A Philadelphia newspaper, on June 9, 1794, greeted him with the following words:

It must afford the most sincere gratification to every well-wisher to the rights of man, that the United States of America, the land of freedom and independence, has become the asylum

of the greatest characters of the present age, who have been persecuted in Europe, merely because they have defended the rights
of the enslaved nations.

The name of Joseph Priestley will be long remembered
among all enlightened people; there is no doubt that England
will one day regret her ungrateful treatment of this venerable
and illustrious man.

Dr. Priestley was sixty-one the year he came to America. His
place among the great scientists was secure, and his writings
on religion well known, but to begin a life of ease now, after
the hard years of struggle, did not tempt him. Still young enough
for adventure, he found the New World a broad and open field
for his crusading spirit.

The United States, now independent, was proving itself
capable of taking its place among the family of nations. The ad-
vances of science and invention were opening new roads of industry and commerce. Education, the arts and literature were
beginning to take root, and there was a growing unrest in religious thinking. Priestley liked these stirrings in society's
thinking.

In Philadelphia, the intellectual center of the country, and
the capital not only of Pennsylvania but of the nation, Priestley
became acquainted with President George Washington and John
Adams, Thomas Jefferson, Benjamin Rush, and other prominent
leaders in national affairs and intellectual circles.

The Universalists in the city were building a new meeting
house but were in debt and threatened with the loss of their
property. Priestley gathered a few Unitarians and at his suggestion they helped save the church. In June, 1794, he wrote to his
friend Lindsey in London:

A place of worship is building here by a society who call
themselves Universalists; they propose to leave it open to any
Christians three days in the week, but they want money to fin-
ish it. My friends think to furnish them with dollars, and engage the use of it for Sunday mornings.

The arrangements were made, the Unitarians advancing

"some hundreds of dollars for completing the building." This is one of the earlier examples of goodwill and cooperation between Unitarians and Universalists.

Priestley preached frequently to the Universalists and stated his agreement with their teaching "concerning the final salvation of all the human race." Under his leadership the First Unitarian Church in Philadelphia was established in 1796. Dr. Priestley's preaching attracted large numbers of persons of independent minds, especially among the young people. John Adams, when Vice President, attended his church but found the sermons too strong for his milder New England religion, and soon stopped coming.

Much of the early history of the Unitarian movement in the United States is in New England, because it was there that the denomination came into being. The earlier growth, however, was in Pennsylvania, where there was a larger degree of religious liberty. There were in New England and elsewhere ministers who held Unitarian views, but they preferred to remain in the orthodox churches and hesitated to take the name Unitarian. Meanwhile, in Philadelphia the courageous Priestley was vigorously exposing whatever he considered false in orthodox views and frankly teaching liberal religion under the Unitarian banner.

After joining his sons in Northumberland, Pennsylvania, a frontier village on the Susquehanna River, Priestley became minister of the Unitarian Church now called the Priestley Memorial. Across the street from the present meeting house is the Priestley Memorial Library. The old Priestley home has been taken over by the people of Northumberland and made an historical shrine.

Soon after moving to Northumberland one of his sons died, followed shortly by Mrs. Priestley, who had never recovered from the nervous shock of the Birmingham riots. Priestley himself died in 1804, after only ten years in America.

At his death Priestley left twenty-five volumes of religious and scientific writings. His discoveries in chemistry were almost the beginning of that important science, yet his contributions to religious thinking in the early years of Unitarianism in England and in America were no less important. He was one of the first to show the world that there is no necessary conflict

19

between science and rational religion.

As a result of Priestley's writings, Unitarian movements were started not only in Harrisburg and Pittsburgh, Pennsylvania, but also in New England. In 1792 an Episcopal minister in Portland, Maine, converted by reading Priestley's books, formed a Unitarian congregation, followed by another in nearby Saco. Furthermore, it was a follower of Priestley, William Hazlitt, who visited Boston in 1784 and persuaded the Episcopal congregation of King's Chapel to become Unitarian.

To understand Priestley's influence on liberal religious thinking, it is necessary to remember the time in which he lived and the type of religious ideas held then. He held some beliefs that have long been discarded by liberals. He appears to have believed in the miracles of the New Testament, in the return of Jesus to the earth, and in the prophecies of the Old Testament as referring to events in the present world. On the other hand, he rejected the doctrines of inherited sin and everlasting torment for sinners. He did not believe in the Trinity, and placed great stress upon the humanity and the ethical teachings of Jesus. In his emphasis on these points, he was far ahead of the New England type of liberalism that finally resulted in the separation of the Unitarians from the Congregationalists.

On many points he held views found among the most advanced thinkers of our own day. He stood solidly for political and religious liberty and for churches free from state control. He was against slavery long before abolitionism was an open issue in America. He believed that reason should be used not only in science but in the discovery of religious truths. Joseph Priestley did more to shape the course of Unitarian thought than any other liberal of his time in either England or America.

CHAPTER THREE

John Murray
1741-1815

A large stone came crashing through the church window, barely missing the preacher's head. It hit the pulpit and bounded to the floor. The speaker picked it up, and holding it in his hand said to the startled congregation, "This argument is solid and weighty, but it is neither reasonable nor convincing." Then, putting it aside, he added, "Not all the stones in Boston, except they stop my breath, shall shut my mouth."

The preacher was John Murray, the place a borrowed meeting house in the city of Boston, the time, late autumn 1774. The religion preached was Universalism. This was not the only time Murray was a target for stones, and for the more deadly poisoned arrows of slander. He had come to America from England about four years before this experience. In his journeys by sailboat and on horseback he had covered much of the Atlantic seaboard from Philadelphia to Portsmouth, New Hampshire. Four years were more than enough to convince the doughty missionary that the strongholds of Calvinism were not easily shaken. People liked his pulpit eloquence, but not his Universalist gospel. Nothing could stay his course, however, nor close his mouth. For fifty-five years Murray preached a religion of the larger hope in America. Today he is called the founder of the Universalist

Church in America because he was the first to see the need to organize the scattered Universalists into a denomination.

John Murray was born in 1741, in the village of Alton, England, about fifty miles southwest of London, the first son in a family of nine children. The Murrays were middle-class people with a comfortable income, which at that time meant opportunity for schooling, meager at best, but denied the children of wage earners. Both parents were Calvinists and all the affairs of the household were regulated according to the stern demands of that religion. John's home life was not happy, but it was not supposed to be. Children and young people were expected to spend their days worrying about their sins, and about the awful punishment in store for sinners. Mr. Murray, self-righteous, rigid, and tyrannical, seemed to the son to be a small edition of Calvin's God; he was afraid of both.

But John, not unlike other children, had a world of his own. Beyond the watchful eyes of his parents were the wonders found in open fields and woods. There was the nearby river Wey in whose clear waters strange creatures swam and crawled. There were trees to be climbed and winding forest paths to be followed, and the great white clouds quietly moving across the sky were fitted by the boy's imagination into the shapes of angels, and sheep, or the Bible prophets in flowing robes and beards. Best of all was the garden where John dug deep into the earth, tended his flowers, and watched miracles of seed and soil. And so, in spite of the fear of his father and his father's God, he grew into a strong, lively lad, eager for knowledge, intelligent, and sensitive to all living creatures.

When he was ten, the family went to live in Ireland in small village near Cork. Here the parents came in contact with the Methodist revivals that were spreading like a prairie fire over the Christian world. The whole Murray family was swept into the movement. Both the father and John became leaders, the latter in charge of forty boys who met twice a week to pray, sing, and rehearse the details of their conversions.

John made friends and readily impressed others with his nimble mind and desire for knowledge. An Episcopal minister who was head of an academy near the Murray home became interested in him, and offered to take him into his own household and prepare him for a university education. Mr. Murray, fearing his son would meet bad boys, refused this offer. But there were other opportunities for education. A Mr. Little was one who saw promise in the young man, and after Mr. Murray died, John went to live in the Little home. Here there was a large library, more books than John thought existed in all Ireland, and free use of them. Until this time his reading had consisted of the Bible and two or three books on the Christian saints and martyrs. Now a new world opened, of history, biography, and poetry.

When John, at the age of nineteen, decided to return to England, he went with Mr. Little's blessing and a generous gift of money. He landed in London with no plans, soon spent the money, and got a job in a cloth mill. Evenings and Sundays were spent at the great Tabernacle where George Whitefield, the popular Methodist evangelist, was preaching to large congregations. Here John met a beautiful young woman, Eliza Neal. She was the loveliest, most captivating creature he had ever seen. He fell in love with her, and she with him. But there were difficulties.

Eliza lived with her grandfather, who hated all Methodists and would not allow one of them to darken his door. John wept and prayed, but it was no use; the more he tried to forget his beloved the more he thought about her. Eliza's older brother, a friend of John's, tried to be helpful by arranging secret meetings of the lovers, but her grandfather learned about this, and in anger tore up his will, which had made his granddaughter his heir. A few months later, when Eliza became of age, she left her grandfather's home, penniless, to become Murray's wife. They were both good Methodists and together entered in the program at the Tabernacle with joy. John became a class leader.

At that time there was a heretic preacher in London named James Relly. Other denominations held that Jesus died to save those whom God had chosen to be saved, but Relly taught that Jesus died that all humanity should be saved. Moreover, he had written a book, *Union*, that set forth this doctrine. Some of the members of the Tabernacle had gone over to Relly's teachings and were attending his services. Murray was sent to a young woman who was among those being "misled," with instructions to show her the error of her belief in universal salvation, and to persuade her to return to the "true faith." Murray's interview with her was a turning point in his life. Not only did he fail to convince her that she was wrong, but she unsettled his own Methodist faith. He now began to think for himself. He also read Relly's *Union*, and with his wife went to hear Relly preach. Then came a long period of mental suffering. On the one hand was the teaching that Jesus died only for "believers," a doctrine that Murray had taught

sincerely; and on the other hand light was breaking upon his searching mind, not only from Relly's teaching, but also from the scriptures
that he now read with new understanding.

He and Mrs. Murray agreed that they would attend the Relly
meetings half of each Sunday and the Methodist meetings the other
half until they could make up their minds. It was not long before this
practice was discovered by members of the Tabernacle. Murray was
called before a committee, questioned, and upon his confession that
he accepted the belief in universal salvation was dismissed from membership.

Freed from their former ties, the Murrays now entered fully and
happily into the religious life of the Relly congregation. In the months
that followed they found a "heaven on earth," both in their life
together and in their new religion. But suffering and tragedy came
swiftly. Their baby died at the age of one year, and the mother, overcome by the shock, soon followed. Murray was thrown into prison
for debts that had accumulated during his wife's illness. On being
released from prison he managed to pay his debts; and this done,
he had no further ambition. Relly urged him to preach, but in his sorrow he felt unequal to preaching. He was broken, his only thought
to get away from London and find solitude in new surroundings
where he would never preach again.

In July, 1770, Murray sailed for America on the brig *Hand in Hand*,
with the intention of hiding himself in the New World. The ship landed at Philadelphia, but because of certain rules at that port it was decided to proceed to New York. By some miscalculation, the vessel was
brought over a sandbar off Cranberry Inlet on the New Jersey Coast,
where it was forced to wait for high tide and a change of wind to
continue its journey. Murray went ashore to find food for the crew,
and there in the New Jersey wilderness he came to the second important turning point of his life.

The following story, in a somewhat more elaborate form, Murray relates in his autobiography. As he made his way through the
woods he came to a clearing with a large house, in front of which
a tall countryman was dressing fish. This man was Thomas Potter.
Murray asked if he could buy some of the fish, to which Potter replied, "No, I do not sell fish. I have them for the taking up, and you
may obtain them the same way." Murray carried the fish to the sailors,
and at Potter's invitation returned to his house to spend the night.

As the two sat before the evening fire Potter told his guest a strange story. He had built a meeting house on his farm, open to all traveling preachers, but with the expectation that God would send him one "of a very different stamp." He had never learned to read, but the Scriptures had been read to him, and he had discovered in them the teachings of a God who would have all people to be saved. He had hoped to hear this gospel preached in his meeting house. He had waited long, and the neighbors had taunted him for the delay. When he saw the ship in the bay it was as if a voice had spoken to him, "There Potter, in that vessel cast away on that shore, is the preacher you have been so long expecting." To Murray's reply that he was no a preacher came Potter's question, "Can you say that you have never preached?" With Murray's admission that he had preached came the further reply that he would never preach again, and that as soon as the wind changed he must be on his way. But Potter, firm in his faith, declared, "The wind will never change until you have delivered to us, in that meeting house, a message from God."

This was Friday evening. Murray had a bad night. It began to look as if God's purpose was somehow within the circumstances that had thrown him into the company of this strange man. On the other hand, what of his own firm plan to escape from an unfriendly world? In the dim, candle-lit upper chamber of the farmhouse he spent most of the night in prayer and tears.

He resolved finally to allow the course of the wind to decide his fate. If the wind remained unchanged he would accept this as a sign from heaven that the lord wanted him to preach. If the wind changed by mid-afternoon the next day he would bring disappointment to his host, but would feel free to resume the journey. This decision, announced to Thomas Potter at breakfast, was received with joy; Potter was certain that the wind was on his side. And it was! All morning and until mid-afternoon the wind never changed its course. Potter was in high spirits. He sent messengers throughout the countryside to carry the news that his preacher had come and services would be held on the morrow.

The little meetinghouse was filled that Sunday morning, September 30, 1770. John Murray was back in the ministry, preaching his gospel of universal salvation, and prophet Potter was not without honor in his own neighborhood. Years before Murray met Potter, the region surrounding Cranberry Inlet had been visited by missionaries from the Spiritual Reformer groups in the Penn colony, and Potter's home and church had been opened to them. Therefore, Murray's restorationist gospel was not altogether new to those who came to hear him. Members of the congregation joined Potter's insistence that Murray remain with them as their spiritual leader. But after Sunday dinner the wind changed, and with tears and a promise of a speedy return to his newfound friend, Murray was on his way.

On board the vessel sailing to New York the crew learned that Murray was a preacher, and insisted that he preach to them. Assured now that he was destined by divine leading to proclaim the gospel, he not only preached to the sailors, but upon landing in New York accepted many urgent invitations for his services. He soon returned to the Potter farm, but not for long. Invitations began to pour in from other New Jersey communities, Philadelphia, and New York. Murray's fame as preacher spread far and wide, even to New England.

His missionary journeys took him to Connecticut and Rhode Island in 1772, and the next year to Boston and Portsmouth, New Hampshire. In 1774, he visited Boston for the second time, preaching to large crowds in Faneuil Hall, and in Croswell's meetinghouse. It was here that the stone-throwing episode occurred. The attack on Mr. Murray made headlines in the Boston newspapers, and it was strongly hinted that he must be a follower of James Relly. Most of the people who read the papers had not the slightest notion who Relly was or what he stood for, but public resentment was aroused, and Murray's life was threatened.

In the midst of his troubles he was invited to visit Gloucester on nearby Cape Ann. Here, to his amazement and delight he found people already converted to Relly's teachings. In 1770, a seafarer named Gregory had brought from London a copy of Relly's *Union*. For four years a group from the First Parish had been meeting in the home of Winthrop Sargent to study and discuss the religious ideas of this book. Murray settled in Gloucester as their leader, with the understanding that he would be free to spend part of his time preaching elsewhere.

Made bold by the backing of the Gloucester Universalists, Murray began more forthrightly to draw the lines between his views and Calvinism. The heresy hunters were not long in finding their prey. Ministers in pulpit and in print assailed both his theology and his character. They succeeded in stirring up sentiment against him until he was looked upon by many as a public enemy. He was accused of being a British spy, and was pelted with stones on the streets of

Gloucester. The Gloucester Committee of Safety ordered Murray to leave town, but he refused.

Upon the outbreak of the American Revolution, Murray became chaplain of the Rhode Island Brigade. Soon after the appointment a petition by other army chaplains asking for his removal was sent to General George Washington, whose reply was brief and decisive: "General Orders, September 17, 1775—The Rev. John Murray is appointed Chaplain of the Rhode Island Regiment, and is to be respected as such." After less than a year in this post, Chaplain Murray was taken ill and returned to his pastoral duties. At this time the people in Gloucester were in financial distress due to the war, which barred the fishing boats and other commercial craft from the seas.

As soon as Murray recovered from his illness he returned to the army to raise money for the relief of his townspeople. The officers responded liberally, with General Washington heading the list of givers. Food and clothing were provided for more than three hundred distressed families, and the town council gave Murray a vote of thanks.

Notwithstanding these services,the clergy continued to hound him, and the people of the community still feared him as a dangerous character. As the opposition grew more furious, however, the loyalty and zeal of Murray's friends increased, and converts, including many of the most substantial persons in the community, supported the cause.

Sixteen members of the First Parish who joined the Universalist group were publicly dismissed from membership. These, with others, sixty-one in all, organized the Independent Christian Church on January 1, 1779. A meetinghouse was built and occupied by the congregation on Christmas Day, 1780. This small building served the congregation until 1805 when the beautiful church now in use was erected.

In Massachusetts, all citizens were taxed to support the Parish Church (Congregational) of the community in which they lived. The Universalists refused to pay this tax, basing their claims on the Bill of Rights in the Constitution of the Commonwealth, and their support of their own church. The tax gatherers of the First Parish enforced their demand by seizing and selling at auction the goods of several members of the Independent Church. One member who resisted this action was taken to jail. The tax case was taken to the courts and the Universalists finally won the right of freedom from taxation to support the church to which they did not belong. This was more than a local victory; it was the first test case of this kind in America to establish an important principle of religious freedom.

In October, 1788, John Murray married Judith Sargent Stevens, the widowed daughter of Winthrop Sargent. Judith Sargent Stevens was a beautiful, gracious, intelligent woman, recognized for her literary accomplishments. She was the first American playwright to have her works performed on the professional stage. She was also a pioneer advocate of women's equality with men. The Murrays began their married life in the beautiful, spacious home built by Winthrop Sargent for his daughter. This house is now maintained as a memorial, the Sargent-Murray-Gilman House.

Murray was now forty-seven and had been in Gloucester fourteen years. His portrait painted at about this time represents him with a round, pleasant face beaming with kindness. He is described as of medium height, of fine presence, "an earnest, effective speaker, a charitable and friendly man who went about doing good."

The last years in Gloucester were not without trials. Trumped-up charges continued to harass both minister and congregation. But Murray remained to build a strong and enduring church with the help of the unwavering loyalty of a growing number of followers.

Outside of Gloucester, there were a few scattered gatherings of Universalists in Pennsylvania, New York, and New England. But there was little communication between these groups, and not much awareness of one another's existence. Murray saw the necessity of organization to strengthen and widen the influence of these forces. At his suggestion delegates, both laity and ministers, came together from eight New England localities for a conference at Oxford, Massachusetts, on September 14, 1785. Five years later, when a more general convention met in Philadelphia, Murray took a leading part in the deliberations. He was always ready to give time and strength to Universalist movements that needed help. He prepared a pamphlet with suggestions for church organization and urged the adoption of a uniform statement of purpose. That he was not altogether successful in consolidating the Universalist forces was due less to his lack of organizing ability than the extreme indifference of local congregations. Early Universalists were fearful that organization would place limits on their personal freedom.

After twenty years in Gloucester, Murray moved to Boston where he served the First Universalist Church there until his death in 1815 at the age of seventy-four. He found the religious atmosphere of Boston somewhat changed since his first experiences there. Calvinism was still the dominating theology, hellfire and brimstone was the message generally thundered from the pulpits. But this sort of religion was being questioned in many quarters.

America had won independence. The declaration that "all men are created equal and endowed by their Creator with certain inalienable rights, including life, liberty, and the pursuit of happiness," was in sharp contrast to the doctrine that the Creator, caring so little about humanity and the principles of democracy, would will that most people should go to hell, regardless of the way they lived.

The liberal religious movement in America sprang not only from the demand for political freedom, but also from the need of a worthy view of God and humankind. The Universalists at this time, although few and widely scattered, contributed much to this movement. It has been said that Universalism and American Independence "were rocked in the same cradle."

John Murray served well the needs of his time. No sacrifice was too great for him, and no hardship beyond his courage. He was not a great scholar, nor a deep thinker; to the end he was a follower of James Relly, teaching what Relly taught. He was not a great preacher, but his message, always of hope, was spoken directly to the hearts of his hearers. He knew his Bible as a familiar book of quotations which he used effectively, bending them with great freedom to his purpose. He lived to witness, not without pain, new emphases in Universalist theology, but his self-surrendering, dream-pursuing devotion to the larger hope for humanity is not outdated.

CHAPTER FOUR

Thomas Jefferson
1743-1826

Thomas Jefferson used to entertain his children with tall tales about the super strength of their grandfather. When grandfather Peter Jefferson was young he could lift two barrels of tobacco weighing a thousand pounds each way up over his head! And one time when three strong men were trying to pull down an old shed, along came grandfather Peter who said, "Stand aside, boys," seized the rope, gave it a mighty jerk, and the shed came tumbling down.

Peter Jefferson, whatever his physical strength, was of solid character and good mind. He was one of the mighty pioneers who tamed the forests and made a place for themselves in the new world. Peter loved seventeen-year old Jane Randolph, who belonged to one of the wealthiest and most aristocratic families in Tidewater Virginia. But with no proper home he could not ask for her hand in marriage. So he took advantage of the low price of forest land and bought a thousand acres east of the Blue Ridge Mountains in Albemarle County. He cleared a portion of it and built Shadwell, a large wooden house about eight miles east of Charlottesville. Then he went to Dungeness, the Randolph estate on the north bank of the James River, and claimed his bride.

At Shadwell there was great rejoicing when, on April 13, 1743, the first son was born; there were already two daughters. He was named Thomas. His young mother was only twenty-three. Wealth in the Virginia colony meant land and slaves, and the Jeffersons had plenty of both. The parents were able to provide well for their children. They were intelligent, hard-working, and serious-minded. In this frontier home there were books, music, and affection as well as good food and good clothes. Jane Randolph Jefferson brought from her family background the traditions and customs of gracious living, and an influence that deeply affected the tastes of her son. The father, self-made and self-educated, took over the boy's education, taught him to read, write, and keep accounts, and guided him in habits of regular study and self-reliance. "Never ask others to do for you what you can do for yourself," the father often said. By the time young Thomas was in his teens he had mastered several languages, both modern and ancient. Yet life on the farm was not all books. He learned to ride horses, shoot wild turkeys, paddle a canoe on the Rivanna, dance, and play the fiddle.

Peter Jefferson, Virginia Colonel, Justice of the Peace, and the wealthiest person in Albemarle County, died when Thomas was fourteen. The good and wise father had given his son a wonderful start in life. The youth, left with his mother, six sisters, and an infant brother, was now the head of the family. By Virginia law he inherited Shadwell, the estate of his father. Of this period he later wrote that "the whole care and direction of myself was thrown on myself entirely, without a relation or friend qualified to guide me." He knew that he wanted more education, to go to college. In Virginia this meant only one college, William and Mary, at Williamsburg, one hundred and twenty miles east of his home, in the heart of Tidewater Virginia.

Three years later Thomas, now seventeen, entered William and Mary College. He was a striking figure, this young aristocrat from the frontier. He stood straight and tall, six feet two, lean, muscular, and roughhewn, brimming with health from his outdoor life. Although he was not handsome, with his freckled face, red hair, and deep-set eyes, there was a rustic charm about him that instantly attracted old and young. Teachers and townspeople liked him from the beginning.

To the country boy from the mountains the small town of Williamsburg seemed like a bustling city. There were about two hundred houses, and a population of around a thousand persons, including a large number of black slaves. There were no sidewalks or sewers. Pigs and goats roamed over the unpaved streets in country fashion. But this was the capital of the largest of the Colonies, and the political, educational, and social center of Virginia. The main thoroughfare was the spacious Duke of Gloucester Street, with some fine homes, the Bruton Parish Church (now said to be the oldest Episcopal Church in America), the court house, the Raleigh Tavern (a center for political and social activities), and the imposing capitol at the end of the street. At the head of this street were the three or four buildings that housed William and Mary College with its seventy-five students, and nearby was the elegant Governor's Palace with its spacious grounds and beautiful gardens.

Within this setting Thomas soon found a lively and interesting world. There were dances at the Palace for old and young. In the beautiful ballroom, lighted by many candles, the cream of Virginia society danced the stately minuet to the soft music of violins and harpsichord. Ladies in their elaborate finery of rich brocades and satins, with billowing skirts; and gentlemen with their fancy waistcoats, knee breeches, silk stockings, and shoes with silver buckles, their powdered hair and cocked hats, copied in their manners and dress the court life of Europe. There was a good deal of fast life, too, in the Virginia capital, cock fighting, horse racing, billiard playing, and not a little gambling and rum drinking. Young Jefferson took part in these sports sparingly, and with little danger of becoming just another idle Virginia gentleman. The lad from Shadwell had come to Williamsburg with a serious purpose, to get his college education. He was well-equipped in body and mind for his course, and threw himself into the work with great zeal. He read everything in sight, did his class assignments, and, in addition, carried on a course of study of his own choosing. Often he studied all night and then ran a mile out of town and back, just for exercise. His teachers had never seen a student like him.

Several of the teachers at William and Mary were of the clergy. They did not greatly impress Jefferson, but there were two persons whose influence was deep and lasting. One was William Small, the science teacher, a person of rare learing. Dr. Small opened doors for his student into the wonders of the natural world. He also introduced him to a small group of scholars who met from time to time to discuss scientific and philosophical subjects. Here was a freer atmosphere than was found in the college classroom. Jefferson listened with open-eyed interest to these teachers who set a pattern of liberal thinking for him. Years later he said that Small "probably fixed the destinies of my life."

The other person who helped shape Jefferson's thinking was a lawyer, George Wythe, the foremost individual in his profession in Virginia. Wythe was a liberal in politics, a believer in democratic principles of government, and like Small, opened new doors to the eager student's mind. Jefferson spoke of him as "my faithful and beloved Mentor." Wythe, years later, was one of the signers of the Declaration of Independence, authored by his pupil and friend.

The most important and impressive figure in the Colony was Acting Governor of Virginia, Francis Fauquier. The Governor was a person of broad scholarship, interested in new ideas of government and philosophy, and a good musician. Jefferson was invited frequently, along with Small and Wythe, to dinners at the Palace. Many years later he wrote, "At these dinners I have heard more good sense, more rational and philosophical conversation, than in all my life besides."

Jefferson always remembered these associations with gratitude. Small and Wythe, many years older than he, saw in his keen mind, his curiosity to know, and his capacity for hard work, the promise of a brilliant future. They did not know of course, the great things he would do for America and for the world. They could not foresee that their young friend in the course of a long public career within an independent nation yet to be born, would be a member of Congress, Governor of Virginia, Ambassador to France, Secretary of State, Vice President, and President twice. This lad was to write the Declaration of Independence, create the University of Virginia, promote the Louisiana purchase, which more than doubled the area of the United States, plan the nation's system of coining money, and found the Democratic political party. The voice of this dancing, fiddle-playing, soft-speaking youth from the frontier would one day become the voice of civil and religious liberty speaking for his countrymen and women for future generations. The stouthearted son of Peter Jefferson was to become known wherever people strove for "Life, Liberty, and the Pursuit of Happiness."

After two years of college Jefferson began the study of law in the office of George Wythe. Here, as in college, he continued his private studies, a rigorous program of reading in philosophy, history, and science. He also continued his social activities about town: music, dancing, and going out with the young ladies. He had an agonizing love affair, too, over a pretty but not very intelligent young woman. All the young men (and some of the older ones) were infatuated with her. Jefferson was only twenty. His "Beloved Belinda" married a handsome older man and the unsuccessful lover managed to live without her.

Jefferson spent five years on his law studies and was admitted to the bar in 1767, at the age of twenty-four. Two years after beginning law practice he was elected to the Virginia legislature, the House of Burgesses. At once he introduced bills which started the conservative old law-makers shaking from their powdered wigs to their silver-buckled shoes. He proposed nothing less than putting democracy into the government. The most radical bill had to do with religious liberty. Since the founding of Jamestown in 1607, the Church of England (Episcopal) had been given privileges as a state institution denied all other denominations. Everyone was taxed for its support whether a member or not, and there were severe penalties for denying its teachings or poking fun at the clergy. Jefferson's idea was not mere toleration; he wanted everybody to be free in religious matters with no interference by the state. The bill aimed, he explained, "To comprehend within the mantle of its protection, the Jew and the Gentile, the Christian, and the Mahometan, the Hindoo, and the infidel of every denomination."

This met with stubborn opposition, but the first-term legislator never gave up. During these years of labor he had need of all his resources: the disciplined mind that he owed to his father, the influence of Dr. Small at college, the support of his friend George Wythe, now a member of the legislature, and above all the courage born of an undying religious faith that all people were made for and deserved freedom. *The Virginia Statute for Religious Freedom* was finally passed in 1779, ten years later, when Jefferson was Governor of Virginia. James Monroe, James Madison, and James Mason, all good friends of his, helped with the passage of this important legislation. It set an example for the whole country for religious liberty and the separation of church and state. Not many years afterwards the principles were written into the nation's Bill of Rights. Before Jefferson's peaceful revolution was over, Virginia had adopted a new code of laws. The prohibition of the trade in slaves, a measure for which he worked, followed two years later.

Often as a boy Jefferson had watched the sun go down behind the highest summit on his father's farm, and he told himself, "Some day I'm going to build me a home on the top of that hill." He cherished this dream, and while in the legislature began to make it come true. The house, which he named Monticello, is a monument to Thomas Jefferson's ability to do well an amazing number of things.

In the creation of Monticello he was architect and builder, landscape artist, engineer, and inventor. He read everything available on architecture in order to become his own master builder. The three-story house of thirty-five rooms on top of the high-leveled plateau had magnificent views in all directions; the town of Charlottesville and the Blue Ridge mountains toward the west, and to the east the beautiful rolling Virginia countryside. Its unusual features included the dome-shaped roof surmounting a large octagonal room, narrow side stairways to save space, long terraces extending from the house with small pavilions at each end, and underneath a basement of twelve rooms housing all the activities usually in plantation outbuildings: the kitchen, servants' quarters and smokehouse, the wine cellars and storerooms, and even the stables, carriage house and laundry rooms. The house was equipped with numerous cleverly designed gadgets, many of them beautiful as well as useful. There was the remarkable clock in the dome room that told the day of the week as well as the time, and a dumbwaiter for serving, both designed by Jefferson. A generous provision was made for his library, to which he constantly added, and which later became the beginning of the present Library of Congress in Washington.

Jefferson fell in love with a charming young widow, Martha Wayles Skelton, a person of rare beauty and grace, who shared his love for music and played the harpsichord. They were married on New Year's Day in 1772, and drove over very bad roads, in a snowstorm, to Monticello. There they began their married life although Monticello was not finished. In fact the building took twenty-five years for completion. It was here that their six children were born. Monticello is owned and maintained by the Thomas Jefferson Memorial Foundation, which, in 1923, purchased the house and the 700 acres of land in the plantation. The purpose of this nonprofit organization is to restore and preserve the house and gardens as Jefferson planned them. Visitors today see Monticello much as it was when Jefferson retired to live there during his last years.

Jefferson would have liked nothing better than to remain at home looking after his family, his fields and flowers, and have time for study and writing. But this was not to be. Strong people were needed in public life, not only in Virginia but throughout the land. The lines were being more and more tightly drawn between the Colonies and Great Britain. Revolution was in the air. Resistance to King George the Third and the British Cabinet was on the increase. In 1773, rebels spilled the King's tea into Boston Harbor, and in 1775 the battle at Lexington was fought. A Continental Congress, a meeting of delegates from each of the thirteen Colonies, was called in Philadelphia to decide what actions should be taken. Jefferson was a delegate from Virginia. He left Williamsburg in the spring of 1775, traveling by horse and buggy, on roads rutted in deep red mud, across streams without bridges, and over forest trails that could be followed only with the help of local guides. He made the three hundred miles in ten days.

The delegates had heard of Thomas Jefferson and his brilliant leadership in the Virginia legislature, and were curious to see him. They were not disappointed when this erect, weather-tanned, redheaded man from the south entered the council chamber. When they rose to welcome him, he stood head and shoulders above many of them. He was thirty-two, the youngest except for two of the delegates. Jefferson was chosen to draw up resolutions setting forth the reasons why the Colonies should break with Great Britain. There were long debates, much speech making, and in the end most of his report was rejected. Some delegates were not yet convinced a revolution was unavoidable.

Jefferson returned to Virginia and his beloved Monticello in August, but not for long. In January 1776, Lord Dunmore, the Royal Governor of Virginia, burned Norfolk. And now the words of Patrick Henry delivered in the old church in Richmond were echoing throughout the land: "Gentlemen may cry peace, peace, but there is no peace. The war is actually begun! . . . Our brethren are already in the field! Why stand we idle here?" In May, Jefferson was back in Philadelphia to attend another session of the Congress. After nearly a month of debate Richard Henry Lee of Virginia introduced a startling resolution: "That these United Colonies are and of a right ought to be free and independent states, that they are absolved from all allegiance to the British crown, and that all political connection between them and the state of Great Britain is and ought to be totally dissolved." John Adams seconded the motion, and Thomas Jefferson wrote the Declaration of Independence.

In his notebook Jefferson wrote: "The Committee for drawing the Declaration of Independence desired me to do it. It was accordingly done." But the task was not as simple as these words suggest. He had rented a bedroom and parlor on the second floor of a bricklayer's house. For seventeen hot June days, at a make-shift desk in the stuffy upstairs parlor, Jefferson labored over the assignment. The finished product not only set forth with crystal clearness the highest of his country's convictions regarding separation from Great Britain, but it was written in language of rare beauty. It was the creation of a political leader, but also of a poet and religious philosopher.

The Declaration, with two or three slight changes suggested by Franklin and John Adams, members of Jefferson's committee, was placed before the delegates. Nothing was added, but some items were stricken out, the most important of these a passage which denounced the King for upholding the slave trade in America. The anti-slavery party in Virginia was strong, but there were delegates from South Carolina and Georgia where the planters profited by slavery, and from New England where the ship merchants who brought slaves to America likewise profited, so the clause was removed.

After Jefferson handed in his report he went shopping. Always interested in new inventions, he purchased a thermometer, only recently placed on the market although invented about fifty years earlier. He also bought seven pairs of women's gloves and made a contribution to charity. Having recorded these transactions faithfully in his diary he settled his account with the bricklayer landlord, and hurried home to his wife and three young daughters at Monticello.

He settled down to the enjoyment of his family, continued the building of Monticello, resumed his studies, created labor-saving machinery for his farm, made scientific experiments, and worked on his book, *Notes on Virginia*. This book, which went to press about two years later, together with his many letters, provides much of what is known of his private life.

Jefferson was not to enjoy retirement long. Mrs. Jefferson had given birth to six children in ten years. Three of them had died, and their mother never fully recovered from the last childbirth. She died September 6, 1782, leaving the stricken father with three small children—Martha, named for her mother and almost ten years old; Mary, four, and the baby Lucy, who lived only about two years. Jefferson took over the care of the children. He had them inoculated for smallpox, a newly discovered protection against the dread disease. Mrs. Jefferson's death had shattered his hopes for retirement. Monticello held too many memories of their happy years together. He took the children to the home of a friend and stayed with them there for several months, not knowing what to do with his future.

The decision was made by his friends in public life. In May of 1784, Congress appointed Jefferson as Ambassador to arrange trade agreements with European nations. He placed the youngest daughter, Mary, with relatives and took Martha with him to Paris where she was placed in school. She described the ocean voyage as a "lovely passage in a beautiful new ship . . . There were only six passengers, all of whom papa knew, and a fine sunshine all the way." Three years later Polly (Mary) joined them in Paris.

Jefferson was in Europe five years, and had no sooner returned home than he learned he had been nominated to the newly created office of Secretary of State. He accepted the post reluctantly because at last there had seemed to be a chance that he might stay at Monticello. After serving nearly four years in this position, and despite President Washington's urging him to remain, he resigned because of differences of view regarding foreign policy. Both the conflict with Alexander Hamilton, Secretary of the Treasury, and the problems of maintaining neutrality in the period of the French Revolution made the position difficult.

Now fifty years old, Jefferson set to work to restore the fertility of his fields. His property had been much neglected, the farm lands were yielding poorly, and, in spite of his 10,000 acres and 200 slaves, he had gone heavily into debt, a condition that never improved. He was glad to be free to attend to his farm.

Meanwhile things were happening in Philadelphia. President Washington, after eight years, was not a candidate for a third term. The two candidates who were uppermost in the public mind were John Adams, a Federalist, and Thomas Jefferson, leader in democracy. In the ensuing election Jefferson lost by a very small margin to his rival, but by the rules of that period became the Vice President. Four years later he was elected President and then was re-elected for a second term.

It was no secret among Jefferson's close friends that he held religious views different from those generally accepted. For one thing, he believed that one had a right to one's own personal religious convictions without interference from church or state. He never regarded matters of religious belief as proper subject for public debate. "I inquire after no man's religious opinions," he said, "and I trouble none with mine."

Although Jefferson in political life met plenty of opposition from several directions, it was not until his campaign for election to the presidency that the religious issue became serious. The two hundred copies of his *Notes on Virginia* had been published in 1781. The book dealt with a variety of subjects, including his observations on religion and theology. It was distributed only among friends, but his unorthodox views became widely known and were used against him by political enemies.

The clergy and newspapers joined with politicians in the charge that Jefferson was an atheist and therefore unfit to be president. Few people in public office have been more slandered and falsely represented. He was called a coward, a thief, a robber of widows and orphans, an anarchist, and an infidel. In New England especially he was feared and hated. Some people during the campaign hid their family Bibles because they were told that if Jefferson was elected his first official act would be to collect and burn all religious books. At a Methodist service of baptism for a child, the father when told to name his son, replied, "Thomas Jefferson," and the minister thundered, "That's no name for a Christian; I baptise thee John Adams."

Throughout the political campaign Jefferson himself answered none of the charges made against his character. He made no speeches, shook no hands, and kissed no babies. But he had the common people with him, those who, having won political independence, now wanted economic freedom. The Federalist campaign appealed to citizens of property and power, but Jefferson's democracy was favored by the less privileged and they were in the majority.

All through his life Jefferson applied certain liberal principles both in private and public affairs: the use of reason as a way to truth, respect for others' religious opinions, and freedom as a natural right of all persons. These are ways of thinking and living by which the best in religious liberalism is known. Jefferson was a religious liberal long before he came in contact with Unitarian or Universalist Churches.

In Philadelphia, he became acquainted with John Adams, Unitarian from Massachusetts, with the free-thinking Franklin, with Benjamin Rush and John Murray, Universalists. He met Joseph Priestley, the English Unitarian preacher and scientist, with whom Jefferson had many common interests. He read Priestley's books on religion and attended his church. There were at that time no Unitarian churches in Virginia. Toward the end of his life in a letter to a friend he wrote;"I must be contented to be a Unitarian by myself, although I know there are many around me who would become so if once they could hear the question fairly stated." Indeed, until Jefferson's reform laws separating church and state were passed, it was a crime in Virginia to be a Unitarian, and the penalty was death.

Jefferson's enemies accused him of being an atheist, but he had never denied the existence of God. He was charged with trying to destroy the Christian church, but he had aimed only at taking from the state-supported churches in Virginia the privileges denied other denominations. He was called anti-Christ, because he did not believe some of the stories in the Bible that many thought were true. But he placed great value upon the ethical teachings of Jesus, and while President he arranged these teachings, scattered through the Gospels, in a book now commonly called *The Jefferson Bible*.

Following his two terms as President there came at long last some years at Monticello. He retired from public office in 1809 at the end of his second term. Always interested in education, he devoted the last years of his life to the building of the University of Virginia at Charlottesville, which he considered the crowning glory of his career.

Jefferson died on July 4, 1826, just fifty years after the signing of the Declaration of Independence. Beside the road leading up the hill to Monticello is the family cemetery where his body was placed beside that of his wife. On his tombstone are these words which he had left for his epitaph:

Here was Burried
THOMAS JEFFERSON
Author of the
Declaration of American
Independence
of the
Statute of Virginia
for
Religious Freedom
and
Father of the University
of Virginia

For these services promoting religious and political liberties, rather than for the high offices held, he wished to be remembered.

CHAPTER FIVE

Benjamin Rush
1745-1813

Benjamin Rush was born on Christmas Eve, 1745, the fourth of seven children in the family of John and Suzanna Rush. His birthplace, a farming community in Byberry, Pennsylvania (now included in Philadelphia), had been settled by a company of Friends almost at the beginning of the Penn Colony in 1682. Benjamin was of the fifth generation of the family to live on the Rush homestead of five thousand acres. His father, a member of the conservative branch of Quakers, besides working on his farm, earned a good living making and repairing firearms.

His father died when Benjamin was five, and the widow took the children to Philadelphia, where she set up a grocery and china shop, "The Blazing Star," on High (Market) Street, near the center of the market sheds district. She purchased a house on the opposite side of the street. Here in the heart of the city Benjamin and his sisters and brothers found much of interest in the busy life around them.

Philadelphia in the mid-eighteenth century, with a population of nearly fifteen thousand, mostly Germans and Quakers, was the largest city in the American colonies. It was the trading post for the surrounding towns, and an important port of commerce, as well as the cultural center of the country. The Rush children, sitting on the marble steps of their substantial brick house, watched the farm wagons carrying produce to the market. Great drays sometimes drawn by four or even six horses creaked past the house going to and from the docks where British ships discharged cargoes and were loaded in the exchange of goods between the Colonial merchants and English manufacturers.

Sometimes Benjamin went with his older brother to watch from a safe distance the black slaves and indentured servants roll the huge casks of sugar and molasses from the ships and reload them with lumber and bales of tobacco. Then there were the street cleaners, organized by Philadelphia's first citizen, Benjamin Franklin. When they appeared with shovels and brooms the children ran into the house to close the windows against the clouds of dust. More exciting than the street-cleaners were the fire-fighters. When a fire broke out in any of the nearby shops or houses they seemed suddenly to appear from nowhere, racing through the streets armed with ladders and water buckets. The fire-fighting organization was another innovation the city owed to Franklin.

Mrs. Rush, with her business duties, was forced to leave the cares of the household mostly to servants. Nevertheless she found time to give careful attention to the education of her children. She had been educated in a Philadelphia boarding school and was a woman of intelligence, energy, and strength of character. She gave Benjamin instruction in the elementary subjects of reading, writing, and English grammar. At the age of nine he went with his brother Jacob to the Academy in Nottingham, Maryland.

This school was founded and presided over by Mrs. Rush's brother-in-law, the Rev. Samuel Finley, a Presbyterian minister. The Academy was especially for theological students, but there was a good deal of scope in the courses offered. Headmaster Finley took special interest in his nephews, and they made rapid progress under his wise guidance. This deep and lasting influence upon Benjamin in the formative period of life shaped his mind and developed his moral vigor for the struggles of later years. In the days ahead he was to become one of the most important figures of the age—a forceful writer on a wide range of subjects, a fearless social reformer, and America's most controversial member of the medical profession.

Benjamin stayed at Nottingham five years, and then entered the junior class of the College of New Jersey (later Princeton University). He studied Latin and Greek, literature, philosophy, and mathematics. There were no classes in science. He showed unusual ability in composition and public speaking. Perhaps it was because of these capabilities that the president of the college urged him to become a lawyer. Mrs. Rush agreed that Benjamin was cut out for this profession, and made arrangements to place him in the office of a Philadelphia barrister. The matter seemed to be settled, although Benjamin himself had some doubts. The choice of one's life work was a serious affair, and he was not going to be unduly swayed by family and friends. His former teacher could be depended upon for sound advice. So he went to see Dr. Finley. The teacher warned him against the law as "full of temptations." After a long and searching conference Finley finally suggested medicine as a possible profession. This appealed to Benjamin, but his uncle said that a decision should not be made without divine guidance. Benjamin, therefore, spent several days and nights searching his soul, meditated and prayed, and came to the conviction that he was meant for the life of a physician.

In 1760, Benjamin Rush was granted the Bachelor of Arts degree. He was only fifteen. Having decided to enter the medical profession, his next problem was how to prepare for it. There was not a medical school in America. Medical books were few and poor, and medical practice was an uncertain mixture of science and superstition. Students preparing for the profession sometimes apprenticed themselves to physicians and learned by practising on the patients. Rush, with his college degree and a reputation for hard work, had no difficulty in making such an arrangement. Dr. Redman, a distinguished physician and member of the staff of the Pennsylvania Hospital, the first public hospital in America, accepted him as an apprentice.

The duties of a medical apprentice were many and varied—running errands, helping with household chores, keeping books, accompanying an employer on visits to the sick, observing surgery, and acting as orderly and nurse. But Rush was eager to learn how to become a physician. In his entire term of service of five and a half years he was absent from work only eleven days, and took only three evenings off. He often burned the midnight oil poring over medical books and making notes for further reference. He also began the study of German, the better to work with his patients, many of whom spoke only this language.

After completing his apprenticeship he stayed on in Philadelphia, attending medical lectures given by the hospital staff and continuing his private studies. Encouraged by Dr. Redman to go abroad for further training, Rush left in the summer of 1766 for the University of Edinburgh. There in one of the chief medical schools then in existence he took all the courses offered. Two years later he received the degree of Doctor of Medicine, after presenting to the faculty a thesis written in Latin setting forth original investigations on the digestion of food.

After graduation he remained abroad for a year, visiting medical centers in England and France, and making the acquaintance of prominent persons in the fields of politics and reform. He seemed to value these contacts equally with his medical studies. Many matters hitherto unexamined claimed his attention—the divine right of kings, political freedom, the treatment of criminals, and relations of church and state. He resolved "never again to believe any statement without question."

Returning to America in 1769, Rush lost no time in setting himself up in practice. He was now in his twenty-fifth year, well-built, vigorous, blue-eyed, and attractive—a young man who could inspire confidence in those he would serve. His practice at first was limited almost entirely to the poorer people, from whom small fees were gathered. Of these patients he had an almost endless supply. His office was filled every morning, and the afternoons were spent in calling upon the sick in their homes. There was now a medical department in the College of Philadelphia. On the basis of his work at Edinburgh, Rush was appointed Professor of Chemistry, the first formal professor of this subject in the country. Rush later succeeded to the chair of Theory and Practice of Medicine. He taught in the college continuously from 1789 until his death. He published the first textbook on chemistry written by an American.

Dr. Rush was more popular with his pupils and patients than with many of his fellow physicians. At Edinburgh he had learned methods which were at variance with those practiced by some of the leading physicians of the city, and he was not backward in pointing out their errors and in making claims of his own superior knowledge. Always cocksure and self-confident, he soon found himself at odds with the older doctors who, with some justification, regarded the young physician as hotheaded and stubborn. For the first seven years not a single patient was referred to him by any other physician. He further cut himself off from his colleagues and others of influence by his championship of unpopular causes. He offended the slaveholders by writing a pamphlet attacking slavery, and later by organizing the first anti-slavery society in America. He caused the displeasure of distillers and tavern keepers by lecturing on the effects of alcohol on the human body, and of the clergy by publicly denying the orthodox interpretation of baptism and communion. Above all, he aroused the enmity of the rich Tories by his persistent agitation for breaking ties with England.

Notwithstanding the strong feelings harbored against him by wealthy and influential citizens, his practice grew and his lectures at the college kept his name before the public. It was not long before Dr. Benjamin Rush was recognized throughout the city as an industrious and successful physician.

In August, 1775, Rush took his first vacation from the daily grind. He spent a few days in Princeton visiting friends. Here he met and immediately fell in love with Julia Stockton, the sixteen-year-old daughter of a trustee of the College of New Jersey. They were married the next winter. Rush's marriage was fortunate for him. Julia proved a capable and devoted wife, and a steadying influence and comfort in the turbulent life of her husband during the Revolution, in the terrible days of the yellow fever epidemic, and throughout his many bitter personal controversies. He wrote that "She fulfilled every duty as wife, mother, and mistress with fidelity and integrity." The Rushes had thirteen children, of whom nine reached maturity. Mrs. Rush lived to the age of ninety.

Rush was one of the first and most unyielding promoters of American independence, and one of the most radical thinkers in the Colonies. Both Rush and his father-in-law signed the Declaration of Independence. While political leaders were discussing conciliation with England, he was writing pamphlets and newspaper articles, some of them anonymous, attacking the principles of colonization and denouncing British colonial policies. He gathered material for a powerful pamphlet aimed at blasting patriots out of their complacency and winning people to the cause of independence. Rush could not publish these revolutionary ideas without losing his practice, so he turned the notes over to a young Briton, Thomas Paine, and named the joint production *Common Sense*. The pamphlet was a firebrand; it inflamed the minds of thousands, and won them to the side of the Revolution. It is an important document in American history.

Impatient with the conservatism of the Pennsylvania Assembly (the legislative body of the Province), elected mainly from the property-owning class, Rush formed a radical political party which in July, 1776, elected him to the Continental Congress. He too signed the Declaration of Independence.

When the guns began to boom Dr. Rush joined the medical

department of the Continental army and saw service in the battles of Trenton and Princeton. After nine months he resigned because he disapproved of the management of the military hospitals. The army was in great need of medical personnel, however, and he accepted appointment to the post of surgeon-general (later physician-general). Inspecting the hospitals, he found them in a deplorable condition. The sick and wounded were crammed into quarters meant for only a third of their number. There were not half enough drugs and surgical instruments. Food was insufficient in quantity, and often not fit for use. Soldiers were dying at an alarming rate of ''camp fever,'' typhus, small pox, and other maladies contracted in the crowded and unsanitary wards. The wounded dreaded hospitalization more than being left to die on the battlefield.

Rush was horrified. He wrote and circulated a pamphlet, *Directions for Preserving the Health of Soldiers,* but it was mostly ignored by the medical department of the army. He then prepared a detailed report on conditions in the hospitals and sent it to Congress. He charged that the reason for the deplorable state of affairs was graft within the medical department. This report stirred up a hornet's nest. Those who were robbing the government at the cost of human lives had friends in Congress. There were counter charges accusing Rush of incompetence and misrepresentation, and he was forced to resign. Finally the chief culprit was court-martialled, but friends in high office came to his rescue and he was set free. Rush fought a losing battle against the heavy odds of political influence. His charges, however, have never been disproved.

After his resignation as physician-general he returned to Philadelphia and again took up his practice. He brought his wife and year-old son home from Maryland where they had fled when the redcoats marched into Philadelphia. There was plenty of work to be done. The British Army had occupied Philadelphia for eight months and left it in a wretched condition. Dr. Rush worked like mad to bring order to the city, to stop the spread of disease, and to patch up the homes disrupted by war. As soon as the classrooms were cleaned up and repaired after their use as barracks by the British, he resumed his lectures at the University.

To Benjamin Rush, the end of the war did not mean the end of the revolution. He wrote a series of articles for the newspapers arguing for reforms that would insure and extend the freedom for which the war had been fought. These writings, later collected in a volume, condemned capital punishment, called for the abolition of slavery, and urged drastic reforms in the treatment of criminals and the insane. He established a free medical dispensary, the first in America. He founded a temperance society that opposed not only the use of alcoholic beverages, but also the use of tobacco as a cause of disease and a waste of money. He estimated that the taking of snuff consumed five whole days a year!

Believing that representative government cannot succeed without universal education, Rush proposed a system of schooling suited to American conditions. His insistence that changes be made in the curriculum of the University of Pennsylvania met with firm resistance from the provost, Dr. John Ewing. The two quarrelled and Rush created a rival institution in Carlisle, Pennsylvania, now Dickinson College. Rush also lent support to the founding of Franklin and Marshall College in Lancaster, Pennsylvania.

Dr. Rush had a migratory church career. Born in a Quaker family he was baptized an Episcopalian, and joined the Presbyterian Church. He was identified in one way or another with several denominations and held pews in a half-dozen churches, attending services wherever most convenient in his rounds. He quarrelled with the Presbyterian pastor and withdrew his membership, then found the Episcopal Church even less to his liking. He could accept no creed and no authority except his own!

It was not until he was thirty-three years old that Rush found a type of religion agreeable to his independent and inquiring nature. In 1781, the Rev. Elhanan Winchester was driven from his Baptist pulpit because of his Universalist views. With some members of the congregation who followed him, a Universalist Society was formed. The group met in a hall at the University until a building of their own was purchased four years later. Dr. Rush joined this group and gave the movement hearty support. "The Universalist doctrine," he wrote, "is not a mere speculation, but a new principle of action in the heart." Universalism seemed so reasonable to him that he thought everybody would accept it if it were made known. When plans were being made for a Universalist convention in Philadelphia in 1790, Rush, with his usual disregard of obstacles, insisted that the call go out to all Christians to come together and frame a common platform based on reason and good works. He was outvoted, and the Convention was entirely Universalist. Rush made his presence felt at the sessions which lasted for fifteen days. He corrected and arranged the Articles of Faith and a Plan of Church Government, making sure that they embodied his principles of religion and social ethics. The hand of Rush is especially revealed in the recommendations voted. They dealt with the reforms for which he had crusaded for twenty years—war, slavery, citizenship, and schools for children where they could be instructed in reading, writing, and singing Psalms on Sunday.

The convention over, Rush went off at once to put this later recommendation into action. He rounded up an Episcopal rector, a Presbyterian elder, some influential Methodists and Roman Catholics, and with their help founded the First-day or Sunday School Association. Schools were set up in various parts of the city, especially for children of the poor and apprentices for whom no other means of instruction were provided. These schools continued for a quarter century or until superseded by the system of public education and denominational Sunday Schools.

Dr. Rush at this time was at the height of his career, recognized not only for his services to the community and to the nation but also as the foremost physician in America. Both his fortitude and medical skill were soon to be put to the severest test of his entire life. In 1793, the yellow fever plague hit Philadelphia with the most appalling disaster ever to come to an American city.

In mid-summer of that year the Doctor observed an unusual number of deaths his patients and those of other physicians. He concluded after careful diagnosis that the disease was yellow fever. He sounded the alarm, warning that yellow fever, which he considered contagious, was spreading fast, especially along the waterfront, where a cargo of spoiled coffee beans had been dumped and where other refuse was allowed to rot. He called for a general cleaning of streets and alleys and vacant lots, believing that the sickness was caused by a "noxious miasma," a poison in the air rising from decayed matter and undrained marshes.

The warning at first fell on deaf ears. Fellow physicians denied the existence of an epidemic; they had seen waves of sickness before and felt there was nothing to get excited about. Other citizens resented the charge that the community was unsanitary, and blamed whatever sickness there might be on the foreigners who were coming to Philadelphia, bringing diseases with them.

Then suddenly the whole city seemed to be dying. Within a week after Rush's warning Philadelphia was one vast morgue. There were not enough well people to dig graves for the dead. Unseen and unexplained, the mysterious power of destruction moved through the air, leaving scarcely a home unbroken. Those able to travel fled to the country districts, but soon were barred from other communities because of fear of contagion. Hundreds perished along the roadsides.

Rush's theory about foul air was generally accepted. To combat the poison in the atmosphere and to fortify the body against attack various remedies were adopted: exploding gunpowder, building smudge fires in streets and yards, chewing garlic and putting it in one's shoes. Housewives sprinkled rooms with vinegar, and women and children smoked cigars from morning until night. One man drank two quarts of blackstrap molasses and got well! So busy were they with their smudge pots and muskets that they had no time to swat the mosquitoes, which were unusually numerous in Philadelphia that summer.

Soon Dr. Rush was one of only three physicians well enough to care for six thousand or more stricken persons. He made 125 calls a day, and his office was filled late into the night. He tried every remedy he knew, he poured buckets of cold water over his patients; he wrapped them in blankets soaked in vinegar. Bloodletting was commonly practiced by the medical profession and Rush used this remedy in moderation. Now in desperation he greatly increased the amount of blood taken and also dosed his patients with calomel and mercury in unheard of quantities. This worked—in some cases. The Doctor was highly pleased with this discovery, claiming that it cured nine cases out of ten. When other physicians expressed doubt of the success of this heroic treatment Rush charged them with ignorance and jealousy. The city was thrown into a furious battle over medical theories, divided into pro-Rush and anti-Rush factions.

Whatever the actual results the tired and desperate Doctor believed in the soundness of his remedies. He kept no records, or perhaps remembered only his successes. He urged that bloodletting should continue until four-fifths of the blood contained in the body was drawn away. Fortunately physicians in the eighteenth century had no clear estimate of the amount of blood in the human body. His sister got the fever, took her brother's remedy and died. His mother refused the treatment and lived. Unfortunately the Rush method of excessive bloodletting not only prevailed then, but also cast its dark shadows across three generations of American medical practice.

The worst of the yellow fever epidemic was over with the first autumn frosts. No one knows how many died or how many deaths resulted from Dr. Rush's practice. But he emerged from these tragic months high in the esteem of his profession and honored by the public he had devotedly, if mistakenly, served.

When in 1813 he was taken ill he insisted on bloodletting. As he grew worse he ordered further bleeding and against the advice of his colleagues this was done. In two days he was dead, perhaps a victim of his own mistaken theory. There is no longer doubt that the purge and bloodletting treatment was a tragic error. But Rush held to it to the end, and won many of the medical profession to his view.

Yet he was a great physician for his time, and at his death was highly esteemed as teacher and practitioner. His lectures and writings served as standard works in medical theory and practice in America for many years. A year before his death he brought out his book on diseases of the mind, the first work on mental illness published in this country. It was used in medical schools for a half-century and marks the author as a forerunner of American psychiatry.

Nor was his fame only in medical science, for it was equally great in patriotic and humanitarian services. A deeply religious nature was the wellspring of his labor for others. Whatever his theological views at any period, he put religion to work. In Universalism he found a faith to match the amplitude of his concern for the good of all people. When Rush died, John Adams, a life-long friend, spoke for the multitude of the great and the humble: "As a man of science, letters, taste, sense, philosophy, patriotism, religion, morality, merit, usefulness, taken all together, Rush has not left his equal in America."

CHAPTER SIX

Hosea Ballou

1771-1852

New England midwinter is not the most pleasant time for an out-of-door baptism. But when a religious revival has been going on, and the devil has been driven from the community and many have been saved, baptism cannot wait for warm weather, lest in the meantime the evil one, routed but hopeful, return and reclaim souls.

And so it was that on a cold bleak Sunday afternoon in January, 1789, most of the people of the little village of Richmond, New Hampshire, and of the surrounding hills, gathered at the river for a baptizing. There were the solid members of the Baptist Church, some of them long since initiated into the holy mysteries. There were the old and the young wrapped in heavy coats, home-knit shawls, woolen mittens, and long tippets. There were children of assorted sizes all so completely bundled in blankets and quilts that only their chilled red noses were exposed to the frosty air. And there were the candidates, most of them girls and boys in their teens, lately persuaded to a fresh examination of the state of their souls, and led to commit themselves to the Christian way of living. Now by the ancient rite of baptism they would be publicly recognized and identified as Christians.

In the middle of the shallow river a great hole had been cut in the thick ice. Near the rim of this open space several people took their stand, with long wooded hay rakes continually stirring the surface of the water to keep it from freezing. The Reverend Isaac Kinney, pastor of the Baptist Church, made his way through the crowd, cautiously let himself down into the waist-deep icy water and, feeling with his feet the stony bed of the river, found a firm place to stand. The candidates for baptism formed a line across the ice, and the minister took them one at a time. With his left hand supporting the back, and taking a firm grip upon the clothing under the chin, he lowered the convert backward until completely immersed, repeating with each operation the ancient, solemn words; ''I baptise thee in the name of the Father, and of the Son, and of the Holy Ghost.''

Whatever hesitation the others may have felt at being immersed in ice-cold water there was one young man in the group for whom this ordeal had no terror. He was used to hardship and even went barefooted in the snow. His name was Hosea Ballou, and at the time of the baptism he was seventeen years old.

Hosea Ballou was the eleventh child in the family of a poor preacher. He lost his mother by death before he was two, never went to school until he was nineteen, and then for only a few weeks. He had no books in his childhood except the Bible, an old almanac, a battered dictionary, and a pamphlet on the Tower of Babel; and he grew up in a religious atmosphere as cheerless as the frigid waters of winter baptism. Yet he became a remarkable preacher, an able theologian, and the leader of American Universalism.

Hosea's father, the Reverend Maturin Ballou, left Rhode Island at the age of forty-five, where he had preached for fifteen years in Baptist churches, and took his wife Lydia and their eight children to the province of New Hampshire. Distant cousins had already settled in Richmond in the Mt. Monadnock region near the southwestern corner of the colony.

Here in the wilderness Maturin Ballou chose to begin a new life as a farmer and preacher. With such help as his children could give, a barn and house were built from timber cut from the forest, rails split for fences, and land cleared of trees, roots, and rocks, for the planting. Six days a week, from dawn to darkness the pioneer farmer labored on his land, and on Sundays preached without pay in the plain little meetinghouse where the members of his own household provided a large portion of the congregation. But with long hours of toil, only the scantiest of living could be wrung from the ground. The soil was stony and the growing season short for a fall crop of corn, turnips, and flax.

More children were born in the Ballou house, Hosea in 1771, about

58

four years after the family came to Richmond. While still an infant, Hosea was deprived of his mother. Worn out with hard work she died without medical care. With the mother gone and children to be fed and clothed, living conditions in the Ballou home did not improve, although perhaps the family was no poorer than others in the neighborhood. The settlement shared the privations common to American pioneer life. Richmond had no schools during Hosea's boyhood; there were few books in any of the homes; and farm work was done mostly with hand tools. The material for every garment worn by every member of the family came from flax field or sheep pasture, and was the product of spinning wheel and loom, and of patient fingers that knit, wove, or sewed.

Hosea, like every child on the frontier, shared the self-reliant struggle for existence, and he probably accepted it as normal, only in later years remembering his boyhood as one of hardship. He learned to milk cows, to drive oxen, to sow and reap, to handle axe and saw, and took his turn at standing watch in the pasture by night for wildcats that came down from the hills to kill the sheep. But Hosea thrived on hard work and plain food. He was remembered in after years as a tall, erect, muscular lad of vigorous health, with dark hair and blue eyes. Early and by himself he learned to read from the Bible, to write, and to do simple exercises in arithmetic.

The rigors of farm life were not more burdensome than the heavy weight of the Calvinist doctrines that Maturin Ballou placed upon his children. He was a person of meager education and gentle heart, and was fond of his family. But he believed and taught his sons and daughters that God willed endless punishment for most of the human race. In the Calvinist Baptist Church, of which Mr. Ballou was pastor, there had been a quarrel among the members about something long ago forgotten. One faction withdrew, started a rival church, and called a minister of its own. Later, in order to bring about a reconciliation, both Mr. Ballou and the other minister resigned, and the two congregations were joined under the leadership of the Reverend Mr. Kinney.

Nobody in the village noticed any change in Hosea's behavior following his conversion; he had always been a good boy. His mind, however, was occupied with a new interest. He had known no religious ideas except those taught by his father and his father's church. But now as a member of the church he wanted to know the reasons for the faith he had accepted. There was no use asking his father questions; he already knew what the answers would be. So he went to the Bible, and was disturbed to find many passages that seemed to contradict what he had been taught.

There was another reason for this new interest. Over in Warwick, about six miles away, a minister named Caleb Rich was preaching a strange doctrine called Universalism. He had come over to Richmond about the time Hosea joined the Baptist Church and had gathered a following, which later built a Universalist Church. There was strong resistance by the Calvinists, especially when some of the substantial members of the Baptist Church were won over, among them a family of Ballous, more or less blood relations of Maturin's. Hosea felt it to be his Christian duty to defend his Baptist faith. He spent hours with the Bible to discover texts to support his position and contended valiantly with the Universalists, but to his dismay was forced more and more to yield to their arguments.

The summer following his union with the Baptist Church, Hosea and an older brother went to New York state to work on a farm. Hosea took with him his Bible—and a heavy heart. At night, after long hours of toil, and on Sundays and rainy days when there was no work, he searched the scriptures for light. While laboring in the fields and in the quiet night hours he agonized over the questions that could not be shaken from his mind. Could it be that his father missed important passages in the Bible? Is the doctrine of "election" true? Is the great majority of humanity doomed to endless suffering? Hosea himself would be happy to have everybody saved; did the Creator feel less kindly toward persons? It was a lonely journey, with no guide except his Bible with its many and often confusing teachings, and his own sense of right.

At last the clouds rolled away. Although there remained parts of the Bible that raised questions for which he found no answers, he could no longer doubt the doctrine of universal salvation. Of this experience he wrote many years later: "Before I returned the next Fall my mind was quite settled in the consoling belief that God will finally have mercy on all men."

On returning home he learned with surprise and joy that his brother David, thirteen years his senior, now married and settled on a farm in Richmond, had joined the Universalists, and had taken to preaching. The father never accepted the faith of his sons. Indeed it must have seemed a deep mystery that with all their careful upbringing they could have strayed so far from "the true faith," and even more strange that they could find support for their heresy in the Holy Scriptures.

One Sunday afternoon as Hosea sat in the corner of the kitchen Maturin asked, "What is that book you are reading?" and Hosea answered, "A Universalist book." "I cannot allow a Universalist book in my house," declared the father. So Hosea walked out to the woodshed and in sight of the watchful parent hid it in the woodpile. After Hosea had gone to bed Maturin went to the woodpile, and discovered that the forbidden book was the Bible!

During the winter when Hosea was nineteen he lived with his brother David. Together they worked in the woods, cutting down the great elm trees and burning them for the manufacture of potash. Potash, used for soap making and other industries, was at this period the only crop that farmers in interior New England could exchange for hard cash. Long winter evenings gave time for Bible study. A private school, the first in Richmond, opened in the Quaker meeting house; and for a few weeks Hosea put down saw and axe to receive instruction in English grammar. This, his first schooling, was all too brief, but it awakened in him a great desire for more. There were so many interesting things to be learned, and he was made aware as never before of the vastness of his ignorance. For several summers after the haying was done at home he had worked for wages on neighboring farms and had saved a little money. Now he decided to spend it to the last penny in the great adventure; he would go to Chesterfield Academy for an entire term. He got his money's worth, absorbing so much from his studies that at the end of the term he was granted a certificate that declared that he was prepared to teach school.

In September, 1791, Hosea went with David to the New England General Convention of Universalists at Oxford, Massachusetts. This was an exciting experience. He had heard Caleb Rich preach in Richmond, and through him had learned that Universalism had gained a foothold in communities on the Atlantic Coast. He knew the names of the preachers, but now he saw and heard them, even the Reverend John Murray, the distinguished minister in Gloucester. At the Convention there were many sermons, eloquent and long, and discussions of plans for extension of the faith. Nobody guessed that for the future of Universalism the most important person present was a silent farm boy from Richmond, in homespun clothes, who came to listen and to see. In Hosea's heart there throbbed a new hope. This was his moment of decision; he had heard the "call" to preach.

In Hosea Ballou's day there were many preachers, even among the ordained, who earned all or part of their living outside the ministry. Hosea followed this practice for three or four years, teaching school during the day and on evenings and Sundays preaching wherever there was opportunity. It was not long before he began to attract attention. His preaching was clear, logical, and, of course, scriptural. He used the simple language of the country people, and never left them in doubt that there were sharp differences between Universalism and the ideas of limited salvation deeply rooted in New England religions. He welcomed questions, discussion and debate, relying upon a knowledge of the Scriptures and his own good sense and sound reasoning. He found time from his teachings to go on missionary journeys, preaching wherever he was promised a hearing, and wherever a meeting place could be found—in churches, schoolhouses, barns, groves, or open fields. It was not long before his labors were brought to the attention of fellow ministers. He was ordained at the New England Convention in Oxford in 1794.

So far as anybody knew, Hosea, completely absorbed in his studies, school teaching, and missionary preaching, never in his young adulthood had a love affair. At twenty-five he was still unclaimed. His friends thought something should be done lest he pass over the brink into habitual bachelorhood. Brother Caleb Rich, always concerned for the welfare of his young friend, came to the rescue. In the town of Williamsburg, Massachusetts, was a young lady named Ruth Washburn. She was intelligent and attractive, and her parents were Universalists. Mr. Rich told her about the roving preacher, a good-looking six-footer of two hundred pounds, a lonely young man who possessed all the qualifications of an ideal mate. He then went to Hosea, explained the hazards of an unmarried minister, and told him that he would miss the chance of a lifetime if he did not woo and win the heart of the Williamsburg maiden. There was, Caleb Rich admitted, one fault in the young woman—she was only seventeen, but, he observed, time would remove this one defect in an otherwise perfect prize.

This questionable matchmaking actually turned out well. Hosea Ballou and Ruth Washburn were married and had a long happy life together. Brother Rich was rewarded with the honor of performing the ceremony. The Ballous went to live in Dana, Massachusetts (then part of the township of Hardwick). He had a circuit of a half-dozen preaching points that together paid a salary of five dollars a week.

Somehow the young couple managed to acquire furniture and to buy a horse and buggy.

Religion during the American Revolution had been at a low ebb, but now a great wave of interest was sweeping over the land. Religious revivals and camp meetings became the chief excitement in every town and hamlet that could attract an evangelist and borrow a tent large enough to hold the crowds. It was a time of fanatical zeal and heated controversy. Hosea Ballou was a controversial figure, not because he was contrary or quarrelsome, but because of circumstances. Wherever he preached he aroused opposition. A common form of attack was through newspaper articles and pamphlets written by ministers. Ballou was a hard person to beat in written argument or in platform debate. He had a keen mind and plenty of scriptural brickbats, and in defense of his religion learned to use both with unusual skill. Yet he was always courteous, never returning the bad names that were hurled at him.

During the six years in Dana, his reputation for forceful speaking spread to the outposts of Universalism and there was constant demand for his services. He made journeys to Rhode Island and Vermont, to Cape Ann in Massachusetts, and to New York state. John Murray, when planning one of his visits to Philadelphia, engaged Ballou to occupy his Boston pulpit for ten Sundays. These two preachers were not in agreement on all theological subjects. Ballou at this time had moved toward a Unitarian position in regard to the nature of Jesus, a view Murray could not accept. They were, nevertheless, friends, respecting each other and united in a common cause.

The young country preacher was well received by Murray's Boston congregation and his unfamiliar teaching was accepted with increasing interest from Sunday to Sunday. At the final service, however, Mrs. Murray, unhappy over what seemed to her a dangerous heresy, sent a message to the singing gallery to be read to the congregation. Just as the minister was about to announce the closing hymn a voice from the choir loft boomed forth: "I wish to give notice that the doctrine which has been preached here this afternoon is not the doctrine which is usually preached in this house." Mr. Ballou calmly stated: "The audience will please take notice of what our brother has said." He then announced the hymn, it was sung, and the people dismissed. That evening a committee from the church called on Mr. Ballou, apologized for the incident, and assured him that the congregation disapproved of the discourtesy that had been shown him.

Early in 1803, Ballou moved his family to Barnard, Vermont. There were then four children. Of the Ballous' eleven children, two died in infancy. The older ministers saw Vermont as a promising field for Universalism and urged Ballou to take up his labors there. Already there were Universalist churches in seven villages in the state, and in other communities meetings were held. The minister in Barnard, where a new meetinghouse had been built, would serve a wide circuit of surrounding towns.

At the turn of the century Vermont was experiencing a real estate boom. Land was cheaper here than in southern New England. Young people with pioneering blood left the settlements in Massachusetts and Connecticut to match their strength against the untamed wilderness. Whole families moved northward with household goods, cattle, and potash kettles. The Green Mountain Boys under the lusty leadership of Ethan Allen had chased the Yorkers out of the New Hampshire grants, beaten the British at their game of political horse trading, and saved the tough little republic for the Union. Vermont had become the fourteenth state twelve years before Ballou's arrival in the little town of Barnard.

This raw new hill country was a congenial place for rugged thinking. Vermonters liked to make up their own minds, whether in politics or religion. Ethan Allen in 1784 had published his *Reason the Only Oracle of Man.* This book, condemned by the orthodox ministers as the work of the devil, boldly and boisterously blasted the doctrine of the Trinity, revelation and election, belief in miracles, and belief in prayer as a means of changing the mind of God, and much else aimed at what Allen called "the ghostly tyranny of the clergy." Allen's book, notwithstanding his bombast and rough words, advanced many opinions that in later years were voiced (in milder language) by Universalists and Unitarians. Because of the limited number of copies available, Allen's book was not read by many, not even by those who roundly assailed it. Its contents, however, became known and were discussed not only in ministers' meetings but also at the cracker barrel sessions in every country store and blacksmith shop in Vermont. Thomas Paine's *Age of Reason,* written ten years later than Allen's book, was widely distributed over the state and won many to the author's deistic doctrines.

The Universalists disclaimed Ethan Allen, although none of them made a stronger argument than he against the belief in endless punishment. Ethan did not accept the Universalists either; when asked if he were a Universalist he said: "No, for there must be a hell, otherwise where would Yorkers go to when they die?"

Hosea Ballou did not escape the free thinking that flourished in Vermont. For several years he had been moving toward a Unitarian position in his view of Jesus. In 1805 he published *A Treatise on Atonement*, in which can be traced the influence of the deistic writings. Ballou's book brought together for the first time in America the points of liberal Christian theology opposing the Calvinist doctrine. It set forth arguments for the rightful use of human reason in understanding the Scriptures, the complete oneness and unchanging goodness of God, and humanity's inability to defeat God's purpose to save all people.

The most radical departure from beliefs commonly held among Universalists of that period was Ballou's theory of the atonement. John Murray and his followers in New England believed in the fall of humanity through Adam and in humanity's redemption through Christ. This redemption was the Calvinist atonement extended to all people. Ballou rejected as unjust the notion that Christ died to pacify an angry God, and argued that Jesus came to bring humanity to God, not God to humanity.

After six years in Vermont, Ballou became minister of the Universalist Church in Portsmouth, New Hampshire. Here he remained for another six years, and then moved to Salem, Massachusetts, for two years. In the meantime, the more progressive Universalists in Boston had set about building a church on School Street. They were restless under the mild teachings of the minister in the First Universalist Church where John Murray had been pastor until his death in 1815. They were ready to hear a strong voice of the Universalist gospel as it was set forth in *A Treatise on Atonement*. Ballou accepted a call to the new church, and began his work on New Year's Day, 1818, at the age of forty-six.

His coming to Boston was an important event, for there was not an outspoken voice for the liberal cause at that time in the city. The ministers and congregations, later to become Unitarian, were still within the Congregational churches. William Ellery Channing, whose Boston pastorate had begun fifteen years before Ballou's arrival, had not yet openly declared his Unitarian convictions. Ballou at once attracted large congregations. The church seated nearly a thousand people. For more than thirty years, it was usually necessary to hold three preaching services on Sundays to accommodate the throngs who came to hear him.

Ballou with his tall straight figure was a commanding presence in the pulpit. The long black coat and wide-brimmed silk hat he wore became increasingly familiar on the streets of Boston as he went about the city, visiting the sick and ministering to all who needed him. He was a good pastor as well as a popular preacher. The Boston pastorate was primarily a teaching ministry. On occasion he spoke out on political questions and was active in reform movements. His emphasis, however, was on correcting ancient theological errors and on making known the larger promises for humanity that he found in the Scriptures. Always he relied upon the Bible for support of his teachings, and never doubted that it contained a revelation from God. Although he moved toward modern Universalist and Unitarian views, he never abandoned the idea that Jesus possessed supernatural powers.

He did not draw all Universalists into the orbit of his convictions. In 1841, twenty ministers and an unknown number of persons who could not go along with Ballou's view that there was no punishment for sin after death withdrew from the denomination, took the name *Restorationists,* and remained apart from the parent body for ten years. Ballou was not the first Universalist to hold the view that there was no punishment for sin after death. Abel Sarjent of Pennsylvania, in 1793, vigorously defended the doctrine of no future punishment. Caleb Rich, from whom Ballou received instruction, openly declared that the consequences of sin were only in earthly life.

In 1819 Ballou became the first editor of *The Universalist Magazine* (later named *The Universalist Leader*). For many years a controversy was carried on in this paper between the followers of Ballou and those who opposed his views. He published both sides, never yielding his own right to set forth his own opinions.

His death in 1852, at eighty-one, brought to a close a long and remarkable career. His fellow Universalists had long called him "Father Ballou," the name still spoken with affection and reverence. Ballou was not the architect of modern Universalism, but he was the craftsperson of Universalism in his generation.

CHAPTER SEVEN

Abner Kneeland
1774-1844

Abner Kneeland is known chiefly for having been thrown into a Boston jail for blasphemy. But there was more to his life than the dramatic conflict with the Massachusetts courts of justice. He was an important as well as controversial figure in Universalist history, and was a stalwart champion of civil liberties. Of more than usual ability, he was carpenter, teacher, preacher, editor, politician, and promoter of the first colony in what is now the state of Iowa. For twenty-five years he served Universalist churches with honest effort, contributed generously to the denomination's output of doctrinal literature, and advanced ideas in the field of religion and sociology that were a century ahead of his time.

The sixth child of Timothy Kneeland and Marie Stone Kneeland was born in Gardner, Massachusetts, on April 7, 1774, the eve of the American Revolution. Originally the Kneelands were a Scotch clan with ancestry dating back to the days of Robert Bruce. They were early immigrants to America. Abner descended from Edward K. Kneeland, who settled in Ipswich, Massachusetts, about 1630, and from Captain John Stone, a member of the Plymouth Colony.

Timothy Kneeland, Abner's father, was the third settler in Gardner, coming through the forests from Harvard by following a trail marked with notches on the trees. He took up land west of the present site of the village and made a comfortable living by farming and carpentry. He served three and a half years in the Revolutionary War.

Northern Massachusetts was mostly wilderness when Abner was born. One afternoon when he was a baby his mother carried him to visit a neighbor. Coming home she lost her way and wandered several miles in the woods. Night came on, and, exhausted, she sat down with the child on a log to rest. Suddenly in the darkness came the crashing sound of some animal coming toward them, perhaps a bear or a wolf. She screamed in fright and was answered by the friendly barking of her own dog, who led the way home.

Abner's childhood was much like that of other children who grew up in the frontier life of America. His parents were plain people who, by hard work, provided a good home for their children. His formal education was limited to what the school in Gardner offered and one term in the Academy in Chesterfield, New Hampshire. He was an ambitious student, however, and by his own efforts learned Latin, Greek, and Hebrew. He was handy with tools, learned the carpenter trade, and at an early age began teaching school. When he was about twenty-one, Abner was given charge of a school in Dummerston, Vermont. Two years later he married Waitstell Ormsbee.

A Baptist Church in the nearby town of Putney was without a minister. Kneeland was invited to supply the pulpit and later was taken on as the regular pastor. In the beginning the people were pleased with his preaching. He spoke well, was interesting and inspiring, and had an impressive manner in the pulpit. Soon, however, they detected a change in his sermons, especially in the Biblical passages quoted, which seemed to stress teachings at variance with sound Baptist doctrine. The fact was that their minister had come across a book by Elhanan Winchester, a Universalist preacher in Philadelphia, and had become convinced of the truth of Universalism. He evaded a heresy trial by obtaining a Universalist license to preach and taking a Universalist Church in Langdon, New Hampshire. He was ordained at Langdon in 1805. Hosea Ballou preached the ordination sermon and, in the name of the Universalist Convention, accepted Kneeland into fellowship.

During the six years in Langdon, Abner Kneeland became known throughout the region as a strong preacher and a ready defender of his adopted faith. He wrote and circulated tracts and preached wherever there was an opening for spreading the gospel of Universalism. Due to his influence four orthodox ministers in adjacent towns came over to the Universalist ministry. Besides preaching and pamphleteering he served two years in the New Hampshire legislature.

In 1807, at the Universalist General Convention in Newtown, Connecticut, Kneeland was elected clerk of this body, an office he held for eight years. He was also named, along with Hosea Ballou, to a committee to produce a Universalist hymnbook. Of the four hundred and ten hymns that came of this effort, Kneeland wrote one hundred and thirty-eight. They were not very good hymns.

The years at Langdon were on the whole pleasant and fruitful. Mr. Kneeland was becoming recognized as an able minister and was growing in favor in the denomination. But while they were there his wife and child died, and he wanted to get away from the scene of his loss. In Charlestown, Massachusetts, a new church had been built by some former members of the First Universalist Church in Boston who found the preaching of John Murray behind the times. Looking for a minister with liberal ideas, they extended a call to Mr. Kneeland. He had subscribed to the views of Hosea Ballou as set forth in *A Treatise on Atonement*, which were quite acceptable to the new congregation. Kneeland was installed, in the autumn of 1811, at the dedication service of the new building as the first minister of the Society. Reverend Hosea Ballou preached the sermon.

The new minister had troubles from the start. The Society was in debt; the members, mostly young people, were severely limited in income. When hard times came with the War of 1812, the congregation fell behind in paying the minister's salary. Kneeland, in the meantime, had married a widow who had been left with a large store in Salem. To provide an income and to help his wife, he went into the mercantile business with her. When he found that business took too much time from parish work, he resigned from the church three years after his installation.

Some of Kneeland's fellow ministers expressed disapproval of him for leaving the church for business. In later years, when he had become an outcast from the church, this old issue was dug up and given an interpretation designed to place him in a bad light. It is possible, however, that these ministers were less shocked by his secular employment than by the heretical ideas that he preached and published freely. For some time he had been plagued by doubt that the Bible was the revealed Word of God. He carried on a lengthy correspondence with his friend Hosea Ballou on this subject, but Ballou failed to put his mind at ease. Kneeland reached the conviction that although the Scriptures contained valuable teachings they came out of human experience and not by divine revelation. This idea in Kneeland's day was heresy among Christians, including Universalists and Unitarians.

According to his own testimony, Kneeland never meant to give up the ministry. After two years in business he was back in the pulpit, this time in a small Universalist Church in New York State. He remained for two years and then, in 1817, was called to the Lombard Street Universalist Church in Philadelphia. Here he had the longest and most successful pastorate of his career.

Abner Kneeland's arrival in Philadelphia began a new era for Universalism in that city. The Lombard Street Church, organized in 1793 by a remnant of the members from the church founded in 1790, had a history of instability and dissension. Members were forever quarreling among themselves. One group had split off and formed a new movement that soon failed. There had been no settled minister for the past six years, and only infrequent religious services.

With Kneeland's pastorate came a new beginning. All his predecessors in the Lombard Street Church were Trinitarians. Kneeland held Unitarian views. Previous ministers believed in punishment after death for sins committed in this world; Kneeland held with Hosea Ballou that there was no future punishment. The new minister began his pastorate with a series of eight addresses proclaiming his religious convictions. A few members unable to put up with his advanced opinions left. Most of them stayed and many others drawn by his liberal gospel joined the church.

Within two years Universalism in the city had prospered to the point where a second church was possible. It was organized in 1820 as the Second Universalist Church, now the Universalist Church of the Restoration, and a substantial building was erected to house the growing congregation. Mr. Kneeland, with the help of an associate pastor, ministered to both churches. He edited a Universalist magazine, went on preaching missions to the south, took on every orthodox preacher willing to debate with him, and in his spare time published a New Testament translated from the Greek. He also created a new kind of spelling book that made an attempt to abolish silent letters. This work was endorsed by teachers and other professional people, but was never accepted by the public.

The Rev. Abel C. Thomas of Philadelphia described Kneeland in the following manner:

He was certainly the most venerable man I ever saw in the pulpit. His commanding presence, slightly florid complexion, all-illuminating blue eyes; his voice never boisterous, his temper never ruffled, not eloquent according to received standards, but wonderfully impressive in calmness and persuasive candor—remarkably self-possessed: All these qualities have fastened him in my memory as a man rarely if ever excelled in the pulpit....Out of the pulpit, also he was remarkable. He was tall and erect, and there was a quiet dignity in all his movements....It is questionable whether even a pursuing mob would have quickened his steps into a hurry; nor can any one who knew him forget his serene courtesy in social life. Besides all this, his moral character was as clear of blemish as we can reasonably hope to see anywhere.

After seven years in Philadelphia, Mr. Kneeland went to New York City as pastor of the Prince Street Universalist Church. One of the most conservative churches in the denomination, it was no place for Abner Kneeland. While in Philadelphia he had asssociated with the followers of Joseph Priestley and others of a liberal mind, and he had grown more and more radical. The congregation at Prince Street, on the other hand, had known no Universalism beyond that of the followers of Murray. In no time at all Kneeland was in trouble with the trustees of the Church. This finally led to a serious division among the members and to his resignation.

After leaving the Prince Street Church he at once became editor of the *Olive Branch*, a Universalist weekly, sponsored by the New York Universalist Book Society, of which he was president. The first page of the paper carried a picture of a dove bearing the emblem of peace. The contents of the publication, however, were hardly designed to give peace of mind to the readers. The editor used its pages to express his extreme views on the backwardness of the churches, and reserved for the Universalists his most scathing words. His denunciations cost him the confidence of many of his Universalist friends. Even so, he had followers, some of whom were from his former Prince Street congregation. They formed the Second Universalist Society, held meetings in Tammany Hall and made Mr. Kneeland their minister. This church had a modest degree of prosperity, but a crisis was just around the corner. Frances Wright, the much-discussed social reformer, came to New York. Kneeland had her speak in his pulpit. Frances Wright, born in Scotland, was a radical philanthropist. In 1825, she came to America and purchased a large tract of land in Tennessee where she carried on an experiment for improving the economic and cultural life of Negroes. At the time Wright was associated with the German community of religious socialists in New Harmony, Indiana, and also with the Robert Owen colony. She was looked upon with suspicion, and her lectures on religious, social, and political issues caused great resentment among the churches and the newspapers in America. Kneeland, who made no secret of his sympathy with the cooperative movements being promoted in several parts of the country, was dismissed from the church.

These were dark days for Mr. Kneeland. Many of the Universalist ministers, some friends of long standing, no longer recognized him as one of them. The year after he was discharged from the Second Church, he attended a gathering of the Southern Association of Universalists held in Hartford, Connecticut. There in the presence of friends and foes he made a clear and dignified statement of his theological position and asked that his Universalist fellowship be continued. This was refused; after a quarter of a century of ministerial labor his fellowship was withdrawn. His dismissal was not without some justification. The Universalists were under constant attack by those who called them fanatics and atheists. Kneeland's extreme opinions, stated in unrestrained language, were an embarrassment and a hindrance that the ministers and churches could ill afford.

He still had sympathizers in the Second Church. They followed him into a new venture, a Free Thought organization called the Moral Philanthropists. They met in a hired hall and Kneeland lectured on problems of the day, philosophy, and religion, not forgetting to point out the errors in Christian doctrine, and the shortcomings of the clergy.

Kneeland called himself a pantheist, never an atheist, although he was repeatedly given this name by others. He was roundly criticized by his fellow ministers for what they termed a fickle nature, "blown about by every wind of doctrine." They had not, however, thought him fickle when earlier he had changed from the Baptist church to Universalism.

In 1831, Kneeland left New York for Boston. There he started a weekly paper, the *Boston Investigator*, the first rationalist journal in America, and became the leader of the First Society of Free Inquirers. The paper and lectures brought him fame among Free Thought people throughout the country. Speaking tours took him south and west. Especially in Philadelphia and New York he was in demand, and his lectures drew a large hearing. In Philadelphia on the occasion of the celebration of Thomas Paine's birthday, Kneeland was toasted as "the greatest obstacle to the New England clergy."

The Investigator, which began with only two hundred and fifty subscribers and never had more than two thousand, nevertheless attracted attention and stirred up trouble. Those were rousing times in the intellectual and religious life of Boston. William Ellery Channing, Theodore Parker, Hosea Ballou, and Ralph Waldo Emerson were speaking and writing in the interest of fresher and broader movements of thought. Kneeland's Investigator, with all its bombast and inelegant language, nevertheless was found on the side of intellectual and political freedom. Its stated purpose was "the protection and development of American principles." It took up the cause of improving labor conditions, advocated a ten-hour working day at a time when men, women, and children worked in factories for twelve or fourteen hours. The editor called for the abolition of slavery and of imprisonment for debt. He championed land reform in behalf of farmers and proposed publicly supported education for all children. He insisted on the rights of women and favored the practice of birth control. Above all, the editor stood for freedom to think, speak, and write; he was against all authority in religion except the authority of reason and conscience.

Kneeland's tirades against accepted Christian doctrines raised wrath among the staid church people of Boston. Even Universalists and Unitarians, some of whom shared his agnostic opinions, were embarrassed by his public statements. Something had to be done to stop this public nuisance, they felt. The Investigator, on December 20, 1833, came out with an issue that inflamed the righteous. It contained three offensive articles. Two of them were copied from the Free Inquirer, a Free Thought newspaper in New York. One was written by Kneeland himself. He had been encouraged by the editor of the Trumpet and Universalist Magazine to state his theological position so that those who still regarded him as a Universalist could judge for themselves. The article in the Investigator was part of Kneeland's letter that appeared about the same time as the denominational magazine. Somebody turned the offending number of the Investigator over to the Grand Jury of Massachusetts. Kneeland was arrested and indicted for blasphemy.

The Kneeland article printed in his paper was as follows:

1. Universalists believe in a God which I do not; but believe that their God, with all his moral attributes (aside from nature

itself) is nothing more than a chimera of their own imagination.

2. Universalists believe in Christ, which I do not; but believe that the whole story concerning him is as much a fable and fiction as that of the god Prometheus, the tragedy of whose death is said to have been acted on the stage of the theater in Athens five hundred years before the Christian era.

3. Universalists believe in miracles, which I do not; but believe that every pretension to them can be accounted for on natural principles, or else is to be attributed to mere trick and imposture.

4. Universalists believe in the resurrection of the dead, in immortality and eternal life, which I do not; but believe that all life is mortal, that death is an extinction of life to the individual who possesses it and that no individual life is, ever was, or ever will be eternal.

Kneeland was brought to trial the following January in the municipal court of Boston, presided over by Judge Peter O. Thatcher, a deacon in the Unitarian Church in Brattle Square. The state's attorney was S. D. Parker, who referred to Kneeland as "a conceited, poor, weak mortal" who was attempting to destroy Christianity, the foundation of civilization. He relied for the conviction of blasphemy upon the single statement, "Universalists believe in a God which I do not." All the other items in the *Investigator* were withdrawn.

Kneeland's lawyer, Andrew Dunlap, a Unitarian, argued that the Massachusetts law relating to blasphemy was contrary to the United States Constitution and that the accused was within his legal rights in publishing his views on religion. The judge in charging the jury left them in no doubt that the law against blasphemy was a good law, that Kneeland had broken the law, and that the verdict should be "guilty." It took the jury only five minutes to find the defendant guilty. The judge sentenced Kneeland to three months in the common jail.

Kneeland appealed his case to the state Supreme Court, where it was tried four months later before Judge Samuel Putnam. The jury reported that a unanimous decision could not be reached. Eleven Christians found Kneeland guilty, but one juror, Charles G. Greene, held out for acquittal. The jury was dismissed and the case turned over to a third trial.

This time the Attorney General of the Commonwealth of Massachusetts, James T. Austin, was prosecutor. His denunciation of Kneeland was even more extreme than Parker's; he declared that no punishment was too severe for such a public enemy. On the final trial Kneeland argued his own case. He claimed that the law against blasphemy, on which the indictment was based, was contrary to the Constitution of Masachusetts, and also in conflict with the First Amendment of the Constitution of the United States. He also maintained that the words in the *Investigator*, when properly interpreted, were not blasphemy, but only a denial of the kind of God in which the Universalists believe. The court had over and over again referred to him as an atheist. This term he refused to accept as a true representation of his views. "I had no occasion," he declared, "to deny that there is a God; I believe that the whole universe is nature, and that God and nature are synonymous terms. I believe in a God that embraces all power, wisdom, justice, and goodness. Everything is God. I am not an atheist, but a pantheist."

After seven hours of wrangling the jury could not agree and was dismissed. The following year a new trial was held before the full bench of the Supreme Court. It took three more years to reach a decision. In March, 1838, this Court, by a majority of one, finally acted to uphold the verdict of the municipal court. Abner Kneeland then went to jail for sixty days.

The imprisonment of Kneeland raised a great furor in Boston and throughout the country. On the one hand were those who, with the prevailing intolerance, regretted that the full penalty of the law was not exacted. On the other hand were those who felt that the state in prosecuting and convicting Mr. Kneeland had been sadly misguided. No one, not even his severest critics who questioned his opinions, ever doubted that he was a person of good character. The editor of the *Boston Advocate* called the prosecution "persecution" and wrote of the action of the Court, "It will stamp another indelible page of shame on the history of Massachusetts, to be added to the record of four Quakers hung in 1669, and nineteen witches in 1692."

The editor of the *Universalist Evangelical Magazine and Gospel Advocate* wrote in the issue of July 20, 1838 a lengthy protest of the treatment accorded Kneeland, saying in part:

The particular words that drew on him the vengeance of an absurd, dangerous and wicked law, fit only for superstitious and ignorant ages and a despotic land were "Universalists believe in a God, which I do not" . . . and on this charge, in this age of toleration and in this land of civil and religious freedom, an aged man was dragged from his family and home, and incarcerated in a prison! Reader, do not your ears tingle and your cheeks burn as you reflect on this melanchology exhibition of our right of speech and freedom of conscience and of the press?

At all events I hope the people of Masaschusetts will demand the repeal of the law—it is a disgrace to the statute book—to the country—the age. Enforcing it will but make cowards, and hypocrites and enlist the sympathies of the noble hearted in favor of bold atheists and skeptics.

Let me not be misunderstood. For Abner Kneeland's opinions I have no fellowship—no charity....but Mr. Kneeland has the same right to his faith, or no faith, that I have to believe in the Gospel of Jesus....his persecution will also give him tenfold influence and importance as an advocate of his theory. On the score of policy—of settled opposition to his views—as well as of humanity and justice—I most solemnly protest against his persecution and punishment.

The Reverend William Ellery Channing drew up a petition to the Governor asking for pardon for Kneeland. It was signed by 170 people who, without expressing sympathy with Kneeland's ideas, nevertheless regarded the affair as an outrage against human rights, freedom of the press, and freedom of speech. The petition was denied. The Reverend Theodore Parker wrote to a friend, "Abner was jugged for sixty days; but he will come out as beer from a bottle, all foaming, and will make others foam."

From his prison cell Kneeland wrote an open letter to his friends:

Fellow-citizens! Countrymen! and Lovers of Liberty!!! Sixty-three years ago a battle was fought on Bunker Hill in plain sight of my window where I now am. But what was it all for? LIBERTY! And what am I here for? For the honest exercise of that very *Liberty* for which our fathers fought and bled.

He decided to go west, to the new territory of Iowa. He was now sixty-five. The east had persecuted and imprisoned him. The denomination to which he had given the best years of his life had rejected him. He would go away where he might find freedom and understanding, gather likeminded people into a new settlement, and live in peace. He chose a place on the Des Moines River, Van Buren County, naming it Salubria, and advertised it as a desirable place for emigration.

Early in the spring of 1839, he set out alone for the western frontier, stopping on the way in Providence, New York, Philadelphia, and Cincinnati to make speeches. He traveled mostly by boat, down the Ohio from Cincinnati, then up the Mississippi. His family followed, arriving in Salubria in July after twenty-one days of travel. At first the family lived in a log cabin as did all the other settlers. But soon Mr. Kneeland designed and, with the help of his stepson, built a large two-story frame house, the finest in the county. He cleared land for a farm, gave lectures on radical religion, wrote for the *Boston Investigator*, corresponded with his lifelong friend Hosea Ballou, and taught school for a while. He also entered politics, was chosen chairperson of the Van Buren County Democratic Convention, and ran unsuccessfully for the upper house of the Iowa legislature, losing because of his reputation as an infidel.

Salubria never became a town, but only a neighborhood of scattered families—people of congenial thought on religious matters. They had large families and were great readers. Home life and wholesome conditions for children and young people were regarded as of first importance. Mr. Kneeland was friend and helper of old and young, and his home was a center for fellowship and edification. All doors were open to this "fine-looking, venerable, white-haired man."

He died suddenly on September 25, 1844, much hated and much loved. With his death, his Salubria community declined, but the influence known in the territory as "Kneelandism" long remained to plague the orthodox missionaries sent from the eastern churches to save the frontier. Abner Kneeland was the most controversial character ever ordained to the Universalist ministry. He anticipated by a century opinions now held without opposition or curiosity in Unitarian and Universalist churches. He would not be considered a heretic today, but in his own day, despite the already radical nature of the Universalist movement, he was ostracized and evicted from ministerial fellowship.

CHAPTER EIGHT

William Ellery Channing
1780-1842

William Ellery Channing, a great leader of Unitarianism, was brought up in the strict religious teachings of the Puritans. When he was a small boy in Newport, Rhode Island, his father took him to a nearby village to hear a Calvinist preacher who was drawing large crowds to revival meetings. This preacher was plainspoken in his sermon, making it quite clear that God was angry with the world, that all people were sinners, and that, except for a very few, they were going to a place of everlasting torture after death.

These ideas, while common enough, were made plain to the young boy for the first time. On Sundays he had often sat in the family pew of his home church and listened, more or less, to the long, scholarly sermons of pastor Hopkins, but was never quite sure what the saintly old man was talking about. Now he knew what he was expected to believe: that the world was bad, the people in it were bad, and the worst was yet to come!

When the long, noisy sermon at the revival meeting was over, the congregation rose to sing praises to God, and the little boy wondered why a being who chose to send souls to hell should be praised. Beside his father in the carriage on he way home, William saw the flowers by the wayside, and looked at the clear blue sky. Frequently, at a turn in the country road, he caught a glimpse of the sea with its rolling waves catching the sunlight. To him the earth seemed not bad, but beautiful. And his father was whistling a gay tune and seemed to be happy in spite of the terrible words of doom they had heard. Furthermore, when they reached home, his father ate a hearty dinner and sat in his easy chair with the newspaper, unmindful of the awful fate which awaited neighbors and friends—perhaps even himself and family!

William was born on April 7, 1780, in the midst of the Revolutionary War. His parents were William Channing, a lawyer, and Lucy Ellery Channing, the daughter of William Ellery, member of Congress and signer of the Declaration of Independence. William was the third child. The Channing home was a large wooden house, with a garden at the back and a broad field that became a playground for the children. There was work as well as play in this Puritan New England household. William had his chores along with the others, helping in the garden, keeping the woodbox filled, and, in winter, clearing snow from the sidewalks and from the driveway to the barn.

Newport was an interesting place for a growing child. The village, built on the hills above the well-protected harbor of Narragansett Bay, overlooked the Atlantic Ocean to the south and east. British soldiers had occupied the town for a time during the Revolution and had destroyed many of the buildings, but there were some fine old houses still standing. Behind the village were farms with their creaking windmills and fertile fields. The inner harbor, filled with fishing schooners and vessels from far lands manned by sailors with foreign language and strange manners, was a never-failing source of interest. William liked best the great cliffs and crags that stopped the huge waves in storms and the long stretch of beach where he played on pleasant days.

William played hard and worked hard. When he entered school, although smaller than the other children, he could hold his own in their games, whether in wrestling, or climbing the tall masts of the ships in the harbor. He was a bright-eyed lad with brown curly hair and friendly ways that made him a favorite among the people in the village.

Often he thought about what the preacher had said about people being completely bad. People did not seem to be as bad as they were pictured in church. Sometimes, as he walked the streets, he heard persons use swear words. There were those who drank liquor, and those who kept slaves, and some ship owners who were slave traders. But not even these seemed to merit the unending punishment the preacher said was in store for them. And then there were those he knew were good, his kind though somewhat reserved father, his gentle and patient mother, and the grandparents he adored. There was the invalid aunt who lived alone, shut out of the busy world, but who was as cheerful as the children who visited her and listened to her marvelous stories of Indians and the adventures of Old Testament heroes. There was Father Thurston, a poor man who did his best to help everyone. He earned a scanty living by fashioning casks and tubs but, when he learned the casks were used for liquor, refused, at severe cost to himself, to make more. Then there were the three friendly blacks who had been slaves owned by Grandfather John Channing. After the Revolution he had given them freedom, but they continued to work for their former master. The Channing children included them in the family circle.

When William thought about persons such as these and remembered the stories he had read of noble, faithful lives, he dared to question, ''Did the preacher know the truth about the world and God and people? Could his father really believe the preacher and then go on as usual enjoying his dinner and his newspaper?'' He could not be certain now of the answers to these questions, but in the years ahead he was to find the answers, not only for himself but for others who doubted, as he was doubting now, the kind of religion they had been taught in childhood.

It was planned that William should go to Harvard College to prepare to take up his father's profession. To enter Harvard more preparation was necessary than the Newport schools could provide. Therefore, he was to go to his uncle, a minister in New London, Connecticut, who would prepare him for college. William was thirteen and had never been away from home. There were now eight sisters and brothers to whom he must bid good-bye, as well as mother and father and a host of friends. It was a tearful parting.

The uncle proved to be an exacting teacher and William studied hard. At the end of the year he was ready for college. His return home was saddened by his father's death. The family was not left destitute, but the capable lawyer with many dependents had saved little. William and his older brother Francis, already at Harvard, talked over the family affairs and agreed that they could best help their mother by doing well at college and preparing themselves for the practice of law. William joined his brother at Harvard in 1794, at the age of fourteen.

In college Channing not only studied diligently, outstripping

many of the older students, but also did a good deal of thinkin
himself and what to do with his life. Before his graduation
he resolved to be a Christian minister. This meant further study, not
of law but of theology.

Unwilling to draw upon the family's financial resources for further education, he accepted a position as tutor to the children of the
wealthy Randolph family in Richmond, Virginia. Mr. Randolph
provided a schoolroom for his children and a few other students who
joined the classes, making twelve pupils in all. Here Channing had
his living quarters.

This period of a year and a half in Richmond was one of great
consequence in his later life. Here he saw the system of slavery close
at hand and observed the aristocratic life of the south that was built
upon the ownership of slaves. The time would come when his voice
would be heard across the land demanding that this inhuman practice come to an end. He spent long hours in study, discovered the
writings of Thomas Jefferson, and read books on the ideas and events
of the French Revolution. Here, far from family and friends and in
the quiet hours of night, Channing formed views that he held all his
life about the natural goodness of human beings and the freedom
necessary to protect and to promote this goodness.

He also got some foolish notions into his head. Among them was
the idea that it was wrong to give attention to bodily needs, and that
he could improve his soul by denying himself sufficient food, clothing, and sleep. He studied far into the night, ate scarcely enough to
keep alive, and slept on the bare floor. During the Christmas season,
there was a continuous round of dinners, dances, and musical concerts in the Randolph home. The children were excused from their
lessons and the teacher was invited to share in the celebrations. But
poor William had spent his salary on books and had no suitable clothes
to join in the merry-making. Probably, also, he had resolved to forego worldly pleasure. At any rate, the forelorn young man spent the
holidays by himself, and, on Christmas Day, felt homesick for his family far to the north.

His term of employment over, Channing returned home. He was
worn out from overwork, and weak because of the unwise neglect
of his health. To make matters worse, he took passage from Richmond
on an old battered coal-carrying sloop because the fare was cheap.
It was leaking and damp and had no place where the lone passenger
could get in out of the wind and rain. Furthermore, the captain and

crew got drunk and ran the vessel upon a shoal, delaying the voyage and adding to the misery of the sick young man. When he arrived in Newport family and friends were shocked to see that the healthy and vigorous youth who had left them eighteen months before was now pale, hollow-eyed, and reduced almost to a skeleton.

Channing spent the next several months at home, happy to be back with his sisters and brothers and to be of help to his mother. He tutored a younger brother and also a son of Mr. Randolph, who had been sent to Newport to be prepared for college. A library in town had some valuable books, and here he spent many hours reading theology. His mother made a study for him out of the room that had been his father's office. Through the quiet night hours William sat at his father's desk, read, and made careful notes on his reading. A few yards from the Channing house, just beyond the garden fence, was the residence of Dr. Hopkins. When William, as a small boy, had awakened on a winter night and looked across to the Hopkins house he had always seen a candle burning, and wondered if the minister was working on the long sermon to be preached the next Sunday. Now, oftener than not, the parsonage was dark when William put out his light.

William's hope of returning to Harvard to prepare for the ministry had not faded, but there was little money left after the needs of the family had been met. Then, about a year and a half after William had returned from Virginia, a letter came from the college offering him a position as proctor. This meant that in return for his services in keeping order in the boys' dormitory he could have free tuition. He accepted this offer in the next mail, and, in December 1801, was back at Harvard enrolled as an advanced student in divinity.

The next year he presented himself before the board of the Cambridge Association to be examined for the ministry. It can be imagined that the Harvard "theolog" approached this meeting with some anxiety. There were distressing stories told of the experiences others had undergone at the hands of this committee of inquisitors. It was said that not only were the candidate's educational fitness and character looked into, but that the inmost secrets must be laid bare and the soul fairly mauled and trampled upon by these guardians of the holy office of the ministry.

Channing was offered a chair at the long table around which members of the board were seated. Only one question was asked: "Was

God the author of sin?'' Whatever answer Channing gave to this profound question, it satisfied the committee. He then delivered the sample sermon required of all candidates, and it was accepted. Willliam Ellery Channing was found fit for the Christian ministry. The ordeal over, he hurried to his room to write the good news to his mother. After all, he had a good record as a student; he had never been up to any mischief in college; he came from an excellent family; and his teachers had drilled him in sound doctrine. What more could be required of a young person looking to the ministry?

Two churches were open to him. One, well organized and with a large congregation, he rejected because he felt unequal to its responsibilities. He accepted the call to the other, the less flourishing Federal Street Church in Boston. The congregation later moved to what is now the Arlington Street Church, at the corner of Arlington and Boylston Streets. This congregation was housed in a gloomy old wooden building, bare and cold in winter, but here the new minister was ordained in 1803, when he was twenty-three years old. Within a few years the growing congregation overflowed the building. The old church was torn down and replaced with a much larger one. From the first, his sincere interest in people and their problems, his ability to speak the truth with clearness in the pulpit, and his single-minded devotion to the work of the ministry drew many people to him.

Channing's mother and the other children came to live with him in the parsonage and remained until his sisters and brothers were settled in life. When Channing was thirty-six he married his cousin, Ruth Gibbs. Then his mother moved to a nearby apartment and, as long as she lived, Channing or his wife called on her every day and cared for her.

When Channing took up his work in Boston, it was a town of about twenty-five thousand. Many fine houses lined the crooked, narrow streets, and there was much bustling trade and commerce, especially along the waterfront, for this was a seaport town. Boston was sometimes called the Modern Athens, for scholars lived there, and many of the great preachers of America could be heard in its churches.

But not all Boston was prosperous and wise. Beyond the big brick houses of the wealthy were the slums, the city's poor, the unemployed, the sick, those able to keep alive only by begging, and not a few who lived by stealing. The new minister, with his scholarly, sincere, and warmhearted sermons, drew a growing number of persons of wealth and distinction. But, from the beginning of his thirty-nine years in this one church, Channing's ministry included the people of the Boston slums.

One winter's day, while making his rounds among the back streets, he was warned by neighbors to keep away from an old couple who lived in an upstairs tenement, because they were dangerous. He went to them at once and found that the old man and his wife had become insane. They were huddled in a small unheated room, half frozen and half starved. For fear of being poisoned, they refused to eat. The minister won their confidence, and they allowed themselves to be fed. He brought them wood and food and cared for them as long as they lived. They were only two among the untold number of forgotten persons befriended, encouraged, and strengthened by the Federal Street minister. His work among the poor grew naturally from his respect for people and his childhood conviction that people were not bad.

To hundreds of people he was friend and counsellor, practicing daily the religion he preached on Sundays. When Abner Kneeland, the radical Universalist preacher, was sent to jail because he had written an article attacking Calvinist doctrine, Channing, although he disagreed with the article, was the first to sign a petition for his pardon.

In Massachusetts after the Revolutionary War liberal religious thinking was beginning to penetrate the hard shell of Calvinism in the staid old Congregational churches. There were not only the issues of how many would be saved, and whether God was three persons or one, but there was the more important question of the right of people to think for themselves.

Outside of New England there were a few examples of Unitarian activity. A church had been established in Northumberland, Pennsylvania, in 1794, the first in America to take the Unitarian name. Joseph Priestley had also founded a Unitarian Society in Philadelphia in 1796. Abel Sarjent, a Universalist minister in Baltimore, had begun to publish *The Universal Magazine* in 1793, proclaiming Unitarian and Universalist ideas. In Massachusetts ministers had been dismissed from their churches because of their Unitarian views. King's Chapel had eliminated all reference to the Trinity in its services, and the controversy over liberal opinions was more and more disturbing to both ministers and congregations.

In the first years of his ministry, Channing took small notice of these controversies. Unlike the Universalist Hosea Ballou, he had no liking for debate. When examined for the ministry he had been found sufficiently orthodox to satisfy the judges. His chief interest was not in theological matters but in people; encouraging them to a deeper understanding of moral rightness, giving them courage to face difficulties, and helping the unfortunate and the wayward to better living. But whenever he was convinced that freedom was at stake, whether in the issues of war, slavery, or religion, William Ellery Channing never faltered. He was, as he once said in later life, "always young for liberty."

A test of his courage came in 1812, when he had been in the Boston church for nearly a decade. The more conservative members of the Congregational clergy were growing impatient over the number of ministers preaching Unitarian ideas, especially Arian views of Jesus, but also other points of theology at variance with Calvinist doctrines. They issued a paper, *The Panoplist,* in which their orthodoxy was set forth and defended. They finally demanded a showdown, calling upon "all true Christians" to separate themselves from those with Unitarian views. Channing wrote a pamphlet in which he pointed out the areas of agreement of the two factions and made a plea for unity and toleration. It was no use; the controversy, more and more heated, raged for the next five years. Then, in 1819, Channing went to Baltimore to preach the ordination sermon for Jared Sparks, in the Unitarian church of that city of rock-ribbed orthodoxy.

Standing in the Baltimore pulpit, this rather young pastor from Boston, with a shock of dark brown hair, large friendly eyes, and a quiet voice, did not look at all like a fiery prophet. But when he had finished the sermon, he had drawn the line unmistakably between Unitarian Christianity and Calvinist theology. Putting aside his distaste for argument, he set forth in no uncertain terms the Unitarian position. He called the Calvinist doctrine of election an "insult to God and man," and made a plea for the return to the teachings and example of Jesus, free from confused theories. He asked for a clearer understanding of "God whose image dwells in our souls."

This discourse, now called the "Baltimore Sermon," marks the beginning of the fellowship of Unitarian churches, and became the standard by which the Unitarian faith was measured for many years. Moreover, it cleared the theological atmosphere in New England and called ministers and congregations to declare themselves on one side or the other. One after another, Congregational churches voted to become Unitarian, until 125 had taken this action. Of these, one hundred were in Massachusetts, and of the ten Congregational churches in Boston, all except the Old South made the change.

In May, 1825, the American Unitarian Association was formed to provide fellowship for the local churches and to promote the cause of Unitarian religion. Channing was the unofficial leader of the New England type of Unitarianism, even though he wanted no new denomination. He proposed no new creed, but stressed the need of minds open to new truths, the importance of reason, and the simple Christian teachings. Indeed, he had no enthusiasm for organizing those with Unitarian views, preferring to be counted among the older ministers who, while interested in public affairs and in maintaining their social positions, were not inclined to look beyond the borders of their own parishes. The demand for organization came almost entirely from the younger Unitarians.

The question of slavery was becoming more and more an issue during Channing's later life. He doubted the wisdom of some of the methods of those who were working to abolish slavery, and for some time withheld his support. But when one of his friends pointed out the desperate need for his voice and chided him for lack of interest, he replied, "I acknowledge the justice of your reproof; I have been silent too long." Until his death he worked for freedom for black slaves and drew into the cause the labors of other able men and women.

In Alton, Illinois, Elijah Lovejoy, a courageous abolitionist, printed and distributed anti-slavery literature. Despite persecution and the destruction of his presses by angry opponents, he continued his publications. One day a vengeful mob raided his shop, broke the presses, and murdered the printer. Throughout the North, indignation was widespread. Dr. Channing, always a champion of freedom, asked for the use of the historic Faneuil Hall for a protest meeting. This request, at first refused by the authorities "for fear of violence" was finally granted. Channing spoke, offering resolutions condemning the lawlessness of the Illinois mob and asserting the right to express one's convictions freely in print. The attorney of the Commonwealth of Massachusetts was in the audience, and he rose at once to condemn the purpose of the meeting. In a burst of patriotic oratory he made the statement that the mob that killed the meddling printer was acting from the same high motives as did our "self-sacrificing boys who gave their lives to make America free." A great uproar followed the politician's outburst. The meeting was saved from riot only by the eloquence of Wendell Phillips. Order was restored and the resolutions were voted.

Channing's friends wondered at his endurance. Physically weak, he still forced himself to long hours of hard work that would have broken a person of greater strength. But the strain of controversy and the burden of parish duties began to tell upon him. He took frequent journeys through the country and abroad for his health. The last was to the Berkshires and the Green Mountains. He died in Bennington, Vermont, on October 21, 1842.

The active life of Dr. Channing was quite different from what might have been expected. He had no taste for agitation, controversy, and political reform, yet he attached himself to the most controversial issues of his day. He was cautious, even timid in regard to social change, yet is recognized as a great social reformer. He entered the ministry a conservative but became progressively liberal as he grew older. His interest in sectarian matters was slight, yet he was the progenitor of a new American denomination.

CHAPTER NINE

Ralph Waldo Emerson
1803-1882

Some of the relatives of the Emerson family thought that little Ralph Waldo would not amount to much. Even his mother held less hope for him than for her other children. He was often ill, sucked his thumb, giggled nervously rather than laughed, and had difficulty learning to write. But he must have had stuff of greatness in his makeup that his relatives overlooked.

Ralph Waldo Emerson was born in Boston, the fourth child of the Reverend William and Ruth Haskins Emerson. His father had been the poorly-paid minister of a quarrelsome, divided congregation in the village of Harvard, Massachusetts. Four years before Ralph Waldo was born, Mr. Emerson brought his family to Boston, where he had been installed pastor of the First Church, which became Unitarian when the American Unitarian Association was established. Here in the city there were opportunities for education for the children. He had the use of the parsonage, a salary of fourteen dollars a week, and twenty cords of stove wood per year.

The Rev. Mr. Emerson had no great liking for the ministry, and had entered it only to please his mother. He liked to read philosophy and novels, to putter around the garden, to play the bass viol, or have a game of checkers. He also liked to wander through the woods of his native Concord whenever he could take a day off, and to hobnob with his friends. His Puritan conscience chided him for these worldly pastimes, and he intermittently shouldered his pastoral burdens, took an interest in public affairs, and became an important figure in the community. His extravagance was books. He found it difficult to pass a book stall without the purchase of a volume or two, no matter how big a dent this made in the too-small family budget. This literary accumulation eventually became the nucleus of the Boston Athenaeum Library.

Whatever influence this sociable, jovial father might have had on Ralph Waldo in later years was precluded when the son was eight years old. Mr. Emerson died at forty-two, leaving the widow with no means of support. The bass viol went to the attic, the books were sold at auction, and Mrs. Emerson faced the problem of feeding, clothing, and educating five sons ranging in age from ten to three, as well as an infant daughter. Another daughter Phebe, and the first born son, John Clark, had died previously. The First Church allowed her to occupy the parsonage for one year, and voted her a small pension. Her Uncle Ripley gave her a cow. She took in boarders. The boys helped, the older ones rising at dawn to saw wood, build the kitchen fire, milk the cow and take her to pasture on Boston Common. Then they were off to the Boston Latin School to learn Latin and to recite English classics. Ralph had trouble with mathematics but got on well with grammar. Even at the age of nine he was writing poetry of a kind, principally on religious topics. Later there were patriotic outpourings inspired by the War of 1812.

Life in the Emerson home was severe, but calm, capable Ruth Emerson managed well. Food was plain, the boys' coarse outgrown garments were handed down, patched and mended, to the younger brothers. Sometimes all five of them successively wore a jacket of durable nankeen, or a pair of trousers made from the same tough material. Ralph Waldo and his brother Edward had only one overcoat between them, which they took turns wearing.

If the children lacked material luxuries they nevertheless had an abundance of intellectual fare. Evenings and Sundays (after church) were spent in Bible study, the reading of good books, and the memorizing and reciting of prayers written by the mother or by her children. Ruth Emerson, for all her remarkable endurance and iron will, was a gentle person given to reading religious literature, and to regular hours of meditation. She did her best to pass these habits on to her children.

The days were not completely taken up with chores at home and lessons at school. Splashing in the shallow water back of the Charles

Street Meeting House, hunting frogs in the mud hole (Frog Pond) on the Common, and gathering shells along the wharves were among Ralph's adventures. Summer vacations were taken at Concord with Uncle Ezra Ripley in the Old Manse. Ralph Waldo was timid by nature and was carefully sheltered from the rough and tumble activities of other children his age. He was not allowed to play in the streets for fear he would get into bad company. Adults admired his solemn smile, his polite manners, and grown-up conversation, but the boys on Summer Street called him a sissy. There were street fights when the tough North Enders invaded the Emerson neighborhood, but Ralph took no part in the fray. Once when he and the younger Edward were walking home from Charlestown they met on the bridge a rough little boy, who on learning that they did not belong in his domain proceeded to punch Ralph in the nose. The brothers put up no resistance, but ran home in tears.

Ralph Waldo's ancestors for generations had been highly literate, and included several ministers. The duty of keeping this important fact before the minds of Ruth's children was authoritatively assumed by Aunt Mary, a younger sister of their father. Mary Moody Emerson, a rigid Calvinist, was an erratic but brilliant spinster. She was almost a dwarf (four feet, three inches), with a sharp tongue and a warmth of heart that she unsuccessfully tried to conceal. Her only means of livelihood were an inheritance of a hundred dollars a year and a small share in a farm. In the periods between cheap boarding houses she lived with various relatives in Maine and Massachusetts. After the death of her brother her visits in the Emerson home were frequent and long. Aunt Mary loved Ruth's children, especially Ralph Waldo, not altogether for what he was, but for what, by the grace of God and her own wise management, he might and must become. She took charge of his education, rebuked, praised, and corrected; and never failed to remind him that he was born for greatness, and sent by the angels to bring light to the darkened ways of mortals.

The Emersons moved to Beacon Street, and were to change residence many more times as Ruth searched out favorable places for her boarding enterprise. Aunt Mary joined the family, helped with the sewing and mending, and enthusiastically set about her mission of shaping the destiny of her nephew, and consequently the world. She liked the house on Beacon Street. Nearby was the State House designed by Bulfinch, and not far away the colonial mansion where

John Hancock had lived. Best of all, from her window she had an excellent view of the Old Granary Burying Ground. Aunt Mary liked graveyards. Even though she found much spice in earthly life she lived in an habitual anticipation of death. She was among the few mortals in good health who wanted to die and go to heaven. At least she thought she did.

At fourteen Ralph Waldo, his head crammed with classical quotations and with book knowledge in excess of entrance requirements, was more than ready for college. He would go to Harvard, of course, where many of his ancestors had studied. Brother William was already there in his senior year. Ralph had grown tall and spindling, long-armed, long-legged, and narrow chested. Not as handsome as his father had been, he still had the aristocratic look of the Emersons, with his large bony nose, shapely head, and kindly blue eyes. He preferred to be called Waldo.

Money was scarce as usual, but the First Church gave him a scholarship, and he was appointed messenger, during his freshman year, to President Kirkland. In a room below the college offices he slept, did his lessons, wrote his verses, and dreamed his dreams. Two short raps on the floor above, and he dropped his pen, grabbed his hat, and scrambled up the stairs to carry the president's message to one of the buildings in the College Yard. By waiting on table at the college Commons and teaching in his brother William's school during vacation, Waldo earned enough so that only infrequently was it necessary to draw upon his mother's scant resources. He also earned money by writing themes and term papers for lazy students with more money than morals. The standard price was fifty cents. Most of his courses he found uninteresting, with recitations based on memorizing, and long tiresome lectures that seemed to him echoes from ancient tombs. He soon concluded that if he were to get an education he must get it by himself. So while other students engaged in sports and various idle pastimes, Waldo stayed in his room and lived with books and with his own musings.

Philosophy and church history, sermons, dramas, the Greek poets, essays on economics, architecture, and religion filled his mind to overflowing. He tried, without much success, to fit the wisdom of the past into some sort of relation to himself and to his world. Through four years of college he continued the practice of private study, guided only by a restless desire to know, and by frequent hints from Aunt Mary. In later years he never regretted these hours of solitary study. After the first year, he became less of a recluse, taking part in debates and competing for honors in public speaking. He won a prize of fifteen dollars for a composition on Socrates, and sent the money to his mother. A group of serious students subscribed to British periodicals, and read and discussed the ideas provided by English and German writers. Waldo joined this circle and found to his delight not the type of thinking embalmed in university libraries, but thinking about the world of the living present. In spite of absorption in studies outside the college assignments, Waldo made a fair showing in most of his courses. He received his A. B. degree at eighteen, and stood number thirty among fifty-nine graduates. He was chosen class poet only after six others had declined the honor.

The young graduate's next consideration was what to do for a living. As with his father, Emerson was being pushed by family traditions toward the ministry. From the beginning of the century Unitarianism had been gaining ground over Calvinism in the Congregational churches, especially in Massachusetts. At Harvard, commanded largely by Unitarians, he had been exposed to the movement, and whatever leanings he had toward the ministry were in this direction. He was not certain what he wanted to do; perhaps he might be invited to teach literature in some small college, or turn whatever artistic gift he had to painting. In this state of indecision William persuaded him to assist in a school for young ladies conducted in their mother's house in Boston. Waldo wrote Aunt Mary that he doubted writing poetry and teaching girls would mix. His native shyness always increased in the presence of girls. With little zest for the job he settled down to it, despite his complaint that he was "a hopeless schoolmaster." After two and a half years, however, he resigned and entered the theological school at Harvard. Aunt Mary distrusted the Unitarian emphasis and would have been pleased if the choice had been the conservative school in Andover.

For a dozen years "a mouse had nibbled" in his chest, Waldo recorded in his diary. The Emersons had weak lungs. His father had died of consumption and the disease was soon to claim his two favorite brothers. Then, after entering theological school his eyes weakened. Uncle Ripley sent him south. This was the first time he had been out of New England. In Charleston, South Carolina; in Washington, Baltimore, and Philadelphia, he met Unitarians and preached in some of their churches. He returned to Cambridge not much improved in health, and after a few months was forced to discontinue his studies.

97

He tutored for a while, took another turn at teaching, and for a season lived on an uncle's farm in Newton. This was a trying period in the life of Ralph Waldo Emerson. He suffered not only from failing eyesight and physical pain but also from too much solitude, too much self-examination, too many undigested books, and too low an estimate of his own worth. Although he would one day be known as the "Sage of Concord," "The Wisest American," poet, essayist, and philosopher, Emerson at twenty-four had not yet found himself.

Then he fell in love. Ellen Louise Tucker was sixteen when they first met in the Unitarian Church in Concord, New Hampshire, where he had gone to supply the pulpit. His shyness suddenly left him, his tongue became loosened in the presence of a young woman. How his dreadful fear of women was overcome no one knew, least of all Waldo himself. At any rate, they were married the next year.

In the meantime, he had been preaching in Unitarian churches near Boston, in western Massachusetts, and as far away as Bangor, Maine. He declined calls to several churches. On a free Sunday he was to be seen in the congregation of the Federal Street Church in Boston, where he listened to the preaching of William Ellery Channing, who, in Waldo's opinion, was the best preacher in Boston.

Despite Emerson's lack of theological training, he was granted Unitarian fellowship, ordained, and installed minister of the Second Church, Boston, in 1829. But ordination could not make him a minister. The routine of parish work tired him. One day he was called to the deathbed of an old soldier who found his pastor awkward and embarrassed. He said, "Young man, you don't know your business; you had better go back home." Emerson knew the old soldier was right.

Preaching he found less irksome. The young people of the congregation liked his plain speaking and simple illustrations, but some of the older members complained that the sermons dealt too much with ethics and too little with doctrine. They were shocked when he reminded them that Jesus was a Jew, and that Christianity had too much of Paul and too little of Jesus. Emerson made a brave effort to meet the demands of the parish but gave up after two and a half years. The immediate reasons for resigning were his unwillingness to administer communion, and the refusal of the leaders in the church to dispense with it.

Ellen had died only eighteen months after their marriage, and he was very much alone. Now withdrawal from the pastorate left him with no plan for the future. Friends suggested that a trip abroad would be beneficial. He sailed from Boston on Christmas Day, 1832, on a trading vessel bound for the Mediterranean. The passage was rough, both in weather and in accommodations—winter storms, beans and salt pork three times a day. But the gales blew the cobwebs from his mind, and his eyesight also improved. Emerson felt like a new person. Always fascinated by people of action and a virility he did not himself possess, he admired the skill of the sailors with their ropes and knives, their tall tales of the sea, and even their salty language, generously punctuated with profanity.

The ship landed at the island of Malta, where Emerson had his first view of the ancient world. He wandered through Greece and Italy, and in Paris dined with the aged Lafayette. What he desired most was to meet some of the living writers whose works he had read. In England he hunted up Coleridge and Wordsworth and was mildly disappointed. He searched out Carlyle, found him on his remote farm in Scotland, and felt rewarded for his trouble. During their conversation lasting far into the night each came to an appreciation of the other, the beginning of a life-long friendship. Emerson left with a new determination to put his talents to work in his own land.

He returned home in September, improved in health. He was thirty and felt that time was running out. If Aunt Mary's hopes for him were to be realized, he must gather the broken pieces of his life together into some sort of pattern for the future. For years his chief joy had been roaming about the fields and woods. He thought about the aliveness of trees and grass and flowers, and the unity of human beings with their surrounding world. He called this oneness the "Over-Soul." Within life itself are the laws that operate in nature and in human nature. People must learn to look to themselves for moral law, to what the Quakers call the Inner Light. These ideas Emerson was to expand and proclaim in later writings and lectures. He had begun to find himself and his mission.

A group of earnest friends by whom Emerson was surrounded, and their followers in New England, were called Transcendentalists. This is a term used to describe people who held many different ideas, but they had in common high ideals of thinking and living. In general they believed that truths came to the individual more by intuition than by experience and reason. They discarded external authorities and put their trust in what their own souls told them was right and true.

THESE LIVE TOMORROW

But Emerson needed anchorage, a place for his books, for writing, and for meditating. And a place for a wife, for he had suddenly become engaged to Lydia Jackson of Plymouth. Naturally he thought of Concord, the home of his ancestors, the oldest inland town in Massachusetts. A vacant house was found on the turnpike, with orchard, garden, two acres of fields, and a barn. The home was large enough for the Emersons and for children that might be born, as well as for Emerson's mother, who came to live with them.

And, of course, there was a chamber for Aunt Mary. Death had passed her by, but she was still hopeful. She had a bed made in the shape of a coffin, and a burial shroud of good strong material. But as time passed and she continued to awaken in the morning to find herself distressingly alive, she took to wearing the shroud about the house, and when she went for the afternoon mail. It was even rumored about town that neighbors hearing hoof-beats on the road at night and looking out their windows saw Aunt Mary galloping by on the Emerson horse, the flowing skirts of her grave clothes trailing in the wind.

Emerson, however, did not go to Concord to bury himself or his talents. He got acquainted with his neighbors, served on committees of the town, and entered his pears at the county fair. Educational and literary institutions called lyceums were springing up all over America. There were nearly a hundred in Massachusetts. Here was a market for his thoughts, connection with the outside world, and an income. And here was freedom of speech, with no board of deacons to pass judgment on the relative value of doctrine and ethics. In a day of limited communication of ideas the lyceum met the intellectual needs of the public, providing a broad course of instruction in many subjects—science, philosophy, and poetry. Emerson gave a course of lectures in Boston, speaking on Great Men, Trades and Professions, History of Philosophy, and Human Culture. Some of his hearers were confused by generalities that he took little trouble to explain and less to defend. Others complained that they did not know what he was driving at. Yet his fame spread and soon he was keeping appointments in country towns and in distant places south and west.

He also did supply preaching in Unitarian churches, preaching for several months in East Lexington. The members there evidently had no difficulty understanding him. One woman remarked, "We are simple folks here, and can understand only Mr. Emerson." He rented a pew in the Concord Unitarian Church, and during the rest

100

of his life attended services there whenever he had a free Sunday.

He was writing too. His first book, *Nature*, came out in 1836 when the author was thirty-three. Other books and published lectures followed. Before he was forty his basic ideas concerning God and humanity and the individual's prospects, duties, and place in life had been stated. Later works were an amplification and illustration of his conclusions set forth in striking poetic phrases that burrow their meaning into people's hearts.

In 1837 Emerson delivered the now-famous oration, "The American Scholar" before the Phi Beta Kappa Society in the Unitarian Church in Cambridge. He charged Americans with too much dependence on European thought and manners, and called for the personal freedom and self-reliance that would match the political independence and unlimited opportunities in their own land.

The next year his "Divinity School Address," given before the graduating class at Harvard College, was a broadside attack on the shortcomings of churches that no longer nurtured but existed chiefly to perpetuate traditions that had lost their meaning. The clergy, the speaker charged, were living second-handedly on the inspirations of former times, neglectful of their powers of reason, and blind to the sources of inspiration all around them. They were challenged to unshackle their minds and to know themselves for what they could become.

These two addresses, spoken without bitterness or bombast, shook conservative New England like an earthquake. They aroused resentment chiefly among the intellectuals—college professors and preachers schooled in the formal systems of philosophy. The common people, however, read the words of Emerson and found hope and cheer for their daily living. They were not always certain of the meaning of some of his phrases, but they felt that he spoke for them when he talked about liberty and cooperation among free people to build in America the greatness of life. They liked his idea that people should be themselves without miserably trying to be someone else.

Emerson had some opinions about Jesus that were not at all acceptable to those who believed that Christ was the only hope of the world. In his youth Aunt Mary had introduced him to some of the Oriental scriptures, especially those of India. He discovered in them many valuable teachings, which led him to the observation that not all religious truths are found in Christianity. Truth is truth whatever its source, he proclaimed, and the worship of Jesus not only obscures his teachings but also sets him apart for a reverence that should be felt toward all souls. This doctrine seemed to the critics, and to many Unitarians, as a belittling or even a rejection of Christianity.

Criticism, no matter how harsh, never disturbed Emerson's serenity. Truth to him was intuitive and self-evident, and he wondered why everybody did not see it. He never argued; he only proclaimed. Once at the end of a lecture at Middlebury College a minister invited to pronounce the benediction prayed that the people be spared ever again hearing such nonsense as they had just listened to. Asked to comment on this public insult, Emerson remarked, "The minister seems a very conscientious, plain-spoken gentleman!"

More and more with the years Concord became a gathering place for persons of distinction: Nathaniel Hawthorne, Margaret Fuller, Sarah Ripley, Henry Thoreau, Bronson Alcott, and others. They were all welcomed at the Emerson home. Visitors came from Cambridge and Boston: Henry Wadsworth Longfellow, William Ellery Channing, and Theodore Parker. Lydia (her husband had re-named her Lydian) was a gracious hostess as well as a wise mother of the four children born over a span of eight years.

Emerson had always hoped that he would not outlive the weakening of his mental powers. But during the last years he suffered lapses of memory that became more and more frequent. One evening his daughter read to him from his lecture, 'Nature.' "I don't know who wrote that," said her father, "but he must have been a great man." He died at the age of seventy-nine, in 1882.

Death had caught up with Aunt Mary nineteen years before. She had fulfilled her mission. Ralph Waldo had amply justified her conviction that he was born for greatness.

In Emerson's later years much of the earlier antagonism toward him turned to adulation. Critics re-examined his teachings and took a second look at themselves. And this practice of estimates and reappraisal has continued with Emerson readers. He is generally counted among the great American authors. Those who look for light in practical experience, and demand proof for convictions find his writings perplexing, illogical, and contradictory. This manner of writing, of recording his insights and feelings, has led to wide uncritical acceptance especially among those who seek short cuts to truth. He was a mystic, a seer, a poet who told the world what he saw and felt and hoped, mixed with a good deal of sound Yankee common sense.

Emerson was not first of all a person of action, although he recommended it to others, and he inspired them to action. Yet his activity in behalf of the Abolitionist movement was sufficient to cause him to be mobbed in Boston and in Cambridge. He summoned America to take courage, to believe in itself and its future. His insistence on the worth of the individual provided an ethical foundation for the political doctrine of American democracy.

From an unpromising childhood, brought up in poverty and handicapped with a frail body, this noble and heroic individual fought his way to health and rose to great heights of creativeness. At the time of his death Emerson was recognized as one of the foremost thinkers and writers in America. But this recognition had come slowly. His departures from the Unitarianism of his time were viewed by many with considerable alarm. Yet today he is rightfully regarded as one who brought into liberal religion fresh insights and a larger liberty in thought and hope.

CHAPTER TEN

Adin Ballou

1803-1890

In the northeast corner of Rhode Island is the township of Cumberland. It is a right triangle, two sides marked by the boundary line of Massachusetts, and the Blackstone River provides the hypotenuse. This small obscure nook is important in Universalist history. Here was the ancestral home of several branches of the Ballou family, which contributed not less than a score of ministers of the Universalist Church, and a host of worthy citizens to the nation. Maturin Ballou, immigrant ancestor of the American line of Ballous, joined Roger Williams in the first settlement of the Providence Plantation in the territory of the Narragansett Indians.

Maturin Ballou raised a family and his descendants multiplied greatly, swarming over Rhode Island and beyond. Many of them settled in Cumberland and in the adjacent areas, until at the beginning of the nineteenth century the Ballous constituted the majority of the region. Cumberland and the nearby towns were known as the Ballou neighborhood. In the Revolutionary War one hundred and thirty-nine Ballous were enrolled as soldiers and sailors from Rhode Island, twenty-seven of them from Cumberland. Early settlers in the township built a church, the Ballou Meeting House. The pastor was Abner Ballou, a Baptist. Nearby was the Ballou cemetery, and the Ballou District School, and not far down the road from the Ballou Meeting House the Ballou Tavern, kept by the rum-selling son of the Rev. Abner Ballou.

Into this neighborhood in 1803 Adin Ballou was born to Ariel and Edilda Ballou. Both parents were natives of Cumberland. Adin belonged to the sixth generation of the Rhode Island Ballous. Ariel had inherited from his great-grandfather the farm on which the family lived. There were over two hundred acres extending over the state line into Massachusetts, but the house and farm buildings were in Rhode Island. Besides the farm Ariel owned a saw-mill, a cider-mill, and a large stock of cattle.

In keeping with the Ballou tradition there were many children, six born to a former wife now dead. All the children were brought up to work, both indoors and out, each given tasks according to age and strength.

Adin, a frail child in infancy, developed under his mother's care into a sturdy and good-looking boy, able to take on his daily chores along with his brothers and sisters. When full grown he was six feet four-and-a-half inches in height.

There was plenty of work on the farm—planting and weeding, harvesting and threshing—as well as the daily routine of caring for the farm animals, and keeping on hand a supply of seasoned wood for cooking and heating the big farm house. There was indeed more work than the members of the family could do, on the farm and at the mills, making necessary the employment of outside help. Adin always made friends with the hired hands. He was especially fond of one called Reuben, an Indian half-breed. Reuben took a great liking to young Adin and instructed him in the mysteries of plant life, the names of birds, and the habits of the wildlife of the woods. Adin went to him for comfort whenever in trouble, and always found this illiterate but wise one a friend and a teacher.

A farm child lives among a multitude of hazards—kicking horses, cross bulls, sharp tools, as well as poisonous weeds and insects. Adin had his share of accidents. One time he fell into the mill pond and was rescued just before the current would have carried him into the great mill wheel that could have torn him to shreds. Another time he tumbled into a ditch and broke his arm.

Adin's father was a stern man who believed hard work was the chief of human virtues. He was suspicious of all amusements, especially country dancing and card playing. These pastimes he regarded as even worse than idleness. The mother, less strict with the children, had a greater influence upon them than their father. But for all the severities of discipline and labor the Ballou home was conducive to wholesome living. There was an abundance of plain food, service-able clothing, and the ordinary necessities of a farm family. Once each year, before winter, the shoemaker came with tools to do the cob-bling for all members of the household. To the younger children this was the happiest time of the whole year, for here was not only a ma-gician, creating shoes and boots out of cowhide, but a storyteller, bal-lad singer, and one who could blow music out of the harmonica.

Adin began school when he was three, at first attending both sum-mer and winter terms, each three months long. Later he went only in winter, since the farm work claimed him during the summer sea-son. The year he was nine the two oldest brothers were drawn into the War of 1812, their absence adding to Adin's home duties and keep-ing him out of school. During the following years his schooling was limited to a few weeks and ended altogether when he was sixteen. He had a quick mind, however, and read everything he could find, remembering and reflecting upon his reading.

Adin's heart was set upon college, and his loftiest dreams were of going to Brown University in Providence. But whenever the mat-ter was brought up, his father disposed of it by saying, "Why, your college courses would cost me three or four hundred dollars, and I'm in debt already." The old man set a very low value on higher educa-tion, frequently reminding his son of a distant relative who went through college and spent the rest of his life in poverty.

The inhabitants of the Ballou neighborhood were on the whole plain, honest, hard-working people, living peaceably with one another; but they were rather indifferent toward other-worldly affairs. They had allowed the Ballou Meeting House to fall into disrepair, and provided for only occasional preaching. But in the year 1815, they were suddenly shaken out of their spiritual lethargy. In September of that year "the Great Gale," as it was called in New England, swept though Rhode Island and Massachusetts. Buildings were demolished, trees uprooted, and orchards laid waste. Nothing like it had ever be-fore been seen by even the oldest inhabitants. Nowhere was the des-truction more serious than in the Ballou neighborhood. The heavy hand of an angry God seemed to be laid upon the people because of their perverse ways. And at the same time a hurricane of a differ-ent character was sweeping through the community. A religious revival was in full swing, led by an evangelist of the Christian Con-nection. The Christian Connection was a group organized by James O'Kelly (1735-1826), in North Carolina, with tenets similar to those of the Disciples of Christ.

"The Great Gale" provided a powerful stimulus to the revival. The preaching went on for weeks, lashing the devil, uprooting old habits of worldly comfort, and laying bare the destruction that awaited the unsaved. Half the people in Cumberland were converted. Adin, his parents, and his siblings all "experienced religion" and were baptized by immersion. A church of the Christian Connection was organized with Ariel Ballou as one of the deacons.

The high winds of excitement subsided in a few months, and many of the converts fell away. But there were some, including young Adin, who continued in the faith and kept the new church alive for a few years. He was deeply affected, and ever after was grateful for the experience that turned his mind toward the religious life.

It was the nature of Adin Ballou that whatever he undertook he did with all his might. He never missed a religious meeting of his church, and he made a heroic effort to order his daily living according to the Christian standards he understood. At nineteen he had an intensive spiritual vision, which he interpreted as a call from God to preach the Gospel. The form of his deceased brother appeared to him in the night saying, "God commands you to preach the Gospel of Christ to your fellow-men; obey his voice or the blood of their souls will be required at your hands." He had never had any desire to be a minister, and shrank from such a prospect, but he yielded to what he considered to be a divine mandate. A few weeks later he delivered his first sermon, in the old Ballou Meeting House. In the autumn of that year, with no preparation beyond his self-directed studies, he was admitted as an approved minister of the Christian Connection.

A number of Adin's relatives had gone over to Universalism, and there were four or five Ballous in the Universalist ministry. The young minister felt it his Christian duty to defend the true faith against the invasion of this hated heresy. His gunning was for big game. He wrote a pamphlet attacking the teachings of Hosea Ballou, a third cousin of Adin Ballou's father Ariel, as set forth in a lecture delivered from his Universalist pulpit in Boston. Adin's chief objection to Universalism was the doctrine that all persons would finally be saved. He accepted the tenet of the Christian Connection that on the Judgment Day the dead would be brought to life and the wicked would be destroyed at once, while the righteous would be given bodily immortality.

When Adin discussed religion with his Universalist neighbors, which he was ever willing to do, he found himself at a disadvantage;

they not only knew the Bible texts that supported their beliefs, but they were also familiar with the literature of their denomination. To overcome this handicap Adin began a closer study of the scriptures, and the reading of Universalist writings. The result was unexpected; he became convinced of the truth of what he had regarded as doctrinal error. He struggled mightily with himself, but finally surrendered to the irresistible appeal that Universalism made to his rational mind. The change cost him the loss of many friends, and deeply wounded his family. On a motion made by his father, he was excommunicated by the Cumberland church.

From the age of sixteen Adin had loved Abigail Sayles, daughter of a Universalist family in nearby Smithfield, but the differences in their religious views had kept them apart. Now with his changed view, religion became a bond of union. They were married, and both his wife and her mother were a source of strength and encouragement. He was cordially received by the Universalists, supplied Universalist pulpits in various places for two years, and in 1824, at twenty-one, was called to the church in Milford, Massachusetts.

An unhappy controversy was going on at this time among the New England Universalists over the matter of punishment for sin. Some thought that there was no punishment after death. Adin Ballou was decidedly of the opinion that after death the souls of persons would suffer for sins committed in earthly life until, tempered and purified, they would be brought into harmony with their Creator. He published a weekly, *The Independent Messenger*, devoted to the defense of this theory, and wrote, preached, and argued his convictions to the end of his life. The Milford congregation respected and loved their pastor, but the issue over future punishment grew more and more heated. When in 1831 Mr. Ballou's party withdrew from the denomination and adopted the name "Restorationist" he was dismissed from the church by a small majority. The Restorationists returned after ten years of separate convention sessions.

The Congregational Church in nearby Mendon at once invited him to be its minister. He accepted and for ten years promoted a vigorous program of social action. In addition to his pastoral work he wrote and lectured on temperance, the abolition of slavery, women's rights, and other reforms, often meeting with bitter opposition.

The dominant trait in the life of Adin Ballou was an intense desire to put religious theories into practice. The wide chasm between the professed faith of Christians and their way of living distressed him.

Should not those who take the name Christian live on a plane above the general ethical codes that made terms with prevailing political and business practices? Did not people act as if the Christian gospel were a beautiful but impractical theory to be talked about in pulpit and Sunday school but not to be taken seriously in industry and international relations?

To put such questions to the test of experience, Ballou conceived and promoted the Hopedale Community. The original name was "Fraternal Community Number One." It was expected to be the first of many such communities. This was a valiant attempt to work out a pattern for a new and better way for persons to live and labor together.

The "Declaration of Faith, Principles and Duties" that was to govern the members of the Community reflects the moral austerity and lofty ethical idealism of the founder. Among the conditions of membership were belief in the religion of Jesus; never in any circumstances to hate anybody; never to take any oath, or hold public office; and never to serve in, aid, or encourage war or the preparation for war.

In March, 1842, twenty-eight persons committed themselves to the exacting code required of them, and began the shaping of a community after the patterns of Christian Cooperative Communism. All property would be held in common, all would work, and all share alike in the profits. Those with means to do so bought stock in the enterprise, but all, without regard to the amount of money invested, had an equal voice in the management. Adin Ballou was the first president, and throughout the existence of the community he was the inspiration and guide of the experiment.

A farm of two hundred and fifty acres was acquired in the Mendon township. The fields were choked with weeds, the pasture land overgrown with bushes, and the farm buildings about to fall apart. Ballou named the place Hopedale, and the members went to work with a will.

The old buildings were repaired. Plowing began as soon as the frost was out of the ground, and a good harvest crowned the labors of spring and summer. The first new building erected provided for a school and a printing ship. Soon a machine shop and a sawmill were added, and cows and other livestock purchased. In time, carpentering, tin and sheet-iron working, hat manufacturing, and boot- and shoe-making were added.

The experiment made a promising beginning. There were many difficulties, however, more than had been anticipated. There was insufficent capital; the first flush of enthusiasm faded; there were problems of interpersonal relations, and of response on the part of some members to voluntary efforts necessary to the success of a cooperative program. Notwithstanding these obstacles, Ballou with unfailing patience reconciled differences and secured financial aid from friends, and the Community experienced a fair degree of prosperity. At the time of dissolution, after fourteen years of existence, six hundred acres had been added to the the farm lands. There were fifty dwellings, barns, stores, and mills, and three hundred residents.

The crisis came in 1856, when the two largest shareholders, dissatisfied because the Community was not making a profit for the investors, withdrew their capital. Those left did not have sufficient financial resources to continue operation. By common consent, the Hopedale Community was dissolved.

To the last, Ballou viewed the Hopedale venture not as a financial failure, but as a moral defeat due to the shortcomings of people in measuring up the principles and demands of the Christian religion. Nevertheless the collapse of the object of his dreams caused him lasting disappointment and grief.

After his death in 1890, a remarkable book he had written, *History of the Hopedale Community,* was published. This is a candid review of the origin, growth, and dissolution of the experiment to which he devoted a large part of a busy, useful life. The purpose was to point out the mistakes that had been made, and to warn any future adventurers into the realm of cooperative living of its pitfalls. The book offers no defense of his methods or management at Hopedale, but strong words in defense of his faith in the possibility of people learning to live together helping one another.

The Community organization, after the industrial features were abandoned, continued only as a religious and educational association. A meeting house was built and the Rev. Mr. Ballou continued to minister to the former shareholders and their families. In 1867, the Hopedale Liberal Christian Parish was organized, and the Community, with its church, cemetery, and meager financial assets, was later merged into it. Mr. Ballou served this church as minister for thirteen years, until his seventy-seventh birthday.

Ballou held his denominational ties lightly. This was so partly because his his fellow ministers did not like his ideas, but more because he thought they failed to put their religion to work. His theology was too conservative for the liberals, and his sociology was too liberal for the conservatives. On the one hand he was a champion of the Restorationists, challenging Hosea Ballou and followers as "ultra-Universalists" and charging them with misleading the denomination. On the other hand he carried the principles of Universalism into areas of ethical idealism and social reform where others of the faith could not, or dared not, venture. His commitment to Universalism was never clouded by doubt or weakened by ill-fortune, but it was a commitment that demanded action. He was immovable in his convictions, would not compromise on matters of principle, but harbored no ill-feeling toward those who opposed him. When the pages of the *Universalist Journal* were closed to him, he published his own paper. When his colleagues shunned him, he went his own way without bitterness. He applied the doctrine of non-resistance to individuals as well as to society.

Under Ballou's leadership and with his willing consent, the Hopedale Liberal Christian Parish joined the "Worcester Conference of Congregational (Unitarian) and other Christian societies." He attended its meetings regularly, but his comments regarding the members are as unappreciative as any he made about the Universalists. "As a religious body," he wrote, "the Unitarians in some respects were quite below my ideal of Practical Christianity." He found them stuffy, crammed with knowledge but without zeal. He talked with Ralph Waldo Emerson once and reported that the Concord Sage was "amiable, harmless, blameless," but not much above the average in practical ethics.

Few have suffered more disappointments in the causes they labored to uphold than Adin Ballou. The denomination of his adoption failed to meet his high expectations in proving faith by good works. The Hopedale project crumbled on the day of its largest promise, and his beloved settlement declined into a typical New England mill village. He saw several peace organizations and non-resistance societies that he had promoted melt away before the hot winds of the Civil War hysteria. He saw chattel slavery abolished by bloodshed but knew that war could not make black Americans free.

Yet his influence was perhaps wider and more enduring than he knew. The Russian philosopher Leo Tolstoi admired him and corresponded with him for several years. Gandhi in turn acknowledged his debt to Tolstoi, and put into practice the fundamental principles-for which Ballou had labored before the great Hindu national leader was born.

The public image of Adin Ballou was of a controversalist in theology, a radical reformer, an unyielding pacifist, an author of books, and a writer of tracts. But in the churches he served he was remembered, loved, and revered as a valiant friend, a wise counsellor, one who lived the religion that he taught. Liberals today think of him as one who worked to build the kingdom of heaven on earth.

CHAPTER ELEVEN

Theodore Parker
1810-1860

Theodore Parker was a country boy. He was born in Lexington, Massachusetts. So was his father, and his father's father, and his father's grandfather. In fact, the Parkers were as solidly rooted in the soil of Lexington as the great oaks and maples on the slope behind the old farmhouse where Theodore's ancestors had lived for a hundred years.

It was Theodore's grandfather, Captain John Parker, who, on April 19, 1775, commanded the company of Lexington Minute Men when the redcoats marched down the Concord Road, and the first shots were fired in the American Revolution. Theodore's father, another John, never allowed his children to forget that, as a boy of fourteen, he had been present at this historic moment, watching the skirmish from a safe distance on the village green, but near enough to hear their grandfather's bold words, "If they mean to have a war, let it begin here."

The Parkers were good, plain citizens—farmers, carpenters, cabinet makers, and storekeepers. They took their turn serving in the small offices of the community, the school board, and committees of the village church. They married from neighboring families and many children were born to them.

Theodore, born on August 24, 1810, was the last of the eleven children of John and Hannah Stearns Parker. His mother was a capable and industrious housewife whose first thought was always for the welfare of her family. She died when Theodore was thirteen. He remembered her as frail, with pale blue eyes, and neatly dressed. She used to read to him from the Bible when he was a very small boy and tried to explain its moral lesson. Theodore liked better the stories about his great-grandfather, Nathaniel, who was captured by the Indians.

John Parker was not a good farmer, but he was handy with tools. He left the fields to the older children and spent the work days in his shop. Here he made all sorts of farm implements for neighbors—pumps and wooden buckets, hoes and hay rakes. He mended their cider presses, put new spokes of ash in wagon wheels, and on a great iron lathe for which he provided foot power turned kitchen bowls and mugs of birch and maple. The shop itself was like no other. It had been the belfry of the old meeting house on Lexington common. When the new house of worship was built, John Parker bought the belfry tower and made it into a workshop. Young Theodore liked to play here among the sweet-smelling shavings, and when he was old enough he learned the uses of saw and hammer and chisel.

He loved the old farm too, with its peach and apple orchards, the cow pasture, and the woods beyond. There was a broad meadow, and a brook that wandered through the fields and woods until it found its way to the Charles River. He had no playmates of his own age; his sisters and brothers were older, and there were no neighbor children nearby. But he was not lonely. Besides the farm animals there were squirrels and rabbits and even foxes and deer in the wooded hills. Fat woodchucks dug their houses in the fields, and down at the pond were frogs and turtles. He learned the habits of the wild animals, and how to recognize the songs of the bobolink, the lark, and the whippoorwill. He brought wildflowers to his mother, who taught him their names.

In winter there was skating on the pond. In his mature years, Parker cherished the memory of these natural surroundings, and felt most fortunate to have been brought up in the country.

And he came to know a wider world. There was the church down at the village where on Sundays he went with the family and sat in the Parker pew high up in the rear balcony. Sermons and prayers were long, and the place was always too hot or cold, but when the meetings were over, if the weather was pleasant the children could run and play on the Common while the women in groups talked about the happenings of the neighborhood, and the men at the horse sheds behind the meeting house discussed crops and politics.

Sometimes on market day, Theodore went to the village in the lumbering, springless farm wagon loaded with apples and peaches. Here were people from Concord, Waltham, and other towns nearby, farmers and their wives in homespun, with produce to sell. Others came to buy, some fashionably dressed, and a few with black servants who carried the market baskets. Lexington was on the road from the northern towns to Boston, and Theodore saw the four-horse teams pulling great loads of hay and grain for the markets in the big city. The teamsters always stopped to let their horses drink at the long watering-trough hewn from the trunk of a giant hemlock. The teamsters themselves found refreshment in the tap room of the Dudley Tavern.

At six, Theodore started school, walking a mile or so down the road to the little brown schoolhouse. The summer terms had a woman teacher, but in the winter, when the big boys came to school, a man teacher was enlisted to keep order. In fair weather a short cut was possible, across the meadow, over the brook, and into the winding road deep with powdery cool dust that pressed between bare toes. When winter came Theodore, in leather boots, found it better to keep to the road all the way. Sometimes there were great snowdrifts, waist-high, made by the winds that blew over the rail fences.

As he grew older the farm claimed his labor, especially in summers, so schooling was limited and ended altogether when he was sixteen, after a short term at the new Academy in Lexington. Brothers and sisters had grown up, married, and moved away to make homes of their own, and the aging father could do little work, so that the responsiblities of the farm fell more and more to young Theodore. With the help of a hired man, he managed to plant and harvest and to take the produce to the markets in Lexington and Boston.

Theodore had more than enough farming before he was out of his teens. His mother had hoped that her youngest son would become a minister, and this was what he wanted to be. But with schooling cut short, and no money, the prospects were not bright. Since there was no profit in farming, he turned to teaching school during the winter months, first in Quincy, then in North Lexington, Concord, Waltham, and in a private school in Boston. His reputation for severe discipline and overloading pupils with work may account for his frequent moves.

During these seasons of teaching, and on summer evenings at home, Theodore used every moment of free time in study. There was

117

no money for books, but he borrowed freely from friends, teachers, and ministers who were glad to encourage a youth with such a burning desire to learn. He possessed an unusual memory, mastered whatever he read, and had the physical strength to endure long hours of study when the day's work was done.

At the end of the haying season, in the summer of 1830 and on his twentieth birthday, Theodore walked to Cambridge, passed the examinations at Harvard College and was permitted to enroll as a nonresident student. By this arrangement, he would not have to pay tuition and would not receive a degree. Years later Parker was offered the Bachelor's degree on condition that he pay four years' tuition. This he declined. In 1840, Harvard gave him the honorary degree of Master of Arts.

In 1832, Parker opened a school of his own in Watertown, in a second story room over an old bakery. It was a dingy place, but he painted the walls, laid a new floor, washed the windows, and with skill acquired in his father's workshop, built benches, blackboards, and a big desk for the teacher. School started with only two pupils, one of whom was too poor to pay tuition, but before long there were fifty-four, most of them paying their way. One black girl was admitted, but parents of the white children made such a fuss that the teacher dismissed her, an act of surrender for which he never forgave himself.

The school venture was financially successful, and it afforded Parker wider associations with people than he had known before. He attended the First Parish Church and found in its pastor, the Rev. Convers Francis, a helpful and life-long friend. Francis was liberal in theology and greatly influenced the thinking of the young man. At the parsonage Parker met important people in church and literary affairs. There was a large library and Mr. Francis was generous with his books.

With the minister's encouragement, Parker became Superintendent of the Sunday School. One of the teachers was a tall blue-eyed young woman of nineteen named Lydia Cabot. She lived under the same boarding house roof with him, and of course, he walked home from church with her and carried her books, and when it rained held her umbrella. She was gentle, well-mannered, admired his talents, sympathized with his ambitions, and was anxious that he not overwork, all of which was not displeasing to Theodore. They became engaged, although it was agreed that marriage must wait until he was established in a parish.

Two years were all that could be spared in Watertown. He wanted to get on with his preparation for the ministry. In April, 1834, he gave up teaching and entered the Divinity School at Harvard, which in 1805 had "gone Unitarian." With money saved, and a scholarship procured by Dr. Francis, he could manage to pay the required expenses of two hundred dollars a year. During the time at Watertown he had learned Hebrew, read Latin and Greek, and under the direction of his minister had aimed his studies toward a broad theological education. He had allowed nothing, not even the courting of Lydia, to interfere with his studies, and had now advanced far enough to be enrolled in the last term of the junior year.

In the Divinity School he was at once recognized by teachers and students as a hard worker, with boundless energy, a will to excel, and a disposition that varied from fun-making to fits of depression. He attended classes faithfully, prepared practice sermons that his teacher thought were rather bad, and joined heartily in the discussions of the Philanthropic Society. But his restless spirit could not be confined within the bounds of assigned lessons and class lectures. He devoured mountains of books: history, philosophy, theology—all fodder for a hunger that could not be satisfied. He studied a dozen or more languages, few of which he could not read with some degree of understanding, and few that he could speak. He tutored students in German, Greek, and Hebrew, taught a class in Charlestown prison, and wrote numerous essays for the student magazine, the *Scriptural Interpreter*, not forgetting to write to his beloved Lydia.

His writings for the *Interpreter* were a compound of theories gleaned from books and his own rash judgments in fields where mature scholars were treading lightly. They were, nevertheless, a forecast of the scholarship combined with independent thinking that characterized his ministry. All in all, Parker in his student days was a rather conservative Unitarian. He accepted the Christian belief in the miraculous birth of Jesus, although he knew that other religions too had their virgin birth stories. Some of the other miracles of the Bible he rejected as unreasonable. He was well within the general Unitarian position of the time; he thought that Jesus was a supernatural being.

Graduation came in the spring of 1836, with Parker in a borrowed gown, sound in body, mind crammed with knowledge, and eager to begin his ministry, get married, and have a home of his own. That he had not undermined his health was due perhaps to a strong body

119

inherited from the hardy Parkers and the wholesome work of his childhood years on the farm. Later years of overwork took their toll of physical strength, but at graduation he was a robust young man, with rapid stride, a tossing mane of thick hair, ruddy face, and blue-gray eyes that reflected a restless and inquiring mind.

After preaching in several churches near Boston and for a summer in the church in Barnstable on Cape Cod, Parker received a call in April, 1837, to the Spring Street Chruch in West Roxbury. He and Lydia were married, and three months later he was ordained. Now in his twenty-seventh year, Theodore Parker, a full-fledged minister, entered upon a professional career that made him the most feared and best hated preacher in America.

He began from the first days of his ministry to turn the raw materials gathered in study into the substance of practical teaching, even preaching a sermon on "The Duties of Milkmen." The parish was small and its duties light, leaving the minister time for extensive study. He now began to build the library that grew to the greatest public collection in America. At his death, his books were given to the Boston Public Library. He wrote for magazines, translated foreign works in theology and Biblical history, and lectured wherever invited and on any subject desired. Despite his preoccupation, he was always ready to drop book or pen to help persons in need.

Four years after he went to West Roxbury, Parker delivered the ordination sermon for a fellow minister in South Boston. It was titled "The Transient and Permanent in Christianity," and came to be known as "The South Boston Sermon." This sermon, while it does not seem extremely radical today, was an explosion that rocked the foundations of Unitarianism, and caused repercussions throughout the country. The transient elements of the Christian religion, he said, are miracles, revelations, creeds, and doctrines. The permanent is found in the moral sense born in the hearts of good person. The truths in the teachings of Jesus are true not on his authority, but because they meet the needs of people in practical living.

Only one person left during the sermon, but the minister who offered the ordination prayer suggested with emphasis that the candidate better not take seriously the heresy he had just heard! The Unitarian ministers in Boson were shocked, angry, and afraid. They knew that Mr. Parker had become radical, and some of them had refused to exchange pulpits with him, but they didn't think he could go so far as to "remove Christ, the Bible, and the Church from Christianity." Some of them explained that Parker was not a real Unitarian; others attacked him in their sermons, wrote reproachful letters, refused his articles in their magazines, and left the room when he entered it. Ministers who were friendly with him were themselves attacked and discriminated against.

Even more violent were the abuses rained upon him by the orthodox clergy. Unable to deal with the matter first hand, they held prayer meetings to ask God's help in punishing him. "We know that we cannot argue him down," they prayed, "but O Lord, put a hook in his jaws, so that he may not be able to speak." The prayers were not answered.

New England Unitarianism at this time was in a state of transition. The formation of the American Unitarian Association, marking the separation from the Congregationalists, had taken place sixteen years before, but many ministers and congregations were timid about cutting loose from familiar moorings. Perhaps they were not aware that the same influences that had drawn them away from their former connection were now causing the more radical Unitarians to advance beyond their conservative comrades. They could take Channing (with some reservations), but Parker was just too much.

Ralph Waldo Emerson and a few other adventurous and kindred souls had formed a discussion group—sometimes called Hedge's Club—for the exchange of views on all sorts of questions—philosophy and theology included. The club was composed mostly of Unitarians of one kind or another, some of whom eventually thought themselves out of the ministry. It later adopted the name "Transcendentalist Club." This group represented the extreme position of liberalism and drew more severe criticism from the conservatives. Not a little of this was aimed at Parker, who had become identified with the Transcendentalist Club.

The controversy Parker had sharpened by the South Boston Sermon was still raging when, in 1846, he left the West Roxbury Church to become minister of the Twenty-Eighth Congregational Society in Boston, preaching in the Melodeon Theater. The church was Unitarian, but like some other New England churches, kept the original name. Newspapers and pulpits were hostile, but there were those determined that his voice should be heard. And it was. Soon the congregation moved to the large Music Hall, where each week he preached to three thousand people, the largest congregation in New England.

THESE LIVE TOMORROW

He was not an imposing figure in the pulpit or out of it. Nature lavished gifts on Parker chiefly above his shoulders. He was five feet, eight inches tall, lost his hair early, and wore a snowy beard. Something of the farmer survived in frame and posture. But his forehead was a dome like the brow of Socrates, and the goodness of his heart shone in his honest eyes. Some of his admirers thought him handsome.

His sermons, while grounded on solid scholarship, were neither sensational nor oratorical, but were fearless discussions of serious issues. He spoke to the conscience of the community on the social evils of the time; low wages, bad housing, inadequate schools, and a press subservient to its advertisers. With the years, he "grew more radical but not less religious," and increasingly threw himself into social reform, urging greater freedom for women, temperance, prison reform, and preaching against capital punishment and war.

In his thundering sermons and public addresses he appealed to the churches to take a positive stand against slavery, but not all of them responded. To him slavery was more than a political issue; it was a religious issue, for it denied to black people the freedom that the Creator meant all people to have. He gave aid to escaped slaves, and was one of the most outspoken among those who protested the Fugitive Slave Law. For his part in "the underground railroad" he was threatened with a jail sentence, but this did not silence him or stop his activities.

Theodore Parker is a pivotal figure in Unitarian history. He was only nine years old when Channing, the accepted leader of the older Unitarians, had preached the Baltimore sermon protesting the Calvinist low estimate of humanity. But a new generation was on the scene. Parker, together with Emerson, ushered in a new era in the development of Unitarianism, more radical, and a greater departure from traditional Protestant Christianity. He appealed to the young to take possession of the churches, to make them instruments of practical religion of the common people. The conservative Unitarians, he said, were aristocratic, exclusive, and smug, proud of their small choice numbers—"A church of old men goes to its grave, one of young men goes to its work."

After twelve years of a ministry of preaching, lecturing, and controversy, Parker's health broke. Orthodox preachers rejoiced and prayed the that great "infidel's" voice would be stopped. A period of foreign travel failed to restore the strength he had spent on truth and freedom, and he died in Florence, Italy, in 1860. His grave was marked by a simple stone with a modest inscription: 'Theodore Parker, Born at Lexington, Mass., United States of America, August 24, 1810, Died at Florence, May 10, 1860.''

Thirty-one years later a more substantial monument was unveiled, adding to the original inscription the words, "The Great American Preacher," and at the end, "His name is engraved in marble, his virtues in the hearts of those he helped to free from slavery and superstition." The addition of these latter words symbolizes the growing esteem and appreciation with which the Great American Preacher is remembered.

Theodore Parker introduced to the Unitarian ministry the liberal views of the Bible, stimulated by the writings of German scholars whose works he translated into English. He, more than any other, turned the course of Unitarian thinking away from its orthodox traditions, and toward the fulfillment of its liberalizing mission. He taught that the books of the Bible were of value as a record of human striving to know God and one's duty to humanity. He held that truths stand justified in their own right, and depend upon no supernatural authority. He broke with many of the formalities associated with the church and saw the church as an institution of worth only as it ministers to the needs of humanity. He claimed that religion is natural to all people and depends neither upon church, nor creed, nor clergy. Above all, he stood for freedom for the human spirit from all outside authorities and indignities, from all except the duties to God and humankind.

CHAPTER TWELVE

Henry Whitney Bellows
1814-1882

The Bellows twin boys looked so much alike that only their mother knew which was Henry and which was Edward. When they were baptized the minister was confused; he named Edward Henry and Henry, Edward. The parents, John and Betsy Eames Bellows, let the matter stand, and the boys grew up bearing the names the minister had given them. Edward perished in a snow storm in the middle west while still a young man. Henry became a Unitarian minister, widely known as a powerful preacher, as a the founder and president of the United States Sanitary Commission for relief work among soldiers in the Civil War, and as a leader in his denomination.

When Henry and his brother were born in Boston in 1814, there were already four children in the family, two boys and two girls. Mr. Bellows was successful in business and the children had the advantages of a comfortable and cultured home life. Before the twins were two years old the mother died, and the children were cared for by Mr. Bellows' sister until the father's second marriage.

The Bellows family in America dated to 1635. Fifteen years after the Pilgrims landed at Plymouth, the first John Bellows arrived in the New World. He came from England as a lad of twelve, and made his home among the Indians and a few white settlers in the region of Middlesex County, Massachusetts. Here he married and raised a family. He and his children helped to rebuild and develop the town of Marlboro, which had been destroyed in King Philip's War. The Bellows were pioneers. They cleared the land, constructed dams for water power, and built mills for sawing lumber, grinding grain, and making leather. The town of Lunenburg, Massachusetts, owes its beginning to Bellow's labor and leadership.

One of the most romantic characters in the family line was Benjamin, grandson of emigrant John. Benjamin was born in 1715, grew up in Lunenburg, married Abigail Sterns of that township, and raised a family of several children. When he was thirty-five, finding little in the settled communities of Massachusetts to satisfy his venturous spirit, Colonel Bellows mounted his horse and took off for the almost trackless wilderness of the north. Following an Indian footpath along the Connecticut River where it crosses the Massachusetts boundary near Northfield, he continued his trek until he reached the Great Falls, almost twenty-five miles north of Fort Dummer. Fort Dummer, built by the province of New Hampshire as a center for trade with the Indians, protected the four or five families that lived within its walls, and was one of the few white settlements along the Connecticut. It was on the site of the present city of Brattleboro, Vermont. To the north, there was only Fort Number Four in what is now Charlestown, New Hampshire.

Benjamin liked this wild country, especially the region of the Great Falls. He obtained, through the royal governor of New Hampshire, large grants of land on either side of the Connecticut and built a fort on a high bluff rising from the east side of the river, about two miles below the falls. Here in 1750 he brought his wife and children and twelve years later founded the town of Walpole, New Hampshire. The town was named for Sir Robert Walpole, Prime Minister of England under King George I. Until his death in 1777, the Colonel lived on his high hill above the river, broadening his land-holdings and widening his influence.

He was a man of great proportions, weighing three hundred and thirty pounds without his boots, altogether fit to match the hardships of frontier life. He built a large house and employed many farm hands, a number of them Indians, to work the ever-increasing acres brought under cultivation. To feed the workers and to entertain his guests an ox was slaughtered every week. Storage for winter supplies included twenty barrels of port and many barrels of hard cider. A great hunter, he found the woods offered plenty of game for his gun—deer and bears, wild turkeys, quails and pigeons. One morning before breakfast he killed two black bears and a catamount.

HENRY WHITNEY BELLOWS

Benjamin Bellows was a proprietor of Rockingham, across the river, and had secured the charter for this township, settled soon after the founding of Walpole. A community grew up near the Great Falls and took the name of the waterfall. In 1791, when Vermont was received into the Union, the name Great Falls was changed to Bellows Falls to honor the individual who had exerted the largest influence, and had been the greatest benefactor in that section of the Connecticut Valley.

Henry Whitney Bellows was a direct descendant of Colonel Bellows. He, too, was a pioneer, not in the untamed forests but in human relations. He, too, was a benefactor of his time, serving his fellow beings out of an understanding of their needs, and with leadership no less powerful than that of his famed ancestor. He, too, led an expansive and generous life.

From the age of seven, Henry and his twin brother were sent to a boys' school in Jamaica Plain, and later to an exclusive and expensive preparatory school in Northampton, Massachusetts. Summer found them spending their vacations in Walpole at the old family homestead, then occupied by Uncle Thomas Bellows.

At the age of fourteen, Henry entered Harvard College; he was graduated in 1832. At an early age he had decided to go into the ministry. In the fall of 1832 he enrolled in the Harvard Divinity School. But there was now no money for his further education; his father had met with financial misfortune. So Henry, who up to this time had found things rather easy, had to buckle down to making his own way in the world. He found a job teaching languages in a school in Cooperstown, New York. The next year he went to Louisiana where he tutored the son of a wealthy family. There was an excellent library in the house and Henry made the most of it in continuing his studies. He saved his money, returned to the Harvard Divinity School, and was graduated in 1837.

Bellows' first pastorate was a newly established Unitarian Society in Mobile, Alabama. He did not remain long, for although the congregation was largely from the north, he could not bring himself to live among those who condoned slavery. He returned north, and on the recommendation of William Ellery Channing, minister of the Federal Street Church in Boston, which Bellows had attended when in college, was called to the First Congregational (Unitarian) Church in New York City.

He had little pastoral experience, and New York was a big place, where a liberal minister would be surrounded by a strong orthodox churches and towering preachers. He shrank from the turmoil and strife of the city, and preferred a pastorate in some quiet New England village. But he was persuaded by those who saw the stuff of leadership in him, and who pointed out that an advocate of the liberal cause was greatly needed in the city. He accepted the position and was ordained and installed in January, 1839.

Bellows was only twenty-four at this time. He feared that the strain would be too much for him, for although of large frame and broad shoulders he had not been strong in childhood, and at times suffered from nervous exhaustion. But he seemed to thrive on hard work and threw himself with great vigor into the new job. For forty-three years he labored in the New York Church with increasing influence and well-deserved fame.

In the summer after his ordination, he was married to Eliza Townsend, daughter of a family in the church. She shared his labors, and until her death thirty years later looked after him and made a good home for their children. There were five children, three of whom died in infancy. In 1874, Dr. Bellows married Anna Peabody, who bore him three more children.

The New York church, founded twenty years before the new minister took over, was a small struggling society in a downtown section of the city. Bellows put new life into it. His down-to-earth sermons covered a wide range of subjects about everyday living. And they were not only wide but long, some lasting two hours. He gave lectures on art and literature, and on government, and when conservative members complained of "politics in the pulpit" he reminded them that religion should be related to all life, and that political affairs were a part of life.

In five years the old church building could not hold the increasing numbers who were attracted to the services. Congregations packed the pews and overflowed into the narrow vestibule. The increasing number of children could not be seated in the cramped quarters of the large Sunday School room. Also, the congregation was moving further uptown, and, except for members who could afford horse and carriage, there was little means of transportation. Horse-drawn cars were introduced in New York in 1831, but were operated only on a few thoroughfares. Whenever the subject of moving was brought up, it was opposed by those emotionally attached to the old building and by those fearful of the expense of erecting a new church. The matter was settled, however, the first Sunday after summer vacation. Just as the minister was closing the service, a great cornice fell from the ceiling, landing on the floor between the pulpit and the pews. One version of the incident says that the preacher had just pronounced the words, "Now let the grace of heaven descend upon us." A new church was built nearer the center of the parish, and named the Church of the Divine Unity. The church later adopted the name Unitarian Church of All Souls.

Bellows' influence reached beyond his church. He spoke and wrote on social issues: slavery, the emancipation of women, and the uses of wealth. He boldly declared his liberal views on matters too controversial for most preachers to discuss in public. His defense of the theater brought harsh comments from fellow clergy and others, who regarded all actors and actresses as immoral and the stage as a gateway to hell. He wrote an article suggesting that the circus offered opportunities to learn about human nature. P.T. Barnum, the circus king and a Universalist, liked it and had copies made, which he pasted to several yards of fence around his Bridgeport menagerie.

There were those who said that the Unitarian minister was always looking for publicity, and he was sometimes accused of sensationalism. Public criticism probably embarrassed members of his church, but none could deny that he brought religion to bear upon the lives of the people. He spoke out for the underprivileged and the deprived, and did more than denounce evil; he gave constructive aid to the reforms he proposed. Both rich and poor found him a warm-hearted, understanding friend.

Bellows' driving force was felt in the denomination not less than in the community. In 1846, he, with other Unitarians in the New York area, started the *Christian Inquirer*, a weekly publication of liberal opinion. Bellows himself wrote much of the paper and for eleven years was its editor. During this time he also was, for four years, the editor of the *Christian Examiner*, another Unitarian publication. With his vivid speech and commanding presence, Bellows was a favorite at denominational gatherings. When there were several others on a program he was placed at the end in order to wake up the audience that the less lively speechmakers had put to sleep.

The minister of All Souls was also a first-rate money raiser. On the principle that people should be glad to share their good fortune, he inspired citizens of wealth to give to worthy causes. In 1854, Horace Mann, president of the new Antioch College in Yellow Springs, Ohio, appealed to him to save the institution from bankruptcy. Dr. Bellows and his millionaire parishioner, Peter Cooper, journeyed westward on a fund-raising campaign. There were not many Unitarians west of the Hudson River, but they responded handsomely and the college was spared. Ten years later, Bellows with the help of Edward Everett Hale, the famous Unitarian minister in Boston, raised an endowment of one hundred thousand dollars for Antioch. He also raised considerable sums for theological education at Meadville and Harvard, and for a theological school in Cleveland that was never built.

The founding of Cooper Union in 1859 in New York was due in part to Bellows' genius in putting other people's money to good use. Peter Cooper, a wealthy industrialist, was a member of All Souls Church and a close friend of the minister. Together the two, in Bellows' study, discussed and made plans for the institution. It was established to provide free college-level courses for laboring people, together with a public reading room and other community services. It is noted for its forum held in the Great Hall where Abraham Lincoln made his famous Cooper Union speech in 1860.

At the outbreak of the Civil War, women in Charleston, West Virginia, in Bridgeport, Connecticut, and in other places in the north formed service groups to sew for the soldiers and to collect medical supplies and other articles to be sent to the military camps and to the battlefields. The women of All Souls Church had such a group. These activities were carried on in a hit or miss fashion, however; there was no central agency, and no overall plan for the collection and distribution of materials. Dr. Bellows saw the need to bring order into the service groups that were rapidly springing up in the local communities. He called a meeting of public-minded persons at Cooper Union, and a committee, including the All Souls minister, was chosen to go to Washington to see what could be done to create an agency for voluntary service to the soldiers.

The committee found much confusion in the capital and little enthusiasm for its plan. Regiments arrived in Washington after long journeys in crowded freight cars and found no preparation for their coming. Most of the army was made up of young men away from home for the first time, and in the charge of untrained officers. Services in the medical department of the army were out of date, and its staff resented outside influence. President Lincoln took a dim view of the proposed organization and said that it would be like "the fifth wheel of a coach."

The committee, except Dr. Bellows, went back home. He stayed on in Washington and talked with the President, and with as many other officers as would listen to him. The most stubborn opposition came from the Army, and from the medical departments. But Henry Whitney Bellows was not one to be turned aside. In June, 1861, the Sanitary Commission was created, with the approval of the Secretary of War. Dr. Bellows was made president and held the office during the war and after.

Bellows and his organization lost no time getting into action. In a tour of inspection he found conditions even worse than he had suspected. Food was scarce and poor in quality. The camps had no drainage or facilities for bathing. The army hospitals were no better. Attendants and nurses, mostly men, were without training, and the medical equipment wholly inadequate for the needs of the sick and wounded. Furthermore, there was graft as well as disorder in the handling of materials; the soldiers were receiving less in food, clothing, and medical supplies than the government provided for them.

Dorothea Dix, a Unitarian already famous for her work in prison reform, had volunteered her services at the beginning of the war, in her sixtieth year, and was appointed Superintendent of Women Nurses. Under the authority of the Medical Department she was allowed little independence, but in spite of this handicap she brought about reforms in the nursing services under her direction. The Sanitary Commission, on the other hand, was independent; it received no financial support from the government and was free from control by the Army and other goverment agencies.

Work was started at once to build temporary hospitals with improved sanitary conditions. Scores of able physicians and hundreds of public-spirited women and men were enlisted in a program to lower the death rate of the soldiers and to reduce the burden of their hardships and suffering. Unsanitary conditions in the camps were corrected, and improved methods were adopted in matters of diet, clothing, and sleeping quarters. Someone remembered that Dr. Benjamin Rush, when he was Surgeon General in the Revolutionary War, had written and circulated a leaflet, *Directions for Preserving the Health of Soldiers*. Bellows had thousands of pamphlets with up-to-date information printed and distributed in hospitals and camps.

The Commission did not confine its activities to camps and hospitals. Bellows, with his usual concern, saw to it that private aid was provided for soldiers and their dependents. Books were distributed among the hospital patients, letters written to families whose relatives were victims of the war, the disabled were visited, and the dead given decent burials. In short, as Mary A. Livermore, a member of the Commission, wrote, ''The object of the Sanitary Commission was to do what the Government could not.''

Backing up the Commission were the contributions of materials and of money that flowed into the treasury from more than seven thousand Soldiers' Aid Societies across the land. The people back home were kept informed of the soldiers' needs and responded generously.

Yet the calls upon the Commission to do what the Government could not, or did not do, were so great that within a year and a half after its beginning the organization was so deeply in debt, and there was danger that its work must come to an end. Bellows appealed for help to Thomas Starr King, minister of the Unitarian Church in San Francisco. King, already involved in keeping California in the Union, and busy undermining the powers of dishonest politicians in the state, nevertheless came to the rescue. He took to the lecture platform and raised one hundred thousand dollars to save the Commission. From then on funds for the work were never wanting.

Now everybody seemed to be raising money for the Sanitary Commission. Auctions, fairs, church suppers, cookie sales, sewing circles, and door-to-door canvassing gathered in the dollars and pennies that kept the wheels turning. A widow in Vermont, when the family cow gave birth to twins, said the Lord must have sent the extra calf for the boys at the front. In a frontier town in Nevada, two men were running for mayor. They agreed that the one who failed the election would tote a fifty-pound sack of flour to the next town, four miles away. The loser kept the agreement. Led by a brass band and followed by a holiday crowd of citizens he carried the burden all the way without once setting it down. He proposed to sell the sack at auction and to send the money to the Sanitary Commission. Each purchaser, in turn, then auctioned it off and soon five thousand dollars was raised. Then the sack was taken from town to town and sold at auction, finally reaching New York City on one coast, and San Francisco on the other. The final returns totaled forty thousand dollars.

The work of the Commission was needed after the war ended, finding jobs for the discharged soldiers, caring for the sick, locating the displaced, securing pensions for the disabled, providing artificial limbs for the crippled, and doing many other things to repair the human waste of war.

From his years with the Sanitary Commission, Dr. Bellows was convinced that there should be a permanent agency for war relief. But the people were weary of everything connected with war, and believed that war was so horrible that there would never be another. Bellows' proposal for a continuing agency was rejected. Years later, however, when the American Red Cross was founded through the efforts of Clara Barton, the services for which he had seen the need were provided.

Following the war, Dr. Bellows gave attention to organizing his denomination. It needed his executive ability. The American Unitarian Association had been founded in 1825 as a voluntary organization by a few individuals, in the hope that it would receive support of all churches in the denomination. But the small program of church extension was poorly supported by local congregations. Wealthy Unitarians gave generously to colleges, hospitals, and to many kinds of charitable and philanthropic institutions but gave little financial help to their denomination. After forty years the Association was still a weak structure. Many of the older ministers had little or no interest in broadening the field of Unitarian influence.

There were others, however, who believed that the time had come to bring the scattered liberal forces into closer union, and to promote a campaign for reaching the unchurched multitudes. A meeting was called in Boston in December, 1864. Bellows came from New York, crammed full of ideas gained from long experience. He proposed that Unitarians make a more serious effort to put their religion to work. The people would respond to a reasonable religion if it were taken to them. This would cost money, but many had prospered during the war and they should be willing to put some of their profits into a good cause. It was voted to raise a hundred thousand dollars for denominational work. Bellows had ready-made money-raising plans in his pocket. They were adopted, and in a few months the amount was surpassed.

He proposed the calling of a convention in New York of the ministers and delegates from all Unitarian churches "to consider the interests of our cause, and to institute measures for its good." The convention was held the next spring in All Souls Church. This was the first time that the Unitarian churches in America were directly represented in an official gathering. At this convention, the National Conference of Unitarian Churches was organized. The Conference put new life into the Unitarian movement, and in its early years greatly strengthened the extension work. After sixty years of varying influence, the Conference was merged in 1925 with the American Unitarian Association.

During the rest of his life, Dr. Bellows was a powerful and steadying influence in the Conference. Sharp differences of theological opinion among the members often prevented full cooperation and at times threatened to ruin the organization. An issue that plagued the Conference for years was whether one could be a Unitarian without being a "follower of Christ." Bellows, while taking a strong stand on the Christian emphasis, nevertheless blocked the effort of the conservatives to make the acceptance of a Christian creed a condition of membership in the Conference. When the names of "radical" ministers were dropped from the Unitarian Year Book, he was the first to protest this action, and continued to protest until the names were restored.

In 1854, Dr. Bellows purchased his ancestral home in Walpole. There he and his family spent the summer vacations, and there he hoped to retire. This was not to be. After a brief illness that came on in the midst of his busy life, he died in his New York home on January 30, 1882. He was buried in the family cemetery in Walpole, near the grave of his famous ancestor.

Henry Whitney Bellows, like his stalwart ancestor of the frontier, was a pioneer. He made his New York pulpit a sounding board for religion in the personal and community life at a time when preachers generally kept aloof from the outside world. Perhaps no other minister served this country with greater distinction during the Civil War. Yet, with all his outside activities he never neglected his pastoral duties. Under his leadership All Souls became one of the strongest churches in the denomination. Religious liberals are indebted to him for his work in the Unitarian movement at a time when, without his invigorating influence, it might have become less a denomination than a loose federation of isolated churches.

CHAPTER THIRTEEN

Mary A. Livermore
1820-1905

The headmaster of the English Department in the Hancock School was plainly in an ugly mood. Calling Mary Ashton Rice to his desk, he demanded, "From what book did you copy your composition?" "I understood that we were to write original compositions, " she replied. "That was the requirement, but you haven't complied with it, it appears," he said with a sneer. Then he added, "I am going to offer a reward to any member of the school who will discover the book or magazine from which you have copied this composition, and someone will find it." Mary's eyes flashed in anger, but she quietly said, "I will persuade my father to double the reward."

The class was called to order and the case stated as if Mary, the accused, were already convicted of the charge of cheating. "Before deciding what to do with this young lady I am going to send her into the lobby with only a large slate and a pencil. She will write a composition on self-government, and at the end of an hour we will hear it. We shall then be able to judge somewhat her ability in English composition." At the end of the hour Mary returned to the classroom and stood before the class. The pupils sat tense and silent as she began to read. The composition, while not remarkable, showed beyond doubt that for a thirteen-year-old she possessed the ability to think clearly and to express her thoughts well in writing. The teacher was not pleased. He stopped her before she had finished, but not until she had read that self-government was important for young people and should be practiced also by the school master who was so entirely ruled by a bad temper that he was both a terror and a laughing stock to his pupils! She took her seat while her classmates applauded and waved their handkerchiefs. The school master had to admit that she had more ability to write than he had given her credit for.

Mary Ashton Rice had a mind of her own, a quick intellect, a retentive memory, a strong body, a sense of justice, and a warm friendly interest in people. These qualities served her well in later life, and helped to place her among the most notable women of America. She became famous as an educator, writer, editor, lecturer, and reformer, active in the national and humanitarian issues of her generation.

She was born in the North End of Boston in 1820, the fourth in a family of six children. Her father, Timothy Rice, was an old-fashioned Calvinist Baptist, and her mother Zebiah Ashton Rice, kind, tolerant, and gracious, was a less rigid member of the same faith. The children were brought up under severe religious discipline. They were expected from the age of six to read the Bible from cover to cover once a year. A blessing was asked before and after every meal, and each day closed with scripture reading and prayers, while the children, under the questioning of the father, gave an account of their use of every hour of the day. Sunday was especially hard on the children. There was to be no work on that day, not even cooking food, and certainly no play. The only reading allowed on Sunday was the Bible. On her eighth birthday, Mary was given a copy of *Robinson Crusoe*. She was caught reading it on a Sunday afternoon and the book was thrown into the flames of the fireplace. Her sense of justice outraged, she said to her mother at bedtime, "I'm glad this Sunday has gone, and I wish we weren't to have another for twenty years."

But the Sundays continued. The family rose early, and every child old enough to walk was marched to the First Baptist Church for an hour and a half of Sunday School, and then to the two-hour preaching service. After a cold dinner at home, the whole family returned to church for another service with longer prayers and a longer sermon than in the morning. Sometimes Mary visited Grandmother Ashton over the weekend and was taken to the Charles Street Baptist Church. She liked this better than her own church, for her grandmother let her sleep during the sermon, a privilege never granted in her parents' pew.

With all its austerities, the Rice family had a good home life. The big vine-covered house with its great kitchen and its many fireplaces, its garden in the back, and the tall elms in the front yard, was comfortable and well-ordered. The children were loved and well-protected, and suffered from neither poverty nor riches. The Fourth of July and Thanksgiving were the chief holidays, when aunts and uncles, grandparents, and a flock of cousins came to share the festivities and joys of the family. The girls, under the direction of their mother, learned to do needlework and to help with household duties, which increased with their years and strength.

Mr. Rice was a generous-hearted man, by nature happy and optimistic, but he was weighed down with a religion that took much of the joy out of his life. His greatest hope was that his children should escape the endless punishment that he believed awaited the majority of the human race. He wept when he taught his sons and daughters the creed of his church.

What happened to people after death was a matter that weighed heavily upon Mary's mind, and aroused fears that marred the otherwise happy years of her childhood. When she was seven she was taken to her mother's room to welcome a newborn sister. As she looked at the baby the thought came to her, "What if she is not elected to be saved?" She appealed to her parents, "Don't let us keep the baby. Do send her back to God!" The father tried to comfort her by saying, "We will pray that God will make her a good Christian." But this was no comfort to Mary; she had learned the doctrine of election too well. Being a good Christian was not enough; one had to be elected in order to be saved.

The problem of salvation was brought home to her by a family tragedy that darkened her life. Its shadow was not dispelled until years later when she came to know and to accept the teachings of Universalism. Her sister, next younger than herself, was an invalid. The child was sweet and lovely and had no fear of death. She died suddenly and without having been converted. The parents accepted the idea that their daughter had died unsaved. Mary rebelled at this monstrous thought, and shocked her family and the pastor by declaring that she would rather go to hell with her good sister than to heaven with God who would damn an innocent soul to torment. The terrible teachings of her religion almost drove her to distraction.

Only complete absorption in study brought relief to her tortured mind. At the time of her sister's death, Mary had graduated from the Hancock School. Now she wanted to continue her education. Education was not considered as necessary for girls as for boys, but Mr. Rice looked favorably upon his daughter's ambition, and she was sent to the Charlestown Female Academy. At the age of sixteen she graduated with honors, and was at once engaged to teach languages in the Academy. But she was restless and was still tormented by the theological riddles she could not solve.

After a year of teaching an opportunity came to get away from the surroundings that continually recalled the tragedy through which she had passed. She was offered a position as tutor to the children of a wealthy plantation family in southern Virginia. Her family was opposed to her going so far from home. Her father even forbade it. "A daughter should live at home with her father," he declared, "and under his protection, obedient to his laws, until she marries, and then she should live under her husband's roof, and be subject to him." For the first time in her life Mary disobeyed him. She was growing up.

Virginia seemed a long way from Massachusetts in 1837, and for a girl of seventeen who had never been away from her family, the journey seemed as venturesome as a trip to the moon. By boat, by train, and by stage coach, she finally reached her destination. Here she taught for three years, and here she came to know at first hand the institution of slavery, the experience that made her a confirmed abolitionist.

The five children placed in her charge were to be taught religion as well as other subjects. Their parents were intelligent, cultured, and well-read. They were skeptical of all religions, but wanted their children instructed in the orthodox Christian faith. Mary complied with their wishes. She still held to her early religious teachings, for she knew no other, although they brought her only sorrow and suffering. There was a well-stocked library in this plantation home, and Mary read for the first time the writings of the Deists, Thomas Paine, and Ethan Allen, and engaged in long theological discussions with the master of the house. Neither the books nor the discussions were helpful; she could not accept the extreme views to which she was introduced, and she could not be reconciled to the doctrines taught by her church and her father. But she learned to live with her trouble, to be outwardly gay, to mask suffering with a smile, and to hide from the world her weariness with life. At last, feeling that she was prepared to face family and friends, she returned home and was soon given charge of a school in Duxbury, Massachusetts. Here Mary Rice found the help which lifted the heavy burden she had so long endured.

One Christmas Eve, too depressed to study, she went out for a long walk alone. With the intention of going to the beach she took the street past the Universalist Church. As she drew near the door opened to receive visitors and Mary heard the singing of a Christmas hymn, more joyous than she had ever heard in a church. She stood in the middle of the street with the raw wind blowing from the sea, attracted to the light and warmth, and singing inside. She crossed the yard and listened at the door. To enter was quite out of the question, she told herself. Her church in Boston looked with disfavor upon any kind of observance of Christmas; it was a Catholic festival, and special pains were taken to treat the day with complete neglect. Besides, this church was a Universalist Church, and she had never heard anything good about Universalists. She remembered hearing her father talking about a preacher named Ballou, who led people astray with his preaching of universal salvation, a man no better than that radical Theodore Parker who gathered the riffraff of Boston to hear his tirades against the respectable business leaders of the society. No, she could not enter a Universalist Church! But just as she was about to turn away the sexton opened the door to let in some latecomers, and she suddenly found herself in the back pew, looking up at the young minister who was just beginning his sermon.

She had never heard such a sermon. The text was from the gospel according to Matthew: "And thou shalt call his name Jesus, for he shall save his people from their sins." "Jesus teaches us how to live," the preacher said, "so that we may avoid the mistakes and wrong-doings to which we are liable. We are taught to forgive others, and God too must be forgiving, otherwise we are expected to be better than God. Even as the shepherd in the parable seeks the lost sheep until he finds it, so God in his love for his children will seek all who stray and finally bring them safely home." It seemed to Mary Rice that the Bible had never been opened to her before. A great peace came over her being.

After the service she lingered to ask the minister for the manuscript of his sermon. He introduced himself as Daniel Parker Livermore, and he not only lent her the manuscript but made an appointment to meet her at the library the next day after school to answer any questions that the reading of the sermon might raise.

She did not intend to be swayed in her opinions by the hearing of one sermon. During the weeks that followed, she read books lent her by her newfound friend, made notes from them, searched the Bible, and discussed religion with the Rev. Mr. Livermore, with the result that the atmosphere was cleared for her. She felt free to develop her own ideas of God.

Mary and the minister evidently did not confine their conversations to theology, for the next year the village school teacher became Mrs. Daniel Livermore. Marriage to a Universalist minister was a blow to the bride's family and friends. She was cut off from the circles in which she had moved; but Mary Livermore was happy, for she had found a religion that appealed to the highest in her nature and satisfied her fine mind.

During the next eleven years, the Livermores moved frequently, serving churches in Massachusetts and Connecticut. Among the churches served by Mr. Livermore were Fall River, Weymouth, and Melrose, Massachusetts; Stafford, Connecticut; Auburn, New York; and Quincy, Illinois. Ministers who had positive views on social problems and engaged in social action had a rough time in those years. Temperance (total abstinence from intoxicating beverages) had been taught as a moral principle by some of the Protestant churches for several years and now was becoming a political issue. Sentiment was growing over the question of Women's Suffrage. And the abolition of slavery was the most debated, most controversial issue of the day. In every congregation were those who took a stand for or against these reforms. The Livermores, active in the temperance movement, championed women's rights, and were outspoken abolitionists. They could not be silent, and although Mr. Livermore was reluctant to withdraw from the parish ministry, he found the position so difficult that he decided to seek employment in some other field.

He became owner and editor of *The New Covenant*, a Universalist paper published in Chicago. In 1858, the Livermores and their three children moved to the booming, sprawling frontier city on the shores of Lake Michigan. Mrs. Livermore for several years had been writing for various denominational and other publications. She now became associate editor of her husband's paper and wrote extensively for it. Mr. Livermore had to travel in the interest of his publishing business, and more and more in his absence she took over the duties of the enterprise, writing for all departments of the paper except the theological. *The New Covenant* became a strong and steady champion of social reform, always with emphasis upon principles of Christian ethics. In addition to editorial duties she was active in church and

Sunday School, and in community affairs, and was one of the founders of the Chicago Home for Aged Women and the Hospital for Women and Children. Of the more than one hundred newspaper reporters in the press section of the Chicago Convention that nominated Abraham Lincoln for president, Mary A. Livermore was the only woman.

During the War Between the States, the United States Sanitary Commission became the clearing house organization for the care and relief of soldiers. The chairperson of the Commission, Dr. Henry W. Bellows, chose Mrs. Livermore as one of his two associates. The other was Mrs. Jane C. Hoge, also a Universalist. Through the entire period of the war Mary Livermore did organizational work, speaking at rallies, keeping records, arranging for supplies to be sent to the front, and raising money. She proposed, planned, and managed the two great Chicago Fairs that yielded nearly a million dollars for the work of the Commission. She made trips to Washington to confer with President Lincoln; visited military camps to supervise the distribution of clothing and medical supplies; and brought back the sick and wounded to hospitals in the north. President Lincoln gave her the manuscript of the Emancipation Proclamation, which was sold at auction for three thousand dollars for the Sanitary Commission.

After the war, Mrs. Livermore gave most of her time to the Women's Suffrage movement, and became one of its most influential advocates. She established and edited *The Agitator* in Chicago, devoted to the cause of temperance as well as to women's rights. After a year this paper was merged with the *Woman's Journal*, a weekly publication founded in Boston in 1870. Mrs. Livermore became editor-in-chief. The Livermores moved to Melrose, Massachusetts, and they resided there for the rest of their lives.

As an editor, Mrs. Livermore was often called upon to speak in behalf of various reforms. Her popularity as a lecturer grew, and the demands were so insistent that after two years with the *Woman's Journal* she gave up its editorship for the lecture platform. This, the last quarter of the nineteenth century, was a period of social agitation and reform movements. Educators, preachers, poets, and professional elocutionists in great numbers took to the American platform. Public lecturers could be heard in almost every village and on every subject under the sun.

Moral courage, idealism, and a wide range of human interest were evident in Mrs. Livermore's lecture topics. Her booking agents warned her against dealing with controversial matters. She listened but went her own way, speaking on the most divisive questions of the day—women's equality with men, the liquor problem, suffrage, the double standard in sexual morality and marital relations. Her power and influence from the platform were tremendous. One of her pleas in behalf of women was that they should receive an education so that married or unmarried they would be able to stand on their own feet, capable of supporting themselves, and helpful to the world. Often men in her audience either protested, or pretended to doze when she advocated such an extravagent freedom for women.

When an audience was listless she would remember with amusement a childhood experience. When she was a little girl she often went to the woodshed to play. Standing on a box she would preach to the sticks of wood arranged in rows to represent her listeners. Her wooden congregation, she observed, was not less responsive than some that she now addressed.

Travel had many hardships and dangers in Mrs. Livermore's day. Hotels often afforded poor accommodations, train schedules were uncertain, and engines frequently broke down. Once, in order to keep a speaking engagement in Cincinnati, she made a twenty-mile journey in a beer wagon. When on another occasion no passenger service was available, she was sent by an obliging official on a cattle train and was billed as "livestock." She was in more than one train wreck, and once nearly lost her life on a ferry boat that caught fire crossing the Missouri River.

In 1878 the Livermores went to Europe for several months. They attended the International Women's Rights Congress in Paris. Mrs. Livermore was a member of the American committee that had promoted this great gathering from sixteen nations. She lectured repeatedly on the Continent and in England, and made the personal acquaintance of important persons in reform, liberal religion, and literary circles. A British newspaper referred to her as "America's Queen of the Platform."

In her long life of public service Mary A. Livermore never neglected her church. During her entire residence in Chicago she taught classes in the Universalist Church of the Redeemer and served on the board of trustees of the Northwest Conference of Universalists. When in 1870 the Universalists in celebration of the one hundredth anniversary of the landing of John Murray set out to raise a Centenary Fund of $200,000, it was found that Mrs. Livermore had raised more money than any other woman in the denomination. Although never ordained, she preached in Universalist and other churches throughout the land.

On May 6, 1895, the Rev. Mr. and Mrs. Livermore observed the fiftieth anniversery of their marriage. They had planned a quiet day of observance in their home, with their children and grandchildren and other near relatives. But friends and neighbors objected, and insisted on a larger celebration. Flags were raised on public buildings. All afternoon from two until seven o'clock the house was thronged with guests. The public schools closed to allow the pupils to share in the festivities and 290 came from the Mary A. Livermore School to pay their respects to the lady for whom the institution was named. Greetings and gifts arrived from all parts of the country and from abroad.

Tufts College, formerly for men only, graduated the first four-year group of women in 1896. At the commencement that year, Mary A. Livermore was awarded the degree of L.L.D., the first honorary degree conferred by Tufts upon a woman.

Mrs. Livermore lived for eighty-five years. Toward the end she wrote, ''False early conceptions darkened my childhood and youth. This faith in Universalism, during the years that I have believed it, has grown upon me, until it is the central thing in me. I do not engage in anything that is not, as I see it, the outcome of this faith. My later comprehension has given me a noble and abiding faith in human destiny.'' And she added: ''I am happy that I may still lend a hand to the weak and stuggling or strike a blow for the right against the wrong.'' When she died in 1905, the *Boston Transcript* proclaimed her ''America's foremost woman.''

CHAPTER FOURTEEN

Susan B. Anthony
1820-1906

Thirteen-year-old Susan Anthony was perplexed over a number of things. It seemed to her as she entered the teen years that women were denied most of the advantages freely given to men. In the district school she had asked to be taught long division, but was told that this was for boys; girls would have use only for addition and subtraction. Then there was the time when an overseer was needed in her father's cotton factory. Sally Ann, from Vermont, the best weaver in the mill, could not be given the position because it would never do to have a woman for overseer. The place was filled by a man. Right in her own family, money from the mill workers who boarded in the Anthony home was turned over to father. Mother, who with the help of her three small girls, Guelma, Susan and Hannah, cooked the meals, did the washing and ironing, and made the beds, kept not a cent for herself. When she needed money she had to ask her husband for it.

Whenever Susan asked her mother why things were this way she was told that men and women had different duties according to their natures. Men carried on the business, managed the affairs of the government, and owned whatever their wives and children earned or inherited. Woman's place was in the home; her duty was to bear children and to care for them and her husband.

These answers did not satisfy Susan. She wondered why only men attended the Town Meetings and were allowed to vote. She wondered why no woman was ever put on the School Board. In her history book she read about the Declaration of Independence and the Revolutionary War, and knew that in colonial America only property owners were allowed to vote. After the war one state after another had removed the property restriction, allowing all free men the franchise. Massachusetts had taken this action in 1820, the year Susan was born near the village of Adams in the Berkshire Hills. Now only black people, Indians, criminals, idiots, the insane, and women were denied the right to vote. Susan wondered why.

It was not strange that she possessed an inquiring and independent mind. Her father, Daniel Anthony, although a Quaker and disciplined in the strict principles of the faith, nevertheless had a mind of his own. Susan had heard about the romance of her parents that led to their marriage. She knew how Daniel defied the authority of his church by taking a woman who was not a Quaker for his wife—lively, attractive Lucy Read, a Baptist.

Two years after Susan was born Mr. Anthony had built a cotton mill of twenty-six looms near Adams and had prospered. Here in the beautiful Berkshire valley the Anthony home was established, and here the first three children were born. Lucy Read Anthony, as the dutiful wife of a Quaker, had to give up her gay dresses for the plain garb, and forego the parties and music to which she was accustomed. She never joined the Quaker Church, but the family attended the meetings, and Susan at twelve years of age became a member of the Society of Friends.

The family had moved to Battenville, New York, forty miles across the state line, where Mr. Anthony was partner in a large and flourishing cotton factory. Susan was only six when they left Massachusetts. But she never forgot the childhood days in the pleasant valley with the big, white clapboarded house, the fragrant purple and white lilacs in the dooryard, and the wide fields beyond, where tall daisies and buttercups waved to her in summer, and snowdrifts piled high in winter. Not far away she especially remembered old Greylock Mountain, with its ever-changing patterns of light and shade made by the moving clouds. On its top the first snow of autumn appeared and there the snow lingered latest in the spring, sometimes for weeks after the lowlands were bare.

In Battenville, Mr. Anthony built a fifteen-room brick house and a company store. He was an advocate of temperance and would not allow liquor to be sold, despite the warning that this attitude would ruin his business. In the house a large room was reserved for a school. In the district school the teaching was limited to spelling, reading, and writing, with sewing for the girls. The Anthonys wanted a better education than this for their children. There were now two more to be educated, Daniel junior, and Mary. A teacher with up-to-date training was found, a graduate of a Female Seminary. She brought new methods, introduced the reading of poetry and nature study, and wanted to teach music. Mr. Anthony balked at this; Quakers were suspicious of music, as they thought it might encourage frivolity. And so the Anthony children grew up without the joy of expressing in song the natural desires of their young hearts.

Mr. Anthony also established a night school for the mill workers, and organized an anti-liquor society in the village. Temperance meetings were held in the Anthony parlor, and while no females were invited, Susan in an adjoining room listened to the testimony of reformed drunkards and to the recital of the evil consequences of drinking. She formed opinions that later made her a strong and active crusader in the temperance movement.

In Battenville, Susan saw black people for the first time. Her father explained that the laws of some states permitted them to be bought and sold like horses and cows. Daniel said that slavery must go some day. Susan faced another perplexing question; why should some people, because of the color of their skin, be the property of another?

When Susan was seventeen she entered a Friends' Seminary near Philadelphia, where her sister Guelma was teaching. Her studies were suddenly cut short, for the greatest financial panic of the century ruined her father's business, and she returned home to Battenville. Daniel had lost everything: the cotton factory, the store, and the house he had built. The cows, pigs, chickens, tools from the barn, and food stored in the cellar were all sold at auction. Susan stood beside her mother and saw their household stripped of everything they held dear: the furniture, rugs they had woven, books, clothing, and even Daniel's spectacles. Lucy wept when her pale blue teacups went. Years before Susan had given them to her mother, having bought them with money earned working a few weeks at the mill. After the auction they learned that Uncle Joshua Read had bid off the most needed and most prized articles, including the pale blue cups. He returned all to the family.

There was no more schooling for Susan Anthony. She must earn money to help her father pay his debts. She taught school in Union

City at a salary of thirty dollars for a term of fifteen weeks. During the following years both Susan and her sisters taught school in various places, never receiving more than two or two-and-one-half dollars a week. Sometimes Susan took the place of a man discharged for incompetency and received only one-half or one-third of the salary that had been paid him. Her sense of justice outraged, she observed that this was another example of the mistaken low estimate of womankind. She wrote home, ''It isn't fair, and sometime I'm going to do something about it.''

Mr. Anthony moved his family down the Battenkill River to a settlement called Hardscrabble, where he operated a grist and saw mill. But people had no money to buy grain or lumber. The next move was to a small farm on the outskirts of Rochester. The first payment on the place came from a small inheritance Lucy had received from her father. Her brother, Joshua, held the property in his name and leased it to Susan's father. If the farm had been held by Lucy, it would, under the state law of that time, belong to her husband, and could have been claimed by his creditors. Susan, home on vacation, joined the family on the journey eastward to the new farm. After several days travel by stagecoach, and by boat on the Erie Canal, they reached Rochester and the farm to begin life anew.

The following year Susan received through the influence of Uncle Joshua an appointment to teach in the female department of the Academy in Canajoharie. She was tired of teaching, but the family needed the money. Her father found that the thirty-two acre farm was too small to yield a living. Eventually he went into the insurance business, a venture that proved successful. The farm was kept, however, as the family home.

Two years of teaching at the Academy were quite enough. Between terms she had traveled to surrounding towns organizing Daughters of Temperance Clubs, and had even made a few speeches in behalf of the temperance cause. This she began to find more interesting than teaching. She wanted a change, something to challenge her thinking and test her strength. She was twenty-eight, strong and good-looking; it was said of her in Canojoharie that she was ''the smartest woman that ever came to this town.''

When friends suggested that it was time she married, her reply was that she would if ever the right man turned up. But this never happened, although candidates for her hand were not lacking. There was probably some dapper young blade in Canajoharie with a flashing mustache and a yellow vest, who would take her buggy riding and top off the evening with a declaration of undying love. And there was the widowed Quaker deacon who tried to tempt her with his one hundred and sixty acres free of debt, a house with running water, and forty Jersey cows! But Susan was choosy, and a bit wary of males and their assumption of superiority.

She returned to the farm in September after two years' absence. The peaches were ripe for canning and the vegetables in the garden ready for gathering and storing. Fences needed mending and a thousand odd jobs required attention. From early morning until sunset she labored in the fields and orchard and found the days too short. On rainy days and in the long evenings when she helped her mother with the sewing and weaving there was time to think about the future and how best to use it.

On Sunday afternoons the anti-slavery group met at the fair. Frequently Frederick Douglass, the black editor for the Abolitionist *North Star* in Rochester, came with his family to dinner, and other noted Abolitionists came to the meetings. Susan was always delighted when the company included the Unitarian minister from Syracuse, the Reverend Samuel J. May. She thought he was the wisest, most friendly of them all.

The Society of Friends in Rochester would have nothing to do with the anti-slavery movement, so Susan, her father, and several other liberal Quakers joined the Unitarian Church. Susan liked the services in the Rochester church with its great pipe organ and choir, features forbidden in the Friends' meetings. Her Quaker upbringing had given her a strong sense of personal duty and high ethical standards. Her new associations added to these qualities a larger concept of human freedom and a clearer understanding of the reaches of religion.

She became absorbed increasingly in the temperance cause, and also attended anti-slavery meetings whenever possible. When the exclusively male Sons of Temperance invited the Daughters of Temperance to its convention in Albany, Susan went as a delegate from Rochester. But when she attempted to speak from the floor on a motion, the presiding officers, amazed that a woman would dare speak in public, announced that "The sisters were invited not to speak, but to listen and learn." Susan and other indignant women delegates left the hall. That evening they held a meeting of their own, which resulted in a new women's organization, the militant Woman's State Tem-

perance Society. Elizabeth Cady Stanton was elected president and
Susan B. Anthony was made secretary.

Several influences were drawing Susan toward the new woman's suffrage movement. The leaders she most admired for courage
and intelligence in the work for temperance and against slavery were
also crusading to give women economic and political freedom. She
especially admired Elizabeth Cady Stanton and Lucretia Mott. Lucretia
Mott, in 1848, had called the first convention on woman's rights, in
Seneca Falls, New York. Mrs. Stanton drew up and published a woman's declaration modeled on the Declaration of Independence. "We
hold these truths to be self-evident: that all men *and women* are created equal." Wherever in the Declaration of Independence the word
"the King of England" appears, the word "man" was substituted,
and the same number of grievances listed. The document created an
explosion that rattled the dry political bones in Washington, and in
every state capital, and brought down upon the head of the author
the wrath and ridicule of conservative newspapers across the country. Susan's parents and her sister Mary had not only attended the
second woman's rights convention, but had also signed this declaration. They still expressed enthusiastic approval of Mrs. Stanton and
her leadership.

It was not until 1852, however, that Susan definitely cast her lot
with the woman's rights movement. That year, at Mrs. Stanton's urging, she attended the convention at Syracuse. She was impressed with
the quality of the leaders, and captivated by the persons she met.
There was Lucy Stone, to whose eloquent speech on the anti-slavery
platform she had once listened, and many others whose names were
often spoken in reform circles. One great delight was in meeting
Lucretia Mott and her husband for the first time. Both of them were
recognized leaders in reform.

Susan came from the convention committed to the cause. Devoted to the programs of temperance and anti-slavery that continued to
claim her labors, she nevertheless was convinced that effective social
reform was possible only with the support of women at the polls. To
give women the ballot, she thought, was to help all people toward
freedom.

Women were held captive with chains forged by the pattern of
the centuries. The Revolutionary War, fought for freedom from
despotic rule, left American women in bondage to the authority and
caprice of men. Men made the laws and enforced them. Men owned

the property and controlled the means of livelihood. This was the way of life passed on from generation to generation. It even had the sanction of religion; in the Christian marriage ceremony the wife must promise to obey her husband. In one denomination she had to promise to fear him! In most of the states money earned by a married woman, or property from gifts or inheritance belonged to the husband. She had no legal claim upon her children; without her consent the husband could will them away, or sell their labor. A husband had the right to beat his wife, although one court ruled that the club used must not be bigger than the thickness of a thumb—a man's thumb of course. Women were barred from most of the professions and trades. If they taught school or labored in a factory they received only a fraction of the wages paid men for the same work.

Such were the conditions, and Susan was fully aware of them when, at the age of thirty-two, she took up the burden of human rights, a burden carried for more than fifty years with an amazing degree of organizing genius and strength of purpose.

She went to see Mrs. Stanton in Seneca Falls and together they planned a course of action. The state capital would be the scene of the first skirmish. A convention would be held in Albany and an attack made upon the stronghold of male privilege, the state legislature.

During the winter, Susan canvassed the towns and countrysides of Western New York, speaking wherever given the use of a hall, and getting signatures to a petition for women's rights to be presented to the legislature. Rowdies often broke up the meetings, poked fun at her on the streets, and women slammed their doors in her face, but there was no stopping Susan Anthony. The hardest part was the indifference and antagonism of the women themselves who seemed to resent any effort to better their condition.

The Albany Convention, lasting two weeks, went off well. Susan made all the arrangements, had posters and handbills printed, and engaged several men speakers of prominence, including Samuel J. May and William Henry Channing, the young minister of the Unitarian Church in Rochester. In Susan's opinion, however, the women speakers did far better than the men. A hearing had been granted to Elizabeth Cady Stanton before the legislature. Susan was in a state of high excitement as they entered the Senate chamber and saw the assembled awe-inspiring bewhiskered, frock-coated makers of the law. Mrs. Stanton made an eloquent plea for legislation permitting married women to keep their earnings, and for woman's suffrage. Miss Anthony presented her petitions with ten thousand signatures. The politicians listened respectfully, but ignored both plea and petition.

Failure of the legislature to act only spurred Susan to greater efforts. During the next two years her campaign covered fifty-four counties in New York, and she sold two hundred thousand tracts. Thousands of names were secured for another petition which was presented to the New York legislature. This document met with ridicule by the politicians in Albany, but when, three years later in 1860, a bill was passed greatly extending the rights of married women, Susan felt amply repaid. The bill gave the right to a married woman to carry on trade, keep her earnings, and to have the guardianship of her children equal with her husband.

It was more and more difficult to arouse interest in woman's rights because of the growing controversy over slavery. One by one Susan's hitherto able workers became absorbed in "saving the Union" or "freeing the slaves." But she persisted even after the fall of Fort Sumter, and President Lincoln's call for volunteers. Susan was a pacifist, with no confidence in violence as a solution in any crisis. She felt much alone and useless in a world gone mad with war.

Throughout the country women were responding bravely to the call for their services. Those with husbands and sons gone to war carried on the work on farms, in mills, and in business. Women sewed and knitted for the soldiers, organized Ladies' Aid Societies to send food and clothing to the army. Mary A. Livermore was raising money for the Sanitary Commission headed by Dr. Bellows, Dorothea Dix, and Clara Barton, while other volunteers were caring for the sick and wounded in the hospitals and on the battlefields. Susan's war services took a different turn. Others could knit and sew, and but somebody should see to it that the slaves were made free as well as the Union preserved. The Emancipation Proclamation was not enough; there must be action by the Congress to make it effective.

Her father, to whom she had always gone for advice, had died suddenly, but there was the ever-faithful Elizabeth Stanton, who had moved from Seneca Falls to New York City. In the spring of 1863, Susan went to see her. The result of their conference was the launching of the women's National Loyal League, whose aim was to arouse public opinion to demand an amendment to the Constitution abolishing slavery. Susan had a busy year with meetings, letters, conferences, and collecting signatures. Four hundred thousand names were enrolled, and within a year the Thirteenth Amendment passed the Senate, and was declared ratified by the states in December of the following year.

The war was over, and the Thirteenth Amendment securely planted. But black people and women still did not have the vote. Mrs. Stanton had believed, Susan had hoped, and the politicians had promised that as a reward for services rendered in the war, women would be given the ballot. Now the squabble was over Negro suffrage, and the matter of women's rights was pushed aside. Party politics clouded the issue. The country was as much divided over giving black people the ballot as it had ever been over slavery.

Susan, with an office in New York, was now publishing a paper fittingly called *Revolution*. She wanted black people to have the full rights of citizenship, but she insisted on the prior claim of women. Week after week the *Revolution* pounded away on this point. The controversy was a factor in the split in the suffrage movement. In 1869, the members who no longer could go along with the Stanton-Anthony policies withdrew from the National Woman's Suffrage Association. After twenty-one years the two associations were united in the National Woman's Suffrage Association, with Susan B. Anthony as president.

There was nothing in the Constitution, Susan Anthony thought, that limited voting to men, but only custom and the notion of male superiority. She decided to test this theory, shared by some lawyers. She went home to Rochester and on election day in November cast her ballot, in a barber shop where the voting took place. She was brought to trial and fined one hundred dollars and court costs, but not before she had given judge and jury a liberal lecture on American civil rights!

When the great Centennial Exposition of 1876 was held in Philadelphia, Susan was on hand circulating tracts to remind people that a century of American independence had not given women their natural rights. When refused permission by the Centennial Commission to hold a meeting to present their claims, the women were given the use of the First Unitarian Church. The new American Association worked mostly for women's rights legislation in the states. Anthony, while she went to help the Rev. Olympia Brown in the Kansas Suffrage campaign, and continued speaking in other states, placed more and more stress on the need of influencing national legislation. For the rest of her life she bent her energies in this direction, sending to the Republican and Democratic National Conventions pleas to include a women's suffrage plank in their political platforms, and also sending petitions to Congress. "We have puttered with States Rights for thirty years," she declared, "without a foothold except in the territories." Only Wyoming and Utah had enfranchised their women. Twice (in 1869 and 1878) a federal Woman's Suffrage Amendment had been introduced in Congress. They were conveniently referred to committees from which they never returned. Many fair-weather friends of Woman's Suffrage said the time was not ripe, but to Susan B. Anthony the time for freedom was always ripe.

At the close of the century Susan Anthony resigned the presidency. She was made Honorary President, and, until her death six years later, continued as counsellor and inspirer of her successor. Her victories came by hard work, sacrifice, daring and endurance, and in the equal suffrage movement they were few. Yet the final triumphant cry of this eighty-six-year-old undefeated woman, the words of her last public speech, were "Failure is impossible." One hundred years after Lucy and Daniel Anthony's second daughter was born under the shadows of Greylock, the belated victory was won. On August 26, 1920, the Secretary of State proclaimed that the Nineteenth Amendment had been adopted and was in effect. "The right of the citizens of the United States to vote shall not be denied or abridged by the United States or by any State on account of sex."

CHAPTER FIFTEEN

Clara Barton
1821-1912

On December 25, 1821, the Barton family had a lovely Christmas gift, a new-born baby named Clarissa Harlow. There were already four children, Dorothy, sixteen; Stephen, fifteen; David, thirteen; and Sally, ten.

The Bartons lived in the township of Oxford, Massachusetts. The father, Captain Stephen Barton, had served in the Indian wars as a young man. He had returned home to Oxford from the western frontier, married Sarah Stone, and had become a successful farmer. The large farm with its cleared acres, big barns, and snug story-and-a-half farmhouse overlooking the wooded hills and valleys of Worcester County provided a wholesome and pleasant home for the growing family. The boys worked with their father in the fields, and in the winter helped cut and haul logs from the forest to fill the woodshed. The girls were taught by their capable and thrifty mother to sew and cook, and generally to be useful around the house.

Clarissa, or Clara, as she was called from the day of her birth, was the pet of the family. Almost as soon as she could talk, her sisters began teaching her to spell and read, and the boys took her to the barns to watch the feeding and care of the farm animals. On winter evenings with the snow piled high against the windows Clara often sat beside her father by the blazing kitchen fireplace and listened to hair-raising stories of his war days, and to tales of the Huguenots who had once settled in Oxford but had been driven out by the Indians.

Clara also liked to hear stories about the Universalist Church in the village. The church had started during the Revolutionary War when old Dr. Isaac Davis, a physician in Somers, Connecticut, had ridden his horse through the wilderness to bring the Universalist message to Oxford. Later, a Universalist Society was formed and, in 1785, the first Convention of the New England Universalists was held there, with John Murray from Gloucester in attendance. It was here in 1791, at the New England General Convention of Universalists, that the young Hosea Ballou had made his life decision to preach Universalisam and was ordained to the Universalist ministry. As a boy, Clara's father had left the Congregational church to join the new Universalist movement.

On Sundays, Clara sat in the Barton family pew, dangling her feet; in winter she nearly froze in the poorly heated room. The five-mile drive to Oxford each Sunday and the services in the plain, white colonial church formed a part of her childhood experience. That God is love, and all lives a precious gift never to be destroyed, were teachings of the church impressed upon her mind at an early age, chiefly because they so fully governed her father's actions.

At the age of four Clara started school, carried a mile through the snowdrifts on the strong shoulders of brother Stephen. She was an unusually timid child, afraid of the wind and thunder, and unhappy when left alone. But Stephen and David did their best to make her more confident, including her in their rough-and-tumble sports, and teaching her to ride horseback. After four years in the local school had not cured her shyness, her parents, thinking that she needed to learn to live with strangers, sent her to a boarding school run by a former favorite teacher. Alas, she was so miserable away from her family that she was brought home at the end of one term. For the next two years she was taught at home.

When Clara was eleven, David fell from the ridgepole at a barn raising and was seriously injured. She took care of him, sleeping on a cot beside his bed, and carrying out the physician's orders. The patient grew steadily worse in spite of pills, mustard plasters, and daily blood letting. Finally the family was told that the case was hopeless, and the physician discontinued his visits. Clara did not give up. She told David he was going to get well, and he did. Yet it was a long two years that she devoted to his recovery. The ordeal had exhausted her physically, but when she was at last relieved of her sacrificial labors she felt lonely and lost.

Then the hired man came down with smallpox. Clara took him on as a patient, and her spirits rose at once. As the sickness spread throughout the community, she forgot herself in caring for others. She, too, caught smallpox, but recovered quickly and returned to her nursing. To work for others was necessary to Clara Barton's nature. This powerful inner urgency drove her in later years to work for underprivileged children, to minister to soldiers on the battlefields, and to labor for the relief of suffering in many parts of the world.

The epidemic over, Clara returned to school. She was now on her own. Sisters and brothers were through school and no longer at home. Clara studied hard, read books recommended by her teachers, and won a prize for the best written theme of the year. She soon passed teaching examinations and received a certificate.

A position in district Number Nine, a nearby neighborhood, was open. The last teacher, a man, had been driven out by the big boys, and the members of the school board had doubts that any woman could handle them. But Mr. Barton was a respected and influential citizen, and his young daughter, only sixteen, was hired.

On the first morning of the term the pupils were surprised to find a woman at the desk. She was not as tall as many of them and younger than some. How could this thin little schoolmarm with her wavy brown hair, innocent brown eyes, and soft-spoken voice manage the tough big boys? It would be fun to see. But at recess when the biggest bully began lording it over the other boys the teacher challenged him to a game of horseshoes and won! Thanks to the coaching received from her brothers she could hold her own in every game proposed by the pupils. Moreover, she won respect and loyalty, even of those who had given former teachers the most trouble, and became known for her excellent discipline.

Barton taught in Massachusetts for fifteen years. During vacations she worked in brother Stephen's cotton mill, in the office and at the loom. She saved money and could now afford more schooling for herself. In her thirtieth year she enrolled at the co-educational Clinton Liberal Institute in Clinton, New York, which later merged with the theological school of St. Lawrence University.

A year later she was back at teaching, now in a small private school in Bordentown, New Jersey. This school was for the children whose parents could afford to pay. The other children of the town had no school, although there was a school committee. Miss Barton went to see the chairperson. He knew there was a law providing for free education for all children in the state, but the leading citizens in the community regarded it a waste of the taxpayers' money to support a school for the riffraff of the town. Anyway parents, they thought, not the government, should be responsible for the education of their children. This point of view was altogether unacceptable to Clara Barton. She informed the gentleman that she was going to start a public school and if the board members wanted any credit for it they had better cooperate. They finally provided a room, desks, and books, and the school opened with six pupils. This, the first free school in New Jersey, was later named for Clara Barton. Soon there were a hundred, then two hundred. When a new model schoolhouse was erected for six hundred pupils, the board said the school was now too large for a woman to manage, and a man was appointed principal. Miss Barton went home to visit her father and brothers. Her mother had died the year Clara was in Clinton.

At the end of the summer in Oxford, Clara went to Washington to visit her sister Sally and family. After a life of thirty-three years in the country and in small towns she found the nation's capital, with its forty thousand inhabitants, an exciting place. Always interested in political affairs, she sat in the gallery of the Senate Chamber through long political debates, looked up congressional representatives from her home state, and wherever she went listened to the arguments for and against slavery, which was fast becoming the major issue throughout the nation.

But it was not Clara Barton's nature to be idle. She got a job copying letters in the government Patent Office, the first woman to be employed in this department. She received the same pay as the men. This the men resented and they made life miserable for her. Resentment increased when, six months later, she was promoted to the position of confidential secretary, and given an assignment to investigate the leaking of secret documents from the Patent Office. She found the leaks and the guilty ones—the men who had been most active in the effort to get rid of her.

Clara Barton was still in Washington when the Civil War began. She was present at the inauguration of President Abraham Lincoln. There were those who believed that peaceful means could be found to free the slaves and to settle other differences between the North and South, but there were selfish interests on both sides. When Lincoln was elected President, South Carolina withdrew from the Union. Other states followed. Their representatives met in Montgomery,

Alabama, to set up a new nation with a President and Congress. Fort Sumter fell in April, 1861. The War Between the States was on. Both sides expected an early victory, but the war lasted four years. A million soldiers were killed or wounded, and the South was in ruins.

Throughout the war women on both sides did heroic work in providing surgical supplies and clothing for the soldiers, and nursing in the military hospitals. Few ever reached the battlefields, considered no fit place for a woman. Among the few was Clara Barton.

Her first service was in Washington. The first regiment to reach the Capitol was from Worcester County. Passing through Baltimore the soldiers had been set upon by Southern sympathizers, and they arrived in Washington bruised, hungry, and without baggage. Among them were young men from Oxford, recognized by Miss Barton as neighbors and some of them as her former pupils. The regiment was quartered in the Capitol, the soldiers sleeping on the floor of the Senate Chamber. Clara went to inquire what they needed. Their chief complaint was the hot sticky air of the city, and their heavy clothing. It was April, and they had left Massachusetts homes in their red flannel underwear! From the vice-president's desk she read to them from the Worcester newspaper, which had a more or less accurate account of the Baltimore incident, then left with a promise to return the next day.

The following morning, a Sunday, churchgoers in Washington saw a strange procession moving up Pennsylvania Avenue—five strapping black men, each staggering under the load of a great basket, and in the lead a prim little woman with arms heaped high with parcels. With her own savings Miss Barton had brought food and clothing, and had been up most of the night stripping her shelves and closets of blankets and linens, and cutting up sheets and petticoats for bandages and handkerchiefs for the soldiers. The were grateful most of all for the generous supply of light-weight underwear!

A notice appeared in the next number of the Worcester newspaper that supplies for the sixth regiment would be distributed wherever the soldiers might be sent. The notice was signed "Clara Barton" with her Washington address.

This was a bold promise. Skeptical friends told her she would never get sufficiently near a battlefield to hear the cannon roar. At that time there was not a professionally trained nurse in America. But one learned by doing, Clara well knew. Had she not nursed brother David? And the hired man? And any number of Oxford neighbors? She would somehow get to the battlefields and to the suffering soldiers who needed her. She bombarded the War Department, wrote letters to Congress, appealed to the Governor of Massachusetts, and buttonholed every politician who crossed her path.

The War Department insisted that her services were not needed in the field, that there was plenty of surgical equipment, and that the soldiers had adequate care. Meanwhile, she continued to collect supplies. In the months of waiting she helped nurse the wounded brought into the Washington hospital. From them she heard stories that made her all the more certain that nursing was needed on the fields of battle. Food and medical supplies transported in slow mule-drawn wagons over rutted roads could not be moved fast enough to catch up with marching troops. The wounded and sick to be sent to army hospitals were often taken to railroad stations or boat landings without medical attention, food, or water. The suffering was appalling; many died from thirst and exposure. Lives could be saved, she argued, if wounds were bound up on the battlefield.

In the spring of 1862, she returned to Oxford to care for her dying father. On the day of the funeral word came that the Surgeon General had granted permission for her to go to the front with the Army of the Potomac. By what means this action was finally brought about is not known; perhaps it was the only way the authorities could get rid of her! She returned to Washington and lost no time getting into action.

Not only was she given a pass for herself into battle areas, but she was also allowed to take others with her. Transporation for her supplies and people to load them would be provided. She was to be free to come and go with no army restrictions. That such broad privileges were granted a private individual was evidence both of Clara Barton's power of persuasion and of the confusion in government and military affairs during the first war years.

Clara had to be careful that eagerness to get to the front did not blind her to the importance of knowing where her efforts would count most. Dorothea Dix, as Superintendent of Army Nurses, was doing pioneer work in setting up nurses' training classes and in improving conditions in the disorganized army hospitals. The United States Sanitary Commission had been created and had initiated a broad program of investigating army conditions and caring for soldiers. Miss Barton conferred with members of the Sanitary Commission in Washington and with medical and army officers, learning what others were doing and what most needed to be done. Already in response to her appeals to friends and notices in Northern newspapers, quantities of clothing, blankets, medical supplies, and food had arrived. Her rooms were overflowing and she had to rent warehouse space.

The Union forces were being destroyed in the Battle of Cedar Mountain, near Culpepper, Virginia, some sixty miles southwest of the national capital. More than two thousand soldiers were killed or wounded. Medical supplies were exhausted, and troops were dying in the fields for lack of care. Word of the battle reached Washington on the second day of the fighting. At midnight of the third day, Miss Barton and her helpers arrived with a four-team wagon piled high with blankets, clothing, food, and surgical dressings. The surgeons, desperate for supplies, welcomed her wagon and her assistance. In the long hours of trial she made soup for the hungry, bound up wounds, and eased the suffering of the dying.

This was only the beginning. For three years this "Angel of the Battlefield," as the soldiers called her, "followed the cannon" into most of the major battles of the Army of the Potomac. Long days under the blazing sun in Virginia and Maryland in the midst of gunfire, long nights of caring for the wounded, braving the weather of the changing seasons, rain and sleet, the almost impassable muddy roads—nothing seemed to daunt her spirit. Following the battle lines meant long journeys—on horseback, in jolting supply wagons, on hospital trains or boats, bringing medical supplies and food needed for the wounded.

When the opposing forces met at Antietam she passed the army's long slow wagon train by travelling all night and arriving behind the Union fighting line hours in advance of the army supplies. The surgeons had run out of bandages and other materials and were using green corn leaves to dress the wounds. Clara and her precious load of supplies saved many lives. The wounded were being brought from the battlefield by the hundreds. Clara Barton worked in the hospital set up in a farm house and she and volunteers from the surrounding country side fought their own brave battles to lessen the horrors of war.

Among the patients were Confederate soldiers who were treated just as the others. In mid-afternoon shellfire reached the farm hospital. As Clara bent to give water to a patient a bullet ripped through her sleeve and killed the man instantly. Another soldier in great pain, waiting his turn for a surgeon, begged her to remove the bullet lodged

165

in his jaw. The thought staggered her. But Clara, who used to hide under the bed in a thunderstorm, rolled up her sleeves, took a long breath, got out her penknife, and dug out the bullet, and washed and dressed the wound.

Toward evening the last scrap of food had been given to the hungry patients. Government provisions were on the way but nobody knew when they would arrive. There remained from her stores only three cases of wine, sent by the people back home. When these were opened it was found that the bottles were packed not in sawdust, but in yellow corn meal! The wounded had New England corn meal mush for supper.

With darkness, the Battle of Antietam ended in a victory for the North. The armies withdrew, leaving behind their wounded, the dying and the dead—ten thousand Northern soldiers and a large number of Confederates. Surgeons, stretcher-bearers, Clara Barton, and the other relief workers carried on in the night. As long as she could be of service, Clara remained at Antietam. Then she returned to Washington, exhausted, and went to bed with a fever.

News of fresh campaigns and of Union victories hastened her recovery and in a few weeks she was on her way to Fredricksburg, Virginia, with six loaded wagons and an ambulance provided by the government, together with eight husky mule drivers. These drivers, with her coaching, became her most able helpers, nursing the sick, binding up wounds, and burying the dead. Fredericksburg was occupied by the Confederate forces. The Union army across the Rappahannock had thrown together a pontoon bridge for entering the city. The first Union squads crossing were easy targets, falling in frightful numbers under the fire of Confederate cannon. A message reached Clara from a doctor begging her to join him at a makeshift hospital on the other side of the bridge. Grabbing her medicine kit, she joined the marching soldiers. A Union officer tried to stop her but she pulled loose from his grasp and swiftly crossed the swaying bridge. A cannon ball tore away part of her clothing and killed the officer who had tried to stop her. She joined the doctor and ministered to the wounded.

From the battle of Fredericksburg in December, 1862, to General Lee's surrender April 9, 1865, Clara Barton, with her kit of bandages and basket of food, was a familiar and welcome figure on the battlefields in Virginia and in South Carolina. Jealousies and opposition, which in the beginning hampered her work, gave way to respect and praise for her services. In 1864, she was appointed Superintendent of Nurses for the Army of the Potomac.

The war ended, but not Clara Barton's acts of mercy. President Lincoln, a few days before his assasination, authorized her project of searching for missing soldiers. Thirteen thousand of the dead at the Confederate prison at Andersonville, Georgia, were identified, and a cemetery laid out with marked graves. Finally more than twenty-five thousand missing people, living and dead, were located.

People wanted to hear Clara tell the story of her experiences. So she went on the lecture platform for several months until her voice gave out and the doctors sent her abroad for rest. She was in Europe four years. In Switzerland, she learned about the Red Cross, founded by twelve nations in 1864. All nations had been invited to send delegates to Geneva and to join by signing an agreement that in case of war aid would be given to all the wounded regardless of which side they were on. The United States was the only large nation that had not joined.

Clara Barton was interested, of course. Her interest increased when, at the outbreak of war between France and Prussia in 1870, she saw the Red Cross in action at first hand. While not allowed at the front, she did relief work at Strasbourg. On returning home she began a campaign to persuade Congress to sign the Geneva Treaty. For thirteen years, between frequent periods of illness, she spoke at public meetings, wrote newspaper articles, and hounded politicians. Finally she suggested that aid in national disasters be included in the purpose of the organization. With this amendment, Congress in 1881 voted for the treaty and the National American Red Cross was born. Clara Barton was appointed president.

She was almost sixty. Throughout the world her name was spoken and her good deeds known. The war years, which had found her sleeping in the rain, broiling in the sun, and spending long nights without rest, had taken their toll. Her lithe frame was still unbent, but her eyes and voice often failed her, and she had recurring spells of pneumonia. But the inner drive was still strong. For more than twenty years she ran the American Red Cross, conducting the business affairs, and carrying on the work of relief in a score of disasters— forest fires in Michigan, the Johnstown flood, the Charleston earthquake, floods in Illinois and Texas, famines in Russia and Turkey, and starvation and war in Cuba. Wherever possible she was at the scene of operation, personally directing the work of saving lives

Others were eager to relieve her of responsibility, and were often critical of her methods of operating. But she held on until she was eighty-three in 1904. She died in Glen Echo, Maryland, in her ninety-first year, on April 12, 1912.

In 1921, the National Women's organization of the Universalist Church acquired the Clara Barton birthplace in North Oxford, Massachusetts. The house had fallen into disrepair, the farm buildings were about to tumble down, and the land had been neglected. The women set out at once not only to restore the homestead, but to equip it and make it a living memorial to Clara Barton. Beginning in 1926 as a "Fresh Air Camp," the homestead became a summer medical colony for diabetic girls, the first in America. Today it and the nearby Joslin Camp for boys, both well-equipped with living quarters and medical facilities, serve several hundred girls and boys every summer. Here in loving remembrance of Clara Barton's service to humanity is carried on the kind of work of which she would have approved.

CHAPTER SIXTEEN

Thomas Starr King
1824-1864

When in 1860 Thomas Starr King arrived in San Francisco, California was the most exciting place in America. Soon after Mexico had ceded it to the United States in 1848, gold had been discovered in the upper Sacramento Valley, and people flocked to the area from all parts of the world. Almost overnight the population increased from a few hundred scattered souls to nearly three hundred and eighty thousand, including four thousand Chinese. San Francisco grew from a small trading center to a sprawling, jerry-built city of fifty-five thousand inhabitants.

Many of the newcomers lived in tents or in makeshift shacks of canvas, planks, or mud. Whether they arrived by boat or in covered wagons they landed in San Francisco. Some stayed only long enough to inquire the way to the gold mines, but they returned to the new city with a fortune in their belts, or failing to find gold, to seek employment. Entrepreneurs from the east saw promise of fat profits in the rising population. They built shops, banks, and storehouses, and as they prospered put up expensive houses and acquired fine horses.

Dance halls, pool parlors, gambling joints, and saloons to catch the money of the easy-spenders kept pace with the growing community. Prices of land and all commodities went sky high. Those unfortunate in mining flocked to the city, swelling the ranks of the dependent. Charitable organizations and soup kitchens were necessary to take care of them. Reformers, revivalists, and temperance workers did their best to stem the tide of moral breakdown among men and women far from home and without moral restraints.

The city was not without cultural interests, provided by schools and churches, music halls, literary clubs, and the lyceum. On the plank sidewalks or in the muddy streets, merchants in tall hats and broadcloth mingled with workers in coarse clothing and Orientals in gay colors. A dozen different languages were heard.

Most of the new population was American, a majority from the southern states. Bringing with them the traditions of slave-holding, states' rights, and strong political interests, these citizens from the south created serious political problems. California had adopted a constitution forbidding slavery, and had been admitted to the Union, but the southerners were determined to bring the new state into line with the slaveholding south. Furthermore, they tried to convince the people that California should be independent of the United States and become a Pacific empire. The promoters of these schemes were shrewd and able, some with more power than principles. To Thomas Starr King goes the credit for their defeat and the saving of California for the Union.

King was born on December 17, 1824, in New York City, the son of the Reverend Thomas Farrington King and Susan Starr King. At the time of the birth of Starr, as he was familiarly known, his father, a Universalist minister, was a circuit preacher in Connecticut. (His mother was visiting her family in New York City.)

The following spring the Rev. Mr. King moved his family to Hudson, New York, where he served the Universalist Church. Here other children were born, adding an extra load to the father's already burdened salary. After four years he welcomed a call to the prosperous Universalist Church in Portsmouth, New Hampshire, where Starr spend the next six years. When old enough he was sent to a private school that, in addition to the usual instruction, offered classes in Latin and French, subjects in which Starr excelled.

Starr liked living in Portsmouth with its great houses and public buildings. It was a leading seaport on the New England coast. Between the hour that school was dismissed and the time for chores at home, he often went to the docks to see the ships anchored in the ample and secure harbor, or to watch the unloading of the great bales of cotton, wool, leather, and other raw materials for the inland manufacturing cities. Sometimes he talked with the sailors sitting about on the wharf, who told him about the far-away lands they had visited. Then he ran home to look up the places in his geography book. He liked the church, too, with its long rows of pews, and the steeple with the weathervane turning with every changing wind. On Sundays, he was allowed to ring the giant bell in the tower. He would hang all his slight weight on the long rope and feel himself lifted upward by it in its swing. These were happy days of school and play, more carefree than any Starr King would see again.

In 1835, when he was eleven, his father became pastor of the large Universalist Church in Charlestown, Massachusetts. Starr attended the Bunker Hill Grammar School, and later the Winthrop School to prepare for college. In both institutions he showed a readiness in learning and a mental maturity far beyond his age. The principal of the Winthrop School later wrote of him: "I well remember the first entrance of that interesting boy, Thomas Starr King, under my charge; his gentleness of manner, his expressive face. His mind grasped every subject presented to his consideration." Another teacher described him as having "a homely face which everybody thought handsome on account of the beaming eyes and winning smile."

From an early age Starr looked forward to going into the ministry. His mother declared that she could not recollect when he did not talk of it. And his father was happy to think of the ministry as a fitting career for his gifted son.

But plans for college were cut short. His father, burdened for months with illness, died in the fall of 1839 at the age of forty-two. Starr, not quite fifteen, had to leave school and get a job to help support his mother and five younger sisters and brothers.

He went to work in a dry-goods store as clerk and bookkeeper. The hours were long and the duties exacting but he did his work faithfully, and in his little free time continued to study. He joined a group of young people of about his own age for mutual improvement though reading, conversation, and debate. A few good books were acquired and circulated among the members, who discussed them and prepared essays on the ideas set forth.

Some of the members of the Charlestown School Committee, observing the serious turn of Starr's mind, urged that he be made assistant teacher in the Bunker Hill Grammar School. There were objections on account of his youth, but the appointment was made and he soon dissolved whatever doubts there were as to his capability. At this time he was not yet sixteen, younger than some of the pupils—a slim bright-eyed, golden-haired, vivacious, lovable lad. He entered into the lives of the students, taking part in their games as well as making learning attractive to them.

The Reverend Edwin H. Chapin was now pastor of the Charlestown Church. Chapin was Starr King's senior by only ten years but was already widely known for his broad scholarship and pulpit power. His influence on the younger man was deep and lasting, and a lifelong friendship grew between them. The pastor lent Starr books, advised him in the selection of reading, and helped him in preparation for the ministry. There were other good and wise friends who recognized his qualities, believed in his future, and helped him with counsel and encouragement. One was Hosea Ballou II, not to be confused with the pastor of the Second Universalist Church in Boston. Hosea Ballou II, as he is generally called, became the first President of Tufts College in 1853.

After two years teaching in Charlestown, Starr became principal of the West Grammar School in Medford, Massachusetts. Ballou was then minister of the Universalist Church in that town. Under his guidance, King entered upon a systematic study that lacked little compared to that offered by a school of theology. While in Medford, he went to hear Theodore Parker in Boston, became familiar with and absorbed the words of Channing, and read the writings of James Martineau, the English Unitarian.

Starr's friends in the ministry, both Universalist and Unitarian, gave him opportunities to supply their pulpits, which he did with credit to himself. He wrote articles for *The Universalist Quarterly*, edited by Hosea Ballou II. Altogether, he used well the two years in Medford, both in his teaching and in his own education. But the salary of the school was inadequate for the needs of the family. He applied for a better position in a school in Roxbury, but was turned down because of his youth. Through friends he landed a job in the office of the Charlestown Navy Yard at double the pay he had been receiving, and with more time for study. Now a little money could be spared for books.

In the fall of 1845, Chapin resigned from the Charlestown Church to be associate minister of the Second Universalist Society in Boston. Starr King was chosen as his successor in Charlestown, and for two years preached in the pulpit where his father had stood. Here he was ordained, his friends, the Rev. Mr. Chapin and Dr. Ballou taking part in the service. The Charlestown parish was not an easy one for the new minister. He was only twenty-two, and in the eyes of the congregation still the former minister's little boy. And his plain unemotional sermons, substantial as they were, when measured by the pulpit oratory of the great Chapin, placed him at a disadvantage. Nevertheless, he had the respect and loyalty of the congregation and was highly regarded in the community.

King brought to his first pastorate a rare combination of gifts, a friendly sympathetic nature, an intellect well-furnished, and a background of association with worldly affairs as well as with great minds. He soon became recognized as a scholarly and effective public speaker on religious, literary, and political subjects. The demands for his services came from many quarters. He developed a rich deep voice, and had the ability to deal with great themes in simple language that even the unschooled could understand. Emerson heard him in the Lyceum in Concord, and remarked that his sermons were not as good as his lectures.

The many calls upon his strength, in addition to parish duties and constant study, brought on a nervous exhaustion that made a period of rest necessary. Through the generosity of a friend Starr King went to one of the islands of the Azores for his health. A few weeks before going away, King had received an invitation from the Hollis Street Unitarian Church in Boston to become its minister. He declined, but during the several months that he spent on the island gave the matter further consideration. After he returned home, he accepted the renewed invitation. In his letter of resignation to the Charlestown Society he made clear that the move from a Universalist to a Unitarian Church was due not to any change in his religious views nor to a weakening of attachment to the Universalist denomination; but was prompted only by personal reasons. He saw that the two denominations were not far apart theologically. The Universalists emphasized the love of God, and the Unitarians the worth of the human soul, or as he himself said, "The one thinks God is too good to damn them forever, and the other thinks they are too good to be damned forever."

Hollis Street was an old church, once strong and prosperous. But it had fallen on evil days. The membership had split over the issues of slavery and temperance. Many members had left the church. Others had moved out of the neighborhood and joined other churches. The few loyal pewholders who remained hoped that with an able minister the church could be revived. It was believed that if anyone could save the church, Starr King was the one to do it. Mr. King was installed on the first Sunday in November, 1848.

A few weeks later, on his twenty-fourth birthday, he was married to Julia Wiggin of East Boston. Their new home at once became a gathering place for Universalist and Unitarian ministers and others, who made up a sort of unnamed and unorganized literary club. Divinity school students from Harvard were welcomed. They were delighted in drawing from the conversations of their elders tough theological questions with which to vex their professors.

Mr. King remained in the Hollis Street Church eleven years; continued his outside lectures; and built up a large congregation. He was sometimes criticized for mixing politics with religion, but this charge never bothered him. It was impossible for him not to deal with the social evils of his day. He saw, as his critics did not, the effect of the organized forces of injustice upon the moral life of people. Religious principles were to be applied to all areas of life, political as well as personal.

When King was chided for frequently speaking on abolition, he replied with the story of a proslavery man of his acquaintance who complained that his minister was forever talking about freedom for the Negroes; when asked "Why did you call him to be your Minister?" the man said, "Well, we found we must have either an abolitionist or a darned fool, and you must feel, Mr. King, that we couldn't have a darned fool, now could we?"

King spent his summer vacations either at Pigeon Cove on Cape Ann, where Dr. Chapin had a summer home, or in the White Mountains of New Hampshire. For nine summers he went to Gorham, which he found convenient for excursions into the valleys and up the heights of the whole mountain region. A series of letters that he sent to the *Boston Transcript*, a newspaper edited by one of his parishioners, became the foundation for a book, *The White Hills: Their Legends, Landscape and Poetry*, published in 1859. The newspaper articles and the book describing the wonders of the mountains and the varieties of trees, plants, and flowers drew attention to this hitherto little known portion of scenic America. One of the high peaks of the White Mountains is named Mt. Starr King in his memory. In the township of Jefferson is the village of Starr King, and on the north side of Mt. Adams a ravine that he discovered is known as King's Ravine.

In the spring of 1860 King accepted a call to the young and struggling Unitarian Church in San Francisco. The Hollis Street members gave him a fifteen-month leave of absence in the hope that by this time he might have had enough of California and would be glad to return to them.

The day before they sailed for the Pacific Coast, their friends gave the Kings a dinner in New York's Fifth Avenue Hotel. Three hundred were present, and the venerable William Cullen Bryant presided. Horace Greeley called at the hotel and said that San Francisco "has the worst climate and is the most infernal hole on the face of the earth." Dr. Chapin and other ministers came to the ship to see the family off. Chapin brought flowers, and somebody gave King a going-away present of a tub of pickled oysters.

On April 5, the Reverend Mr. King, his wife, and little daughter Edith, with a thousand passengers on a ship built to accommodate only five hundred, steamed out of New York harbor bound for San Francisco by way of the Isthmus of Panama. They were in for a rugged voyage, "packed like cattle in a stock train" as King put it. Eight days on the Atlantic brought them to the Aspinwall harbor, where the passengers were herded into railway cars to cross the Isthmus to another crowded steamer for the last lap of the journey. The trip from New York to San Francisco required twenty-five days

San Francisco was a long way from Boston, by distance, communication, and ways of living. It was two thousand miles west of the settlements in Minnesota and Kansas, and five hundred miles from the new settlement of the Mormons at Salt Lake, Utah. The nearest railroad ended somewhere in central Missouri. Mail came once in twenty-six days, when roads were not washed out. The cost of sending a letter to Boston by Pony Express was five dollars in gold. The city, with its flimsy shacks spread out over the hills, housed the families of ever-increasing newcomers from the south and east. A few had quickly grown rich not only by finding gold but also by the rapidly rising trade and speculation in land. Law and order were loosely administered, those with quick triggers walked the streets, and thieves and beggars mingled with pleasure-seekers in the halls and saloons along the waterfront. Yet there were people of literary interests, too, some of them in King's congregation, who made the new minister feel at home, and who found in him a charming companion.

Mr. King threw himself into his new labors with great zest. He found the church in a weak condition and in debt, but from the first Sunday the congregations filled the small auditorium, morning and evening. Except for families who came from the east, few people in the community had even heard of Unitarianism, and King's was the only liberal voice in the new city. Before crowded audiences in the church he gave twelve lectures of more than an hour each on the distinctive nature of liberal religion. Within two years the church debt was paid and money was raised for a larger building.

In coming to San Francisco it was Starr King's intention to give up lecturing and to devote himself entirely to extending the influence of the liberal gospel on the coast. His reputation as a platform speaker, however, preceded him. Hardly had he planted his feet on California soil than invitations to address various groups began to pour in. He took on a few engagements at first, in order to become acquainted with the people. But the grave political situation was soon forced upon his attention. The war clouds that darkened eastern skies were drifting across the mountains. Secessionists were taking every advantage to swing California into the Southern cause. They were known to be well-organized, armed, and desperate. A secret society, the Knights of the Golden Circle, paraded through the streets of San Francisco, broke up meetings of their opponents, and spread terror among those who raised their voices in favor of keeping California in the union. Most of the political offices were held by those from slaveholding states. The politicians were hand-in-glove with the most lawless elements throughout the state. The Union cause needed a leader, one who could plead for it, who could strengthen the timid and speak out for those who were afraid to speak for themselves.

Almost before he knew what was happening, King was in the thick of the fight, turning his lectures into an aggressive political and moral compaign. Large crowds came to hear him whenever he spoke, paying a dollar or more admission fee. Receipts were turned over to the campaign or given to some other good cause. The people loved oratory and King now added an emotional appeal to his speeches which, with his eloquent voice, flowery language, and patriotic sentiments, made him irresistible. On horseback or by stagecoach, he went up and down the state, wherever an audience could be gathered in halls, churches, barrooms, or village streets. Miners, farmers, stockraisers, and traders—all were brought under his hypnotic spell. They caught his vision of a nation united to preserve and to extend freedom to all its people. Hired thugs tried to break up his meetings and his life was in constant danger, but somehow this pale young man of small stature managed to disarm violence by the power of persuasion and fair mindedness.

Nothing could stop him. More calls came than he could answer, from Hangtown, Hell's Delight, Gospel Swamp, Dead Wood, Rough and Ready, Scott's Bar, Mad Mule, Piety Hill, and Skunk Gulch, as well as from less romantically named places. But day after day and night after night his voice was heard. All through the summer and fall of 1861, except for time required by his church, King devoted himself to his patriotic mission. In October he was able to write to friends in the east, "The State is safe from Southern tampering." The political contenders, southern in their sentiments, were defeated for public office, and Leland Stanford, backed by a Union legislature, was elected Governor.

Mr. King now turned his attention to raising money for relief for the war. A letter from his friend the Rev. Henry Bellows, President of the United States Sanitary Commission, told of the critical need for money in order to continue the work. King responded at once, traveling up and down the coast and as far as Vancouver Island. His appeals to audiences and personal solicitations raised over a million dollars. His efforts allowed the commission to continue its important services to those in the armed services and their families.

The first summer after coming to San Francisco, Starr King took his vacation exploring the natural wonders of the state. He visited the Yosemite forest with its giant trees and the valleys and ravines with their views of the great mountain ranges. As often as he could spare the time thereafter he went on expeditions to the north, even into Canada. Sometimes he combined lecturing with sightseeing. He delivered the first Unitarian sermons ever heard in Oregon and Washington. The *Boston Transcript* printed articles describing the places Mr. King visited. He planned to write a companion volume to his *White Hills*, on the forests and mountains of the Pacific Coast, but early death came before he could undertake this project.

Above Yosemite rises a lofty snow-capped peak in the Sierra Nevada range. This is Mount Starr King, named in memory of the lover and interpreter of the grandeur of the great state that he helped keep in the union. One of the giant sequoia trees of the Mariposa Grove in the southern part of Yosemite Park is also named for him. The Pacific Unitarian School for the Ministry, founded in Berkeley, California in 1906, was later renamed the Starr King School for the Ministry.

The new church building in San Francisco was dedicated in January, 1864. With this accomplished and the future of the state secure, Mr. King looked forward to a much-needed rest and a change of scene. But he suffered a complete physical breakdown after only six Sundays in the new church. Never in the best of health, the four years in California had taken more of his vitality than he could spare. He died on March fourth at the age of thirty-nine.

At his death a deep sense of loss was felt throughout the nation— nowhere more deeply than among the Unitarians and Universalists. He served both denominations with honor and both are proud to claim him.

In the spacious city park of San Francisco, overlooking the Golden Gate, is a bronze statue of Thomas Starr King. It was erected by the people of the city in 1892 in grateful memory of his service to the state of California. The inscription reads:

In Him Eloquence, Strength and Virtue
Were Devoted with Fearless Courage
To Truth, Country and Fellow-Men
1824-1864.

In 1931 the state of California placed a statue of King in Statuary Hall in Washington, D.C., as one of the two people chosen to represent the state.

CHAPTER SEVENTEEN

Jenkin Lloyd Jones
1843-1918

On a cold November night in the year 1844 an immigrant mother aboard a Hudson River steamboat bound for Albany huddled her children close to the great smokestack on deck to keep them warm. The captain of the boat urged her to take the children to the cabin provided for them, but she could not believe that the luxury of comfortable quarters was meant for poor folks. She and her husband and their six children had landed in New York from South Wales a few days before and were now on their way to the west to seek whatever fortune the New World had in store for them.

Richard Lloyd Jones and his wife Mary were Welsh farmers of small means in Cardiganshire County on the west coast of Wales. For years they had dreamed of living in America. By scrimping and saving they had saved money for steerage fare, and a little besides to begin life in the new land. Both were of old Welsh Unitarian stock, and they looked forward with bright hopes to breathing the air of religious freedom on the American frontier. Many hardships were to be endured, however, before the end of the overland journey. At Albany the Joneses joined a wagon train going westward, but severe winter storms stopped them near Steuben, New York, where they remained for several weeks. Here the children were taken sick with diphtheria and three-year-old Nannie died.

Jenkin, the baby, a year old on the day the family landed in New York, was seriously ill, but of tough fiber, and pulled through. This boy, Jenkin Lloyd Jones, lived to become a great American, a builder of lasting good works, and a strong leader in the Unitarian movement.

In late May the family reached the Rock River Valley in Wisconsin Territory, forty miles west of the growing trading center Milwaukee. Land was cheap, a dollar and twenty cents an acre, and was being taken up rapidly by immigrants from Europe—Germans, Scandinavians, French, and Swiss. Richard Jones purchased one hundred and twenty acres, a yoke of oxen and two cows, corn and potatoes for planting and seeds for a garden in a newly made clearing. There were as yet no buildings, but before winter a crude shelter for the livestock was thrown together, and a one-room log house with a stone fireplace and chimney built.

To win a living on the frontier required intelligence, self-reliance, and much hard labor. There was little money, but the Wisconsin soil, cleared of trees and brush, yielded abundantly, and the acres of wilderness were steadily transformed into a productive farm. Nature provided much in the surrounding country, fish in the cold clear streams, plenty of game in the forest, and wild fruits to be had for the picking.

The Jones family had few near neighbors but a steady stream of visitors—immigrants of strange speech coming to the valley in search of homes, or on their way to lands farther west. The wayfarer was never turned away even though members of the family sometimes gave up their beds to sleep in the haymow.

Not all the inhabitants of the Rock River Valley were farmers. Indian hunters, some of them unfriendly and resentful of the white people's invasion, roamed the forests and were a constant source of fear among the settlers. There were trappers, mostly French, who caught fur-bearing animals, especially the badger, and carried their pelts to distant trading posts. The Valley had its share of bad folk too, gamblers, whiskey makers, outlaws from the cities, and a few horse thieves. To deal with them, the two-gun sheriff and a brave band of deputies were always on call.

The forces of law and order were well supported by the churches that sprang up at every crossroads. From the old Jesuit Mission founded on Green Bay, the Catholic priests travelled through the settlement to baptize, marry, confess, warn, absolve, and bury, according to their ancient rites. Protestant churches, mostly Lutheran, were patterned after the religions brought by the settlers from their homelands.

Besides the ministers of established churches there were the Baptist and Methodist revivalists—powerful, leather-lunged exhorters, proclaiming a gospel of hell-fire for the wicked, and a heaven of easy living for the converted. Preaching was aimed to move the hardest drinkers, the boldest fighters, the toughest gamblers, and the meanest sinners. Great camp meetings drew families from near and far for a season of singing, preaching, and testifying; and many were periodically saved. The ceremonies often overflowed into shouting, dancing, fainting, and other excessive evidences of "getting religion."

The Joneses took no part in these meetings. In the home, the children were taught from the Bible and joined the parents in discussions of religion. The country school, held in a log schoolhouse, had an English-speaking teacher and the children learned to speak the new language, sometimes mixing it with words picked up from their German neighbors and with their native Welsh. Jenkin did well in his studies, and in whatever time he could find from his work on the farm read every printed word that came into the home.

The damp soil of Rock River Valley was good for farming, but bad for malaria. Every member of the Jones family suffered from the disease, believed to be due to breathing poison air arising from the bogs and marshlands. Armed only with quinine, which they swallowed in great doses, they fought a losing battle for eight years. In 1856, Richard Jones set out to find higher ground and more healthful surroundings. In Sauk County he came upon a farm for sale and to his liking—cleared rolling fields, substantial barns, and a large comfortable frame house. The farm in the Valley was sold and the family moved the hundred miles west to the new location.

Jenkin, now thirteen, was sent to a school in the growing village of Spring Green for the winter months. During the summers he worked hard on his father's farm. Farming at this time was mostly with hand tools. The chilled steel plow and the mowing machine that revolutionized agriculture in America had not yet been invented. Plowing was done with the heavy, back-breaking, horse-drawn implement little changed since Biblical times. The hoe, the hand rake, the sickle, and the scythe were the farmer's chief tools of the field. Jenkin knew how to use them all.

But work on the farm and at school was cut short by the Civil War. The Wisconsin farmers, like all Americans, were drawn into the tragic conflict that at the time seemed to many, North and South, to be inevitable. For months the boys at the Spring Glen School had been drilled in the business of killing: learning to march in step, shoot, and use the bayonet. In the summer of 1862, in his nineteenth year, Jenkin joined the Army of the North, and was sent to training camp in northern Mississippi.

He was a soldier for three years; saw action in eleven battles; and received a foot injury that made him lame for life. Throughout the war he kept a diary in which he recorded not only the routine of army life and an account of military engagements, but also his observations on the waste of the war and what it did to the people involved in it. He hated war but the diary contains no complaints of his own hardship, only regret that his schooling was being interrupted. The diary shows the uncertainty he felt about his future—in what field to spend his life, and how he could "attain the highest good." Of one thing he was certain—he wanted an education that would fit him for some useful service.

Jones received in army pay for the first three years $604.97. Of this amount he sent home $445, and he came home with a hundred dollars. Discharged from the army, he reached home on July 3, 1865, and the next day made his first public appearance. From a flag-draped platform on the village green of his home town he read the Declaration of Independence at a Fourth of July celebration.

Released from the army, Jenkin had his mind set on an education. But he was needed on the farm. His aging father could no longer do a full day's work; older brothers had married and settled on lands of their own; and the farm had become run down during the war. All summer while he worked in the fields, mended fences, and made repairs to the buildings, he dreamed of college and the thought of the state university founded at Madison just before the war. During the winter he taught a country school near home, but was back at the farm in time for the spring planting.

Then one day in late summer he came from the field, hung his rake in the woodshed, and announced to his mother that he was going to Meadville Theological School in Pennsylvania to learn to be a preacher. His parents were pleased with the prospect of having a Unitarian minister in the family. They said they would get along without him. After all, the younger children were growing up fast and could take over his work. No financial help could be promised however: he would have to shift for himself. Jenkin still had the one hundred dollars' war pay. With it securely sewed into his jacket pocket, and with mixed feelings of sadness at leaving home and soaring expectations for the future, he boarded the train for Meadville.

186

He was just under twenty-three when he entered the school, and, except for his limp, was in perfect condition, iron-muscled and self-reliant, with many homebred skills. Ravenous for the graces of learning beyond the rim of life on a farm, he was ready for hard work, and determined to absorb all the knowledge the school could offer. He waited tables, sawed wood, washed windows, and was janitor of the dormitory where he had a room. Despite all his outside labors he made a good record in his courses, and became familiar with the English classics and mastered the essentials of American history. He was graduated in 1870.

At Meadville, Jones fell in love with Susan Baker, secretary to one of the teachers. They were married the day after his graduation, and spent their honeymoon at the meetings of the Western Unitarian Conference, held in Cleveland. The Western Unitarian Conference, founded in 1852, comprised the Unitarian societies of the mid-west and at times included others farther west and east. They arrived in time to witness a heated discussion between the two factions in the conference. One group, disturbed over the radicals whose ideas were at odds with Boston Unitarians, insisted that a creedal test be imposed upon all ministers as a means of weeding out the undesired ones. The other group opposed all doctrinal statements, and argued for freedom of belief and an open mind with respect to the historical view of the Bible, non-Christian religions, evolution, and the application of religious principles to social reform.

Jones' sympathy was with the radicals. He liked books, philosophy, and poetry, but he liked people more; and he valued religion as a means to helping them meet their problems, and to improve the quality of their lives. His long ministry was marked by the principles of applied religion, working with all kinds of people of whatever background or condition.

His first charge was the Liberal Christian Church in Winnetka, Illinois, a village north of Chicago on Lake Michigan. Here he was ordained. A year later he moved to Janesville, Wisconsin, where he served the First Independent Society for nine years. In this parish the nature of Jone's ministry took shape. He looked upon the church as a character-building institution. He got street corner loafers to come to classes to study all sorts of subjects from the Old Testament prophets to Shakespeare. He rounded up the young people of the town and gave them lessons on moral values. And he widened the interests of the church women from putting on bean suppers and making crafts for the annual fair to attending courses on Women's Rights and the great world religions.

Dissatisfied with the teaching materials in use in Unitarian Sunday Schools, he began *The Sunday School*, a weekly publication "for all those who seek to work for practical Christianity, liberated from creeds and dogmas, based on Love, Service, and Devotion." He advocated giving up the practice of memorizing Bible verses, singing "jingle" hymns, and writing "preachy" children's stories. He recommended class discussion and lessons on practical Christian living. His work was well-received, especially by the churches in the Western Conference. He was encouraged to prepare courses of study on the Bible, on leaders in the non-Christian religions, and on nature. Songs, responsive readings, and poetical selections were woven into the lessons, and these were later collected in *Service of Song* for youth and adults.

As if parish duties and preparing Sunday School materials were not enough to keep him busy, the Janesville minister took on the work of State Missionary, rallying small struggling churches and helping to start new ones. He also was Secretary of the Western Unitarian Conference, and in 1879 became editor of *Unity*, a liberal religious periodical. This post he filled for forty years until his death.

Both as secretary and as editor Jones was a mighty power in the Western Conference. Differences of opinion regarding official statements of belief that have risen again and again among Unitarians and Universalists were the chief cause of what is known as the Western Issue. On the one hand were those who wanted some kind of statement of belief, binding upon the members, and identifying Unitarians as Christians. On the other hand were those who demanded complete freedom of societies and individuals in the matter of theological opinions.

This controversy was most acute among the western Unitarians, owing to the distance from New England with its cherished traditions, and the freer atmosphere of the denominational frontier. The two factions are most easily designated as conservative and radical. The conservatives insisted that Unitarians must stand squarely on belief in a personal God, with allegiance to Jesus Christ as Savior of the World, and should make these convictions the basis of their work and worship. The conservatives said that unlimited freedom would invite persons with all sorts of crazy ideas to call themselves Unitarians, and would bring grave danger to the cause. The radicals claimed that an official statement of theological belief, if made a condition of fellow-ship, would close the doors of the church to liberal-minded persons to whom ethical principles, not theology, were central in religion.

The controversy raged for several years, earnest, painful, and sometimes bitter. Neither faction would yield an inch. The officials of the American Unitarian Association in Boston favored the conservatives. Contributions to the denominational program were extremely slender, with some of the wealthy churches in the East giving nothing. Their unwillingness to support missionary work was attributed to fear that money would go to advance radicalism. To allay this fear a policy was adopted at denominational headquarters that provided financial aid only to the societies committed to Theistic Christianity. The American Unitarian Association kept its own missionary agent in Chicago in competition with the Western Conference.

Finally in 1886 the radicals won by voting to revise the constitution to read "The Western Unitarian Conference conditions its fellowship on no dogmatic tests, but welcomes all who wish to join it to help establish Truth, Righteousness, and Love in the world."

The conservatives were very unhappy: not a word about Jesus, God, the Bible, or even religion! They saw this action as a deliberate invitation to every Tom, Dick, and Harry, agnostic and atheist, to take the name Unitarian and to undermine the structure of the Church built on the foundations of the Christian faith. There was nothing they could do except to withdraw from the Western Unitarian conference.

And this they did. They organized the Western Unitarian Association with the purpose of "a more definite cooperation with the American Unitarian Association in its Western work to diffuse the knowledge and promote the interests of pure Christianity." A new magazine, *The Unitarian* appeared to represent the views of the new organization and to counteract the influence of Jones' *Unity*.

Although the differences between the two camps were partially resolved eight years later by a compromise statement that pleased neither side, Jones, in his church and in his paper, never accepted any theological pronouncement as a measure of religion. And the societies of the Western Unitarian Conference never ceased to stress the ethical character of practical religion.

Susan Jones was her husband's chief assistant and counsellor. She kept the parsonage in order, economized so that he could buy books, made his shirts, and built the first desk he ever owned. Often she conducted Sunday service when he was visiting outlying churches. One evening Jenkin confided in her that ever since he had decided to be a minister he had wanted a church in Chicago, but none was offered him. They agreed that since no opening had been provided they would make one.

In November 1882 they packed up the many books and their two children and went to Chicago. Jenkin hired a large hall over a store at the corner of Cottage Grove Avenue and 35th Street on the south side of the city. A placard nailed on the door announced to the passersby that the next Sunday, the Rev. Jenkin Lloyd Jones would preach. Twelve persons showed up, nine adults and three children. The following Sunday there were thirty-three, and at the third service, sixty-six. After the sermon the preacher told them that with their help a new church, to be called the Church of All Souls, would be built. No subscriptions would be asked for until the worth of the church should be proved to them. Out of what they put in the collection plate all church bills would be paid, and anything left over would be accepted as salary. For several weeks there was little left over.

Soon, however, word got around that a new kind of preacher had come to the neighborhood. He was making the church a center of religious education for all people—black people, Scandinavians, Orientals, and others who did not feel at home in ordinary churches. In a few years the hall was so crowded on Sundays and weekday evenings that it had to be abandoned for larger quarters. In 1887, the congregation moved to a new church building on Oakwood Boulevard. It was a structure designed by Mr. Jones for practical uses, with no frills but plenty of light. The first floor contained an auditorium, several classrooms, kitchen, office, and study. On the second floor an apartment was provided for the minister and his family. Again, in another two years, more room was needed. The auditorium was enlarged to include the entire ground floor; the minister moved to a new parsonage, and the second floor was used for parish activities.

The Joneses liked company. There was always a spare room for ministers visiting or passing through Chicago. Frank Lloyd Wright, the famous architect, was Mr. Jones' nephew. When Frank was a boy he ran away from home and lived with his uncle while serving his apprenticeship.

To extend his church program, Jones acquired land on the Wisconsin River near his boyhood home, and established the Tower Hill Community for summer vacationists. Here, at low cost, came families from his Chicago church and others in the Western Unitarian Conference, for a season of simple living and solid thinking.

Jones put his religion to work in civic affairs. He was president of the Illinois State Conference of Charities and an officer of the American Humane Society, served on the Council of the Municipal Voters League, helped organize the Associated Charities of Chicago, and founded the first Browning Society in America. For several years he lectured on English literature at the University of Chicago, and throughout the country, on the University's extension program. A group of leading citizens rented Central Music Hall and engaged him for a series of Sunday evening meetings for downtown residents and strangers in the city.

When plans were being made to hold the World Columbian Exposition in Chicago in 1893, Mr. Jones thought that with the celebration of material progress there should be also recognition of the religions of humanity. Largely through his efforts the World's Parliament of Religions was initiated and carried through to a brilliant success. As Executive Secretary he made arrangements to bring to Chicago leaders of all the religions of the world, as well as speakers from the several branches of Christianity. A Roman Catholic Cardinal led in the reading of the Universal Prayer at the opening meeting, and a Rabbi led in the recitation of the Lord's Prayer that closed the last session. The World Parliament of Religions was the most representative religious assembly ever brought together at one time in one place. Nothing like it has happened since.

In 1904, Mr. Jones made a pilgrimage to Abraham Lincoln's birthplace in Hodgenville, Kentucky, and was shocked at what he found. The cabin where Lincoln was born had been carried off to New York for exhibition in a Broadway museum and only a stake marked the spot where it had stood. The fields had been taken over by weeds and underbrush, and the farm itself was to be sold for taxes. The next number of *Unity* carried an editorial on "The Neglected Shrine." Other papers took the matter up, with the result that the birthplace was rehabilitated and both the cabin and farm dedicated as a national memorial. Paid for chiefly by the pennies of American school children, the shrine was accepted for the nation by President Woodrow Wilson in 1916. The next year Jones organized a pilgrimage by chartered train from Chicago to the restored birthplace.

The year after Jones made his first visit to Hodgenville another memorial came into being bearing the name of Lincoln—the Abraham Lincoln Center in Chicago. All Souls Church had long since proved too cramped for its extensive program. For ten years the minister and congregation had been making plans, raising money and dreaming of a great church center of cultural life in the community. On Easter Sunday, 1905, the seven-story brick building across the street from the old church was dedicated as "a proving place of worship unhampered by creed or dogma, or denominations, a place of study, and a platform for every honest message."

It was one of the most complete churches for educational work in America. The building contained a large chapel and auditorium for religious meetings, lectures, and concerts, classrooms, large and small diningrooms, gymnasium, workshops, art gallery, music room, library, guest rooms, and apartments for the minister and family, and for other residents. The facilities were in use seven days a week. Jones believed in education for the whole person, physical, mental, and moral.

For the remainder of his life he made the Center a training school for effective living. Under his guidance thousands were given the only opportunity they ever had to think and to appreciate the rich heritage of humanity's cultural achievements. He preached, lectured, taught classes, and always had time for those who needed his counsel. He seemed to be everywhere at once, yet never in a hurry. At public gatherings in the city he was a familiar figure, with his cane, stocky frame, shaggy hair, long white beard, and deepset eyes.

Speaking engagements often took him to the college campuses of the mid-west, where he never failed to leave with students and teachers a measure of wisdom not found in their text-books. The University of Wisconsin gave him an honorary degree.

Mrs. Jones' death in 1911 took from her husband his chief helper and from the Center a staunch friend and supporter. Dr. Jones held unshakeable convictions about war and peace. War was wasteful, inhuman, and, as a means of settling disagreements, ineffective. For three years he had seen war at first hand, and ever since that experience had labored to heal the wounds of hatred and division that victory for the Union forces did not and could not cure. When, in 1897, preparations were being made for war with Spain, he denounced the imperialistic ambitions of the United States, and advocated the purchase of the Spanish possessions as more honorable and less costly than war. Again, in 1914, he opposed military "preparedness" as a danger that would involve his country in the war raging in Europe.

In December, 1915, Henry Ford brought off his Peace Ship Expedition to Europe with the object of organizing a peace conference to end the war. Jones accepted an invitation to join the party. The world was not in a mood to think about peace. The effort failed to stop hostilities abroad, or to win favor in America, where peace talk was becoming increasingly unpopular. Yet in spite of editorial ridicule and public scorn, Jones was glad to be counted with those who made a sincere, if unsuccessful, bid for peace.

After the United States entered the war, he continued in the columns of *Unity* to plead for understanding and goodwill among the nations. To authorities in Washington such sentiments were subversive, and, in 1918, *Unity* was denied the use of the United States mails from the first of July to the end of August. The editor, ill at Tower Hill, received a copy of the first number after the ban was lifted. He read it, then fell into a deep sleep from which he did not waken. He died on September 12.

On a plain tombstone in the old Welsh Burying Ground at Tower Hill are lines from Lincoln, chosen by Jones, "He sought to pull up a thistle and plant a flower wherever a flower would grow." Jenkin Lloyd Jones, immigrant, gave much to the land of his adoption. He left his mark upon the city of his choice, labored in it and for it for thirty-six years, and at the time of his death was the oldest and best known settled minister in Chicago.

He, more than any other, was responsible for giving shape and direction to the Western Unitarian Conference, which he served as secretary for eleven years and continued to guide throughout his life. Under his leadership the Conference made secure its position as the most liberal wing of Unitarian religion. With missionary zeal and organizing genius he started new movements and tied them into state and regional relations.

The Western Conference came close to being a denomination by itself, with its expanding empire, and proud independence of the conservative Unitarianism to the east. It had its own state conferences and Sunday School Society, published tracts and other literature, raised its own missionary funds, and employed its own missionaries.

Jones, as editor of *Unity*, made the paper an outspoken herald of liberal opinion and applied religion as well as the organ of the Conference. The Abraham Lincoln Center, carrying on the traditions of its founder, remains the visible witness of his faith and works. Unseen but no less real is the vital strain of liberal thought and action that Jenkin that Jenkin Lloyd Jones gave to his church.

CHAPTER EIGHTEEN

John Murray Atwood
1869-1951

When many people of Universalist or Unitarian background think of St. Lawrence University, they think of John Murray Atwood. During most of his eighty-two years he was associated in one way or another with St. Lawrence—as a student, teacher, trustee, and dean of the Theological School.

His father, Isaac Morgan Atwood, was president of the Theological School for twenty years. John Murray Atwood's children, two daughters and a son, were graduated from the university, as were a long line of nephews, nieces, in-laws , and grandchildren—thirty-four in all. The name Atwood is ploughed deep into the life of St. Lawrence as well as into the history of the Universalist Church.

Isaac Morgan Atwood, born into a poor family in western New York state, had little schooling. He went to work at eleven to help support the family, was successively farm hand, stable hand at a village tavern, and mule driver on the Erie Canal. At seventeen he organized and taught a private school. He was self-educated, and by diligent use of every spare moment managed to acquire the equivalent of a college education. He became a master of English expression and prepared himself for the Universalist ministry, to which he was ordained at the age of twenty-three. Besides serving several Universalist churches as pastor, he was editor of *The Universalist*, the denomination's leading journal, and was the first general superintendent of the Universalist church.

It was while he and his wife, Almira Church Atwood, and their three small daughters were living in Bridgewater (now Brockton), Massachusetts, that their son John Murray was born in the Universalist parsonage. Later the Rev. Mr. Atwood's pastoral changes took the family to Chelsea, Massachusetts, and then to Cambridge.

When John, or Murray as the family called him, was ten, his father was made president of the Theological School at St. Lawrence University, and the Atwoods took up their residence in Canton, New York. This was a pleasant village on the Grass River, the county seat of St. Lawrence County. The area had been settled mostly by Vermonters who brought with them native political ideas and frugal habits. At the time the Universalists founded the University in 1856, a local newspaper proudly stated that St. Lawrence County was the strongest Republican county in the state. The first permanent settler, a man named Stillman Foote, from Middlebury, Vermont, purchased the square mile of land on which Canton is built, swapping one horse equipped with bridle and saddle for the land. The Universalists had come early to the region, and at the time St. Lawrence University was founded had several thriving churches in the North Country. The Universalist Society in Canton was organized in 1828 and incorporated in 1836.

John Murray was a spirited lad, strong, quick of action, and a fast runner. Canton was a good place in which to grow up. Nearby there were deep woods and broad fields to be explored, and opportunities to work on farms in haying time. In winter there was coasting on the long hills, and skating on the Grass River. Of all sports John liked baseball the best. The Atwoods kept a cow and chickens and John Murray took care of them. He had no taste for his charges, since the chores too frequently conflicted with more important engagements on the baseball field.

He was graduated from Canton Academy in the spring of 1885, and that fall enrolled as a student in the University. I.M. Atwood set a high value on college training. Denied the advantages of formal education himself (he wanted to go to Yale), he saw to it that his children received the best that the University provided. John Murray was encouraged to take courses in the ancient languages, and in all classical subjects offered. He was graduated with Phi Beta Kappa honors, in 1889.

During his four years of college he played on the varsity baseball teams, mostly in the outfield. At that time players in the outfield used no gloves. Consequently Murray had banged-up knuckles and crooked fingers throughout adult life, evidence of his skill in bare-handed catching. He also had had his nose broken by a ball he failed to catch.

After graduating from the University he got a job as reporter on the *Rocky Mountain News* in Denver, Colorado. The work brought him into contact with people and conditions quite unfamiliar to one ac-customed to the shelter of a minister's home and the routine life on a college campus. As a cub reporter he was given the less desirable assignments. He heard and saw much of the shady side of life—ward politics, vice, and crime. He was sent to sordid neighborhoods and bad homes to gather news of accidents, fires, and murders. He learned many things that were not taught in college classrooms, but the press as a career was not for John Murray Atwood. After a year on the newspaper he returned to Canton and enrolled in the Theological School.

He entered into the student life of the University, and into the social affairs of the town, coached baseball, taught a class in the Canton Universalist Church, and played cards with the younger set. During the Christmas recess a student, Mary Ford, entertained her sister Addie fom Middleville, a small village a few miles east of Utica. Addie was nineteen, petite, vivacious, and attractive. John met her at a whist party, looked into her laughing gray eyes, and trumped his partner's ace. Later he took her snowshoeing, skating, and to dances in the town hall.

The theological students were given opportunities to do supply preaching in the churches of the North Country for pulpit experience and for money to pay their term bills. Murray frequently managed to be sent to Middleville. He always stayed at the Ford home over the weekends. Addie never missed a service on the Sundays when he preached. Usually he came down by train on Saturday night, and returned to Canton on Sunday evening. One Sunday afternoon he borrowed the family horse and buggy to make a call on a member of the church far out in the country. Nobody informed him that old Dobbin would not allow himself to be tied. Murray anchored him se-curely to a hitching post in the farmyard. After the call he discoverd that Dobbin had already gone home, taking the hitching post with him. After the long four-mile walk to Middleville it was too late to catch the train for Canton. Murray and Addie had a long evening together in the Ford parlor.

Graduating from the Theological School in 1893, he was engaged as minister of the Universalist Church in Clifton Springs, New York. Here he was ordained, in the same little wooden church where his father had been ordained thirty-two years earlier.

John was now twenty-four. He was tall and lean, with well-developed muscles. He danced gracefully and his walk had the lightness of a seasoned athlete. He was not handsome, but seemed it when his dancing blue eyes and flashing smile lighted up his plain features, reflecting the warm-heartedness of the man.

At this time the Young Peoples' Christian Union of the Universalist Church was in its early years of rapid growth. Unions were springing up in the Universalist churches across the land, and were nowhere more flourishing than in western and central New York. The first annual convention of the organization was held in 1890 in Rochester. John was present and when he came to Clifton Springs he brought to the church the enthusiasm of that gathering. The young people were full of plans to strengthen the local churches and to raise money to start new movements in the southern states. Area meetings were held for the exchange of ideas, for mutual encouragement, and for the promotion of fellowship among the members. The new minister at Clifton Springs gave freely of his time to the activities of the Union, speaking at meetings in the region and widening his acquaintance with the young people in the state. By judiciously arranging pulpit exchanges with the minister in Middleville, and with others in nearby towns, John was often a guest in the Ford home. Nobody was surprised when he and Addie were married in the summer of 1894.

The next year they moved to Minneapolis, where John was minister of the Third Universalist (later called the Tuttle Church). This was a young organization started by the First Universalist Church. John was also in charge of a mission church in the city. Two daughters, Ruth and Helen, were born in Minneapolis.

In the autumn of 1898, following his father's resignation as head of the Theological School, John went back to Canton to teach ethics and logic, and to complete work for a Master's degree. At the end of the academic year he accepted a call to the Universalist Church of the Messiah in Portland, Maine. Westbrook Seminary, a coeducational preparatory school founded by Universalists in 1834, was nearby. The minister, with his characteristic interest in young people, formed strong ties with the students. They came to church services and sang in his choir; he spoke at their meetings and could always be counted on to give support to their athletic activities. He and Mrs. Atwood were regular guests for Sunday buffet supper at the Seminary, and then joined the students and teachers in their weekly worship and discussion in the school parlor.

The Atwoods were in Portland six years. Their son John was born there in 1901. The Messiah pastorate was a happy experience, but John Murray had a deep devotion to St. Lawrence. He liked the atmosphere of the college campus, and he liked to teach. Therefore in 1905, when he was invited to join the faculty of the University, he was glad to return to his alma mater. He taught sociology and ethics in the Theological School, and was made Professor of Greek in the University. During the following years Atwood taught a wide range of subjects. There were never enough teachers in either the Theological School or the University. At one time or another he taught education, psychology, and philosophy in the College of Letters and Science, and most of the courses offered by the Theological School.

John Murray Atwood was a superior teacher. He was an eager student himself, who enjoyed probing the depths of new scientific theories, and exploring the trends in philosophy and theology. Any undergraduate with an inquiring mind could hold genuine conversations with him. He did not ask that his ideas be accepted, but that the students in written examinations give evidence of independent thinking and of having arrived at some opinions of their own. "The purpose [in education]," he said, "is not to make the youth the preconceived kind of being we may want him to be, but to help him fulfill the promise of his own inherent powers. The great object of education is to assist the individual to be what it is in him to be."

He lectured to his classes as little as possible, preferring to investigate the subjects at hand with his students, stimulating their thinking and leading them in free discussion. Often teacher and pupils became so absorbed in these exercises that when the chapel bell rang to end the period, they failed to hear it. Then Bonnie, the Atwood collie, would stretch, walk to the door, and whine until she broke up the discussion and the students would dash for their next class.

Atwood delighted in the brilliant student, yet showed infinite patience with the slow to learn. It was not his habit to prejudge immaturity. Of the poor student he would say, "He will learn." He liked to recall the names of former students who, with only passable academic records, gave good accounts of themselves in their vocations.

These Live Tomorrow

The Atwoods, in their large frame house on the edge of the campus, kept open house throughout the college year. Always there were
one or more theological students living in the home. In return for room
and board they took on certain domestic responsibilities. All students
felt free to drop in at any time, for consultation, a friendly chat, or
even a meal. The house had a much-used side entrance. The custom
was to knock and walk in with a loud "Hello." Mrs Atwood might
answer from the kitchen or living room, or John Murray might call
out, "Come on up," as he looked down from his study door, over
the railing of the broad and open stairwell. Students, teachers, neighbors, visiting lecturers and dignitaries found in the Atwood home
equal and informal welcome. The wide hall, flanked by living rooms
on either side, could accommodate fifty guests on Thanksgiving Day
when the Atwoods and the Theological School professors and their
families had the students for dinner, music, and dancing. In the long
living room comfortable chairs around the fireplace invited relaxation
and discussion. During the long, cold winter evenings of the North
Country, students or guests would gather before the crackling fire
to enjoy the lively conversation that was always a part of the Atwood
home. Outside the winds might howl and snowdrifts pile high, but
inside there was warmth and good cheer, friendly debate, spirited
disagreement, and the problems of the universe to be considered, argued, and settled.

Dr. Atwood became the head of the Theological School in 1914,
following the death of Dean Henry Prentiss Forbes. Under Dean Atwood's administration new courses were introduced into the Theological School and academic standards for the degree of Bachelor of
Divinity were raised. Now for the first time a college degree was made
a prerequisite for a degree from the Theological School. In the earlier
years courses were aimed primarily at preparing students to preach
the Universalist gospel. This was now changed. They were no longer
indoctrinated in theology, but were encouraged to think for themselves and to inquire after truth wherever the search might lead them.
Students preparing for the liberal ministry were made acquainted with
the theological positions of their denomination, but they were led to
examine critically and discuss these points of view.

The Theological School operated on a slender budget, and the
tuition was kept low to favor students with small means. But Dean
Atwood somehow managed successfully to meet each financial emer-
gency as it arose. In the days before the university had large dormi-

tories, accommodations had to be found in the village for the new students. The Dean canvassed the town for rooms and jobs for those who needed to earn money. Not infrequently he helped needy students out of his own small salary. In addition to the executive burdens, he continued to carry a heavy teaching load. In 1919 he was made a member of the Board of Administration of the University, a position he filled to the end of his life.

Dr. Atwood always took an active part in the local Universalist Church and in denominational affairs. He served on the board of trustees of the Canton Universalist Church and taught in the church school. Always on Sunday mornings he was in his regular place, listening with interest and critical attention to the sermon of the day. At various times he was on the board of the New York Universalist Convention as trustee or as president.

In 1923 at the Universalist General Convention in Providence, Rhode Island, Dr. Atwood was nominated from the floor and elected president. This was the first time in Universalist history that a president outside the nominating committee's slate was voted into office. The campaign was engineered by the enthusiastic support of his former students and friends. He served as president of the denomination and as chairman of its board of trustees for four years. The office demanded many hours of additional work, traveling and speaking. The "Five Year Program of Advance," brought into being during this period, included the raising of a large fund for service projects abroad and for the building of the Universalist National Memorial Church in Washington.

The Dean's life was not all work. In addition to his lifelong devotion to baseball he played a smashing game of tennis, and when the St. Lawrence nine-hole golf course opened in 1926 he became an ardent golfer. Another favorite hobby was gardening. In the wide plot behind the house (with a corner reserved for Mrs. Atwood's flowers), he could be found on an early spring morning or between classes during the day, spading, hoeing, and planting. His pea vines bore fruit a full week earlier than any in the village, and he shared sweet corn with the neighbors long before their own was ready for use. He was accused of getting a head start by sprouting seed corn in the cellar during the winter and then transplanting the young shoots into the garden when the frost was out of the ground, a charge he denied.

Dean Atwood found in his garden laws of nature, which he said applied to education. If a plant is to be brought to is finest flowering and fruitage its nature must be studied. The kind of soil, climate, and culture it requires must be known. Just so, if the educative process is to be of greatest help to the people, their native capacities, the kind of moral, social, and other environment and the laws of development must be considered.

Dr. Atwood was a thorough-going liberal. He called himself a theist, but his theistic views were tempered with the solid conviction of humanity's dependence upon itself for the attainment of the good life. His God was not a vague, elusive, supernatural being, but the force of living, active, human love. God is demonstrated by those who labor with ''good will and sacrificial spirit for the good of their brothers.'' ''This means,'' he taught, ''that if human society is to be delivered from selfishness and savagery this must be by human efforts.'' The spirit and power of God are found and seen only in the good works of human beings.

He was in the forefront of the generation of Universalists who, moving away from belief in miracles, supernatural revelations, and special providence, made a rational religious adjustment to the findings of science. With John Murray Atwood any theological idea had to stand the test of reason. He was somewhat distrustful of set forms in public worship, lest ritual become a substitute for the rigorous confronting of living issues. One Christmas Sunday at the Canton Universalist Church he saw a lighted candle in the chancel, turned to a lady beside him in a pew, and jokingly whispered, ''Are we going high church?''

The right of individuals to grow in the direction indicated by their own capacities, and to hold convictions reached by their own honest thinking were principles that the Dean applied not only to his students but to all people. He was ever quick to come to the defense of any fellow minister under attack because of radical views or minority opinions.

Herbert Philbrook Morrell, professor of Christian Ethics in the Theological School, was a pacifist. When World War I came he took the stand that the entire German population should not be condemned for the evil deeds of their political leaders. For this he was bitterly assailed both on the campus and throughout the community and demands were made for his dismissal. In this time of emotional tension and hysteria of war Dean Atwood stood by Professor Morrell, defended his right to hold unpopular opinions, and refused to yield to public clamor.

JOHN MURRAY ATWOOD

Years later when an editorial appeared in a denominational journal saying that there was no place for a black minister in a Universalist pulpit John Murray raised a shrill cry of impatience. He contended that if this statement were true, then Universalists had better search their consciences to discover if they really believed in equality or were only giving this doctrine lip service. The congregation of a Universalist Church in New Jersey ousted its minister (who had engaged radicals to speak at the Sunday evening Forum) on the charge that he neglected parish duties. Dr. Atwood brought the issue out of the shadows, revealed the real reason for the minister's dismissal, and challenged the forces of reaction in the denomination.

In 1949 a Universalist Church was established in Boston as a venture into untried ways of worship and the use of the religious arts. The minister came under suspicion among some of the other Universalists because he was a humanist. Dean Atwood defended him with articles in the *Universalist Leader*, spoke in his behalf, and invited him to Canton to talk with the theological students.

A champion of freedom, an inspiring teacher, a vivid preacher, a capable administrator, and a constant seeker of truth—Dr. Atwood was all these. But here was also the man himself. For forty-seven years as teacher and dean he devoted his life to St. Lawrence and its Theological School, giving himself without stint to the successive line of students. Not all of them justified his high hopes for them, but perhaps none went out from the institution untouched by the quality of his nature. Very likely they forgot much of the subject matter of his teaching, but they remembered his concern for their future usefulness, and his sympathetic understanding for their doubts and dreams.

The Dean's iron physique served well his bustling days and buoyant spirit, but it was not proof against the creeping years. In 1949 he suffered a heart attack. At eighty he had hardly known a sick day. Those accustomed to seeing him pushing a lawnmower in the hot sun, shovelling snow in zero weather, and sprinting across campus could scarcely believe the report of this sudden illness. He made a partial recovery and insisted on resuming his work, but in October 1951 he was stricken again. Now at Dr. Atwood's request he was relieved of administrative duties. The trustees of the Theological School made him Dean Emeritus. To the last he continued to meet with his classes, some of them held at home. On Sunday morning, November 4, 1951, Dr. Atwood died suddenly in his home while at breakfast with Mrs. Atwood and their daughter Helen Atwood Harwood.

A few weeks after his death, Fisher Hall, the main building of the Theological School, was completely destroyed by fire. Plans were immediately made to raise money for a new home for the school. The cornerstone of the new structure was laid by Mrs. Atwood on October 17, 1955. The building was formally opened and dedicated a year later, bearing the name Atwood Hall in grateful memory of John Murray Atwood and his father, Isaac Morgan Atwood. With the closing of the Theological School in 1965 the building became the property of St. Lawrence University.

CHAPTER NINETEEN

Clarence Russell Skinner
1881-1949

Young Clarence Skinner made two important decisions before he finished college. One was to win the affection of Clara Ayres, an intelligent, quiet, charming young woman. They had entered St. Lawrence University in Canton, New York, in the fall of 1900. Clara was from Long Ridge, Connecticut, and Clarence from Brooklyn, New York. They were in some classes together, frequently met in the library, and discovered that they had interests in common. They attended the Universalist Church in Canton. Clara played the pipe organ. Clarence never missed a Sunday service. He was attentive to the organ music and to the organist.

The other decision was the more difficult to make. Should he choose the stage or the ministry? Both of these professions were in the Skinner family tradition. His father's brother Otis had won fame as an actor, and his own brother Harold had chosen the theater as a career. His father, Charles Montgomery Skinner, on the editorial staff of the *Brooklyn Eagle*, was a writer of plays as well as dramatic critic for the paper. And Clarence himself had strong leanings toward the stage. In Erasmus Hall High School in Brooklyn, where he prepared for college, he had taken part in plays, and he had continued his interest in dramatics at St. Lawrence.

On the other hand, there was the pull of the church. For several generations the Skinners had been prominent in Universalist religious and educational affairs. Grandfather Charles Augustus Skinner, and greatgrandfather Warren Skinner were Universalist ministers, as were more distant relatives. Another Universalist minister, Otis Ainsworth Skinner, had raised money to establish Tufts College and was later president of Lombard University.

When Tufts needed money to open the college to women, Clarence Skinner's grandmother, Cornelia B. Skinner, asked the Universalist women of Massachusetts to raise the $100,000 for this purpose. She gave her camel's hair shawl and her diamond ring. The proceeds from the sale of these articles helped to create the fund which provided scholarships for women students at Tufts University.

With this impressive family background it is not strange that Clarence finally chose the ministry. His decision gave the Universalist denomination a genuine liberal, a wise teacher, and a brave champion of human rights. One consideration in Skinner's decision was the more satisfactory home life that the ministry offered.

Clarence Russell Skinner's lifespan placed him in one of the most critical periods of American history. Born in 1881, he lived through three of his country's wars, two of them of world-wide scope. Throughout his life he remained a confirmed pacifist and suffered the special public contempt that in times of war is reserved for such individuals. His insistence on the application of religion to social problems caused him to be looked upon with suspicion by conservatives, even in his own denomination.

Clarence Skinner's revolt against social wrong sprang not from any outward conditions of deprivation, but from his complete identification with the underprivileged and the victims of evil forces. He carried no scars on body or mind of personal struggle with poverty. In economic advantage and cultural level his family belonged to the American upper middle class. He grew up in a good home, with reading and good conversation. His parents took him to see plays and to hear good music. His father introduced him to the wonders of the natural world in their walks together in parks and woods. He was endowed with a fine mind and early learned how to use it. In high school and college he stood high in scholarship, and he was a student all of his life.

Clarence and Clara graduated together in the spring of 1904. Clara went abroad and Clarence spent the summer at his grandfather Skinner's place in Proctorsville, Vermont. In the fall he went to New York City to assist in the work of the Universalist Church of the Divine Paternity. He had charge of the church school and the youth program, and sometimes preached when the minister was absent. The city offered many opportunities and Skinner made the most of them, going to lectures, attending the theatre, and using the public library. He joined a group of interesting people at the University Settlement on the lower East Side, where he taught evening classes in current public affairs and took part in the study and production of social problem plays. The settlement, the first institution of its kind in America, was established to bring together trained and sympathetic persons to study the needs of the community, and to serve individuals, families, and groups through programs of education and other activities. The two years in New York were profitable and pleasant. His family and childhood friends were in nearby Brooklyn, and Long Ridge was not far away.

Skinner was ordained to the Universalist ministry on April 8, 1906, in the Church of the Divine Paternity. The following summer he accepted a call to the Universalist Church in Mt. Vernon, New York. He and Clara were married in October, and went to the city of Washington on their honeymoon.

The work at Mt. Vernon prospered. A new church edifice was built, the church school was brought up to date in lesson materials, and classes of young people and adults were formed for the study of social problems. Mr. Skinner continued to be active in the University Social Settlement, making frequent trips to New York. He attended summer sessions at Columbia University and completed work for a master's degree, which he received from St. Lawrence.

About a year after Skinner settled in Mt. Vernon, John Haynes Holmes came from the Unitarian Church in Dorchester, Massachusetts, as one of the ministers of the Unitarian Church of the Messiah, now the Community Church of New York. The two had much in common and a warm comradeship was established that grew throughout the years. Both were convinced that Christian churches, with their traditional individualistic emphasis, must be reformed to meet the needs of the time. Religion, they believed, must not be limited to saving a few souls within a bad society; it must help create a society in which all people could have a good life. Religion must be brought to bear upon the whole range of human affairs—in education, politics, industry, and international relations. This stress on social ethics, or the Social Gospel as it was commonly called, was a vital movement when Skinner came into the ministry, and it continued to gain momentum up to the beginning of World War I.

The movement was spearheaded by men and women of intelligence and deep convictions, and accepted by many who had only a faint idea of what it was all about. Congregations were reminded of the injustices found in public life—low wages, bad housing, corrupt politics, poverty and crime. They were exhorted to become socially conscious and to share the guilt of social sins. The fiery words of the Old Testament prophets and the stern demands of the Sermon on the Mount came to life with fresh and compelling meaning when applied to the task of Christianizing the social order.

Adult classes for the discussion of urgent issues sprang up in churches of all kinds across the country. Ardent reformers, some of them on university teaching staffs, produced quarterly or weekly publications for use in study groups. These periodicals carried facts about such evils as corrupt political practices, the use of the police by powerful corporations to put down labor strikes, the scandal of large profits and low wages, the adulteration of food, and the unholy alliance between big business and government.

There were specific suggestions for action to secure worker's compensation for accidents and sickness, the abolition of child labor in factories, the eight-hour day in industry, and labor's legal right to strike for higher wages and better working conditions.

The public forum came into being with its program of reform, supplanting the lyceum, which was devoted to personal intellectual development. Even theological schools were persuaded to add courses in applied Christianity to meet the growing sentiment that religion should be related to the conditions under which people live and labor. At no time in America had the Kingdom of Heaven seemed so promising, or had Christians been so confident that it could come by the application of the Gospel to social reconstruction. This high optimism was not by any means shared by all people in all churches, and it was felt less by the laity than by the clergy. Yet the central idea of the Social Gospel that to create wholesome conditions for daily living is an ultimate aim of religion was accepted by leaders of most denominations—Protestant, Catholic, Jewish, and Liberal.

Clarence Skinner, Universalist, and John Haynes Holmes, Unitarian, were leaders in their respective denominations, fostering an ethical sensitiveness within the entire range of human relations. Holmes in 1908 formed the Unitarian Fellowship for Social Justice, and Skinner in 1910 was one of the founders of the Universalist Social Service Commission and its secretary for six years. In 1917, he formulated a Declaration of Social Principles, which became a platform of social ethics for the denominations.

In 1911 Mr. Skinner moved to Lowell, Massachusetts, to be pastor of the Grace Universalist Church. In this manufacturing city on the Merrimac River, with its giant textile mills, crowded tenements, and labor troubles, the minister had close-range experience with social problems. He brought representatives of labor and management together for discussions and for mutual understanding, and conducted a Sunday afternoon forum with outside speakers on public questions.

Skinner's interest in education was based on the conviction that information was necessary to intelligent action. In classes that he taught at summer institutes he frequently warned against "zeal without knowledge," against rushing into social action without knowing all that could be learned about the situation. He insisted that facts are as important in religion as they are in science. He was a constant reader, and out of a well-furnished mind wrote for several religious journals. While in Lowell he was made president of the Massachusetts Universalist Sunday School Association.

In the fall of 1914 Mr. Skinner was appointed Professor of Applied Christianity, in a department that had recently been established in the Crane Theological School at Tufts College. The school at this time was passing through a crisis. Former teachers had died or retired. There were few students, and they had been deprived of their classroom building to make room for the female students of the recently established Jackson College. But with the appointment in 1912 of Dr. Lee S. McCollester, pastor of the Universalist Church in Detroit, as dean, prospects for the school were beginning to brighten.

The coming of Clarence Skinner to the faculty met with warm approval in liberal circles. At the same time there were those who had misgivings over the appointment; they thought Skinner's radicalism would be a bad influence on students preparing for the Christian ministry.

Professor Skinner brought to the school a high valuation of the ministry and positive ideas about the breadth of education ministers needed to serve their generation. From the first the students hailed him as an excellent teacher, thorough in scholarship and able to make learning an exciting venture. His reputation as a sympathetic and inspiring classroom leader never diminished in his more than thirty years at the school.

The next year after coming to Crane, Skinner brought out his

book, *The Social Implications of Universalism.* This small volume was
as revolutionary in practical Universalism as was Ballou's book, *A Treatise On Atonement*, published more than a century earlier, in the field
of Universalist theology. Skinner dealt with the application of Universalist principles to the organized life of humanity.

World War I had already begun in Europe when Professor Skinner came to Tufts. Germany had declared war on Russia and France,
and Britain on Germany. Soon most of the nations of Europe were
at one another's throats. Treaties were broken, secret alliances revealed, poison gas used for the first time in history, neutral nations
overrun, and humane practices in warfare formerly observed by civi-
lized people thrown overboard.

As the slaughter continued sentiment grew in the United States
for this country's entrance into the war. Financial and other interests
were at stake. Neutral nations were being pressed hard by the war-
ring powers. There were also strong feelings that the United States
should remain neutral. Peace organizations carried on active campaigns. These feelings faded, however, before the overpowering
events that finally pushed the country into taking sides against Germany and its allies. After President Wilson had protested in vain
against the sinking of ships without warning, and the Lusitania was
sunk by a German submarine, with the loss of one hundred and
twenty-four American lives, the war spirit prevailed. Congress
declared war on Germany on April 6, 1917.

When the hostilities broke out in Europe, the churches in America generally favored neutrality, and in conventions passed resolutions
against war. But more and more religious leaders shifted their position. Once the country entered the conflict, with few exceptions, they
threw their weight into the war effort. They saw the war, which now
involved the whole world, not as a struggle for territory and commercial power, but as a righteous cause, a battle between the forces
of good and evil. This was, they believed, "a war to end all wars,"
a moral crusade to establish democracy for all people. Waves of hysteria swept over America, affecting every institution, including the
churches and colleges.

Ministers who were lukewarm about the war or who were suspected of pacifism lost their pulpits. In one denomination local
churches that received aid were warned that if they harbored ministers
not in favor of war, financial support would be cut off. A New England college abolished the chair of English when the pacifist head

212

of the department refused to resign.

Everything German was taboo. Schools stopped teaching the German language, German-American banks became Liberty Banks, and German measles were called Liberty measles. A man in Buffalo was refused a license for his German police dog Kaiser until he changed the dog's name.

Tufts went all out for war. Students joined the armed forces. The Navy took over the theological school buildings. The few theological classes that were continued met in Dean McCollester's home. The story told by students who were in Tufts during the war years illustrates the frenzied atmosphere of the time. A German liner in Boston harbor, impounded by the United States government, threw the president of the college into a panic. Fearing that the sailors would break loose from the ship and seize the towns of Greater Boston, he called the students together, warned them of the danger, armed them with Indian clubs from the women's gymnasium and announced that in case of attack the chapel bell would be rung, and that it was the patriotic duty of all students in college to defend their country by routing the enemy.

At Tufts, as elsewhere, persons were classified either as patriots or as pacifists. It did not take the patriots long to identify Professor Skinner. He was opposed to the war, and was unmoved from his position under the pressure of patriotic appeals or public opinion. Faculty members shunned him. He was generally held in contempt on the campus and was a source of embarrassment to the administration. These were dark and lonely days for Clarence and Clara Skinner. Dean McCollester and two or three other members of the college faculty stood by him and defended his right to hold and to express his minority opinions. Among Skinner's colleagues in the ministry in accord with his views were Dr. Edwin C. Sweetzer of Philadelphia, Dr. Levi Powers of Gloucester, and Professor H.P. Morrell of Canton Theological School, all men older than he, and a few young ministers. To these young ministers, Professor Skinner's uncompromising stand on the war was an inspiration, and his composure under attack a rebuke to their hotheadedness.

Hostilities ended in the fall of 1918, but wartime conformity, intolerance, and brutality continued after the fighting ceased. The country became conservative. Many people had prospered by the war and did not want to be disturbed. Reforms were a nuisance, and reformers were dangerous agitators. The reasons for getting into the world war were conveniently forgotten. The political control of the country was in the hands of conservatives who opposed progressive legislation, gave comfort to extreme nationalists and rejected the League of Nations. In the name of Americanism the hooded Ku Klux Klan fanned the flames of religious and racial hatred. Liberals and radicals were labeled Bolsheviks and Communists.

In this period, as in the war years, Professor Skinner stood like a rock. In public speeches and magazine articles he called for cooperation between nations, and for total disarmament. Complaints came to the college about what he said, or what others thought he said, but these communications were dealt with in a fair-minded manner by John A. Cousens, the new President who had come to Tufts in 1919.

Few churches anywhere measured up to Skinner's idea of what they ought to be. So he started the Community Church in Boston. In his theological school classes, at summer institutes, and in his writings he had continually stressed the need for the churches to relate themselves to the problems of the community and to national and world issues. The new church would demonstrate the practical nature of his theories.

A further motive behind this venture was to create a church for people whose religious needs were not met by the churches of any denomination. He was well-known for his firm pacifist position during the war period and for his devotion to the cause of civil liberties. Those who helped in the creation of the new church shared these views. Dr. John Haynes Holmes of the Community Church in New York, out of his long experience and generous spirit, supported the project both by his counsel and by frequent trips to Boston to speak to the growing congregation. The first service was on January 11, 1920, in Steinert Hall. As more space was needed meetings were held in Copley Theater, and then Symphony Hall, with seating for twenty-six hundred.

Skinner conducted the services and frequently brought to the church speakers of national and international fame. From the beginning, Community Church maintained a free pulpit where any subject related to good government and good citizenship could be discussed. Speakers denied a hearing in other churches or halls were given an opportunity to be heard if they had something to say that was worthy of public attention. For seventeen years Clarence Skinner presided over the programs of this church, building into the life of the city an enduring and vital influence on the principles of responsible freedom and democracy.

In 1921, Nicola Sacco, a fish peddler, and Bartolomeo Vanzetti, a shoe factory employee, were accused and convicted of killing two men in a payroll holdup at Braintree, Massachusetts. They were radicals, and many believed that their arrest was a trick devised by those interested in getting rid of them. They became the objects of a six-year campaign for release on the grounds of lack of evidence and prejudice of the court. Skinner was convinced that they were victims of persecution. He followed the case closely, attended sessions of the trial, spoke his opinions, held protest meetings in Community Church, and reported the court procedures to liberal periodicals. Up to the last minute he had hopes that their lives would be spared. When the men were executed he felt that a grave injustice had been done. His interest in this case was typical of his concern and his ready response in the defense of those whom he believed were wronged.

Professor Skinner was made vice-dean of Crane in 1929. Three years later Dean McCollester resigned. Under his administration, the school's enrollment had grown from a half-dozen students to forty-five. Crane Chapel and Library and the Fisher Arcade had been built. Altogether the institution was in good condition. It needed a capable leader. Dr. McCollester let it be known to the trustees of the college and to the school's alumni that he considered Professor Skinner best fitted for the office. President Cousens also favored Skinner. Some of the trustees wavered in making Skinner the dean, and few of them had any enthusiasm for the appointment. There was also considerable opposition in the denomination. The board of trustees of the Universalist General Convention had a plan to recommend to the trustees of Tufts. If it had been carried out, a candidate other than Skinner would have been placed in the Dean's chair. The plan fell through; Skinner was appointed dean.

The theological school grew under his management both in the number of students and in its scholastic standing, and continued to do so throughout the twelve years of his administration. His responsibilities as head of the institution never interfered with his teaching. He continued his classwork and added courses to broaden the outlook of students and faculty. Those who took his course in comparative religions were made aware of the value in non-Christian cultures. To Skinner, Universalism represented more than a denomination; it was a recognition of the religious elements that unite humanity in common aspirations. He presented Judaism and Buddhism as sympathetically as if he were a follower of these religions. One of his students, at the end of an examination on Confucianism, wrote: "Professor Skinner almost thou persuadest me to become a heathen."

When he became dean the Skinners moved from Cambridge to College Hill to be near the students. Here on Sawyer Avenue students and teachers came to know the gracious hospitality of Dr. and Mrs. Skinner. In 1938 the Dean was supposed to have a sabbatical year, but he took a vacation of only four months. He and Mrs. Skinner drove across the country, put their car on a boat, and came back by way of the Panama Canal in time to teach summer school at Harvard University. Several summers were spent in foreign travel, especially to observe the new governments and national realignments that came after World War I. In 1922, he had tried to visit India to study the work of Gandhi but was refused admission by the British government, presumably because of his sympathy with the great nonresistant revolutionist.

World War II put him under severe strain. Again facilities of Crane were taken over by the military, and students went off to war to be injured or killed. Leadership of the Community Church had been turned over to a younger person, but there were still heavy demands upon the Dean's time and energy. He was writing and speaking constantly, in addition to carrying on his classes and administrative work. So much needed to be written and said when humanity was lost in the madness of hate and war!

Skinner never weakened in his stand against war. The aftermath of both world conflicts proved him right in his contention that war is no answer to world problems—that peace can be secured only as the causes of wars are removed. America's spirit was less vindictive in World War II than in World War I; thus Skinner was not a victim of intolerance. Also, many of his severest critics, even though they could not agree with him, learned to respect his stubborn honesty and unyielding convictions. At the end of the war he resigned as dean, due to failing health, which surgery could not restore.

Dr. Skinner hoped to have years for writing and for travel, to visit places and to do the things he and Mrs. Skinner had planned to do together but that had been impossible during his busy life. He continued to write, attend ministers' meetings and church gatherings, and speak publicly. But he had used up his physical resources. Four years after his retirement from Crane he died, on August 27, 1949, at Long Ridge, Connecticut.

Skinner received honorary degrees from Meadville Theological School and St. Lawrence University, and was a member of the boards of trustees of St. Lawrence and of the Civil Liberties Union. The building on Mt. Vernon Place in Boston that was acquired in 1962 by the Unitarian Universalist Association has been named Skinner House.

Clarence Skinner left a wealth of writings, a half-dozen books and numerous articles published in *The Universalist Leader*, *Unity*, the *Survey*, and other journals. Perhaps the most important of his books was *Social Implications of Universalism*, because it was written at a time when Universalists were desperately in need of a fresh vision of their mission. It gave socially-minded ministers a chart and compass for their perilous navigation amid the shoals of conservatism.

Several unpublished manuscripts were left, three of which were combined after Skinner's death into one volume, *Worship and the Well-Ordered Life*. This book represents Skinner's deep reflections on the role of the liberal church, and the place of worship as the wellspring of religious experience. It is the summation of his own well-ordered life, and the final gift of one of the most courageous prophets of liberal religion.

CHAPTER TWENTY

Frederick May Eliot
1889-1958

Frederick May Eliot was a city boy, well-born, well-bred, and well-educated. He was born in the Dorchester area of Boston, Massachusetts, on September 15, 1889, the first child of the Reverend Christopher Rhodes Eliot and Mary Jackson May Eliot. His father was pastor of the First Parish Unitarian Church in Dorchester. Two daughters, Martha May and Abigail Adams, were also born while the family lived there.

The Eliot children were birthright Unitarians. Their great-grandfather, William Greenleaf Eliot, helped establish All Souls Unitarian Church in Washington, D.C., in 1821. His son, William Greenleaf Eliot, Jr., went west in 1834 as a young man, and became the first settled minister of a new Unitarian Church in St. Louis, Missouri, and with missionary zeal helped start several churches in that part of the country. Among his important civic activities was the founding of Washington University in St. Louis. Christopher Rhodes was an incorporator of the St. Louis Church, and when Frederick's father was born he was named for this devoted layperson.

Frederick's uncle, Thomas Lamb Eliot, went in 1867 to be minister of the Unitarian Church in Portland, Oregon. His name is written large in the history of the developing northwest United States. Others, both ministers and laypersons, in this family were prominent in the annals of Unitarianism. There were also Unitarians on the mother's side, one of them the Rev. Samuel May, Eliot's distinguished uncle, and another a cousin, Joseph May of Syracuse, New York.

With these strong family traditions it is not strange that Frederick was led to take up the Unitarian ministry. Nor is it strange that, favored with rich natural gifts and a well-trained mind, he became one of the foremost leaders in liberal religion of our time.

When Frederick was four the family went to England, where his father studied for a year at Oxford University. Here the Eliots were initiated into the ways of English life. Poorly heated rooms and too much mutton were defects offset by the privilege of dwelling for a time in the cultural atmosphere of this ancient seat of learning. Mrs. Eliot read and shared her husband's studies, and on warm days romped with the children on the college greens. Frederick was never allowed to have toy guns, but now he had a football. He was fascinated by the colorful academic regalia he saw, and his mother made him an "Oxford" cap and gown, which he wore in the grand manner of a giant of learning.

On returning to America, Mr. Eliot became minister of the Bulfinch Place Church on the back of Beacon Hill in Boston. This church had inherited the spirit and the philanthropic activities of Joseph Tuckerman. The family lived a few blocks away on West Cedar Street. The four-story brick house, with basement kitchen and sub-basement cellar, was one of a long row of dwellings built with continuous frontage close to the sidewalk. The many rooms were heated by a coal-burning furnace in the basement and lighted by gas. Frederick's room was on the fourth floor.

The Eliot children were not allowed to play in the street. The only outdoor space the premises provided was a small, grassless, almost treeless back yard, with a brick floor. However, Boston Common and the Public Garden, popular playgrounds for children on the Hill, were not far away. The wide grounds with their trees and rocks, winding trails, and Frog Pond provided a world where the young Eliots could work off their surplus energies. Their mother warned them always to be very careful crossing Beacon Street because the horse cars came down the hill at terrific speed.

Frederick and his two sisters went to the public grammar school at the corner of Exeter and Newbury Streets. It was a mile away and in good weather a pleasant walk. In spring, across the Public Garden, sometimes following the crooked paths but often ignoring the "Keep Off the Grass" signs, skirting the clumps of forsythia, beds of tulips in their many colors, and the Japanese tulip trees with purple blossoms, the three little Eliots would reach the school house out of breath. It was pleasant, too, in autumn to scuff through the fallen leaves. Sometimes they tried, without much success, to memorize the long Latin words that told the family names of the many kinds of trees in the Garden. In winter the sidewalks cleared of snow were preferable to the Garden paths. Dashing wildly into the traffic they would steal rides on the back runners of the sleighs and pungs, risking the danger of losing their grip and being trampled by the horses of oncoming vehicles.

Mrs. Eliot and the children went to Grandfather May's farm in Dorchester on Saturdays. Early in the morning Philip the coach driver arrived at the house on West Cedar Street with a span of horses hitched to a black surrey with polished brass lamps. With mother and the girls in the back seat, and Frederick up front with the driver, the party drove out through the crowded parts of Roxbury and finally reached the shaded roads of Dorchester.

The farm with its wide fields and woodlot, orchard, barns, and domestic animals was a never-ending wonder and delight to the children. The hours were always too short before nightfall when Philip brought his passengers home.

Grandfather May was a retired merchant of wholesale purchases, and he carried the practice into providing for his family. Flour, sugar, crackers, and vinegar were purchased in large quantities. Vegetables were bought by the crate or barrel. The cellar looked like a miniature warehouse with provisions, barrels of dishes, and unused household articles. Grandfather, an abolitionist who had helped in the activities of the underground railway, was a big-hearted man with unfailing generosity, but with over-developed habits of New England thrift. He saved everything. In the attic were three decades of the *Atlantic Monthly* and the *Boston Transcript*, together with miles of accumulated string.

After the exhausting day at the farm the Eliot children were allowed to sleep late on Sunday mornings, sometimes until half-past seven. Bulfinch Place Church was a city mission type of church. In the midst of a lodging house district the church carried on a program of religious education for all age groups, as well as general social activities for the citizens of the West End of Boston. Many of the Howard Sunday School teachers and other workers came from Unitarian churches in and around Boston.

Services were held in the afternoon because the working people of the congregation, some of them employed at night, needed to sleep on Sunday morning. In this atmosphere of friendly human relations, the Eliot children grew up without the handicap of national and racial prejudice. Frederick always remembered with deep gratitude his Sunday School teacher, Miss Porter, who during his growing years helped him understand how religion, to be real, must be applied to personal living and public affairs.

After grammar school, Frederick entered the Roxbury Latin School, going back and forth by electric street car. He did well in his studies and was active in dramatics, an interest that he continued later at Harvard University. While in grammar school he took piano lessons, and continued them for several years. He played well, but gradually did less as the demands of his work increased. Later he took up painting, a field in which he showed considerable talent.

In 1903, when Frederick was fourteen, his father bought fifty-four acres of land on the east shore of beautiful Lake Memphremagog in Canada as a vacation site for the family. Here, five miles north of the village of Georgeville, a log cabin and tents housed the growing Eliot clan and friends. Later, cottages were built.

When school was out, Mr. and Mrs. Eliot and the children would take the Montreal Express from Boston to Newport, Vermont, where they would spend the night. The next morning they would board the side-wheeler steamer the *Lady of the Lake*, bound for the northern end of the lake. This was the best part of the journey. The boat was a wood-burner, broad in beam, but a creation of beauty and luxury to the children with its gleaming white paint, roomy decks, red carpets, and polished brass. And Captain Bullock, its master, was equally distinguished with his long white beard and blue uniform with gold braid. At eight miles an hour, the vessel steamed past the green islands and Owl's Head Mountain, and crossed the international line into Canadian waters.

Summers were never long enough. There were fields to roam, woods to explore, and raspberries and wild strawberries to pick. The lake provided boating, swimming, and fishing. And there were good books to read in the swinging hammock under the maples, and during the long evenings of northern summer. Frederick loved this retreat, and continued to enjoy it throughout his life.

Frederick Eliot then went to Harvard. Frederick's father was a graduate of Washington University and the Harvard Divinity School. Frederick entered Harvard after graduating from Roxbury Latin in

1907. He was interested in government, and majored in it at the University. On graduating *summa cum laude* in 1911, he went abroad on a fellowship to study the governments of European cities. The next year he served as instructor in municipal government at Harvard, and received his Master's degree.

During his years at the University, Frederick attended the First Parish Church in Cambridge, where Samuel McChord Crothers was pastor. It is likely that Dr. Crothers' influence helped turn the younger man's mind toward the ministry. At any rate he decided to enter Harvard Divinity School.

The year 1915 was important in the life of Frederick May Eliot; he not only was graduated from Divinity School, but was ordained, became assistant to Dr. Crothers at the First Parish Church, and was married. Elizibeth Berkeley Lee left her Universalist home in Brunswick, Maine, to become Mrs. Eliot. She entered upon what proved to be a long and interesting future, sharing with her husband the trials and triumphs of the liberal ministry, and helping to maintain a happy home life. They had two sons, Richard and Christopher Rhodes II.

After two years at the First Parish Church, Frederick was called to Unity Church in St. Paul, where Dr. Crothers had been minister before coming to Cambridge. For twenty years the Eliots made this thriving mid-western city their home. Both the church and its minister became identified with the best in the life of the community. Patrons of good causes looked to Mr. Eliot for moral support, and he gave generously of time and labor to the social service agencies of both city and state. At a time of crisis in city affairs, friends outside the church strongly urged him to run for mayor, but be declined. His first duty was to his parish.

His was a well-balanced ministry. He was a forceful figure in the pulpit, with his tall husky frame, strong features, heavy dark hair, brown penetrating eyes and rich, pleasing voice—altogether a well-constructed trumpet for prayer and song, and for the words of challenge and comfort. Parish work was fitted to the needs of his people. He knew his parishioners in their homes and they grew to rely upon his counsel and to trust his confidence.

One area received more attention than others — the religious education of the young people. Never willing to turn over to others the ministry to children, Eliot insisted on conducting the worship services of the church school and supervising its teaching program. He found on taking up the work in St. Paul that in Unity Church, as in many other churches, the adults were well provided with spacious quarters for their worship services—an artistic sanctuary, pipe organ, stained-glass windows and cushioned pews. The children had none of these luxuries. They met for worship in the basement, and went to classes in corners, and in dingy cubby holes—wherever there was unwanted space. Mr. Eliot set out at once to correct this situation. He persuaded the people to add an education building to the church. Light, airy classrooms were provided, and a children's chapel with suitable furnishings and an artistic threefold window of stained glass.

The twenty years in St. Paul were happy, productive years for the Eliots. Lasting friendships were formed both within and outside the parish. Unity Church became known as a center of good influence, whose circumference encircled the progressive interests of community and state. Carleton College in Northfield, Minnesota, gave Mr. Eliot the honorary degree of Doctor of Divinity, and the University of Minnesota gave him an honorary Doctor of Laws. Later, both Meadville Theological School and Mount Holyoke conferred degrees upon him.

Among Unitarians, Dr. Eliot was known as an able minister, effective in leadership of his church, and devoted to the welfare of the denomination. In 1934, when a Commission of Appraisal was set up to make a study of Unitarian organizations and agencies and to make recommendations for change, Dr. Eliot was named chairperson of the Commission.

The 1930s were a trying period in the churches of America. A nationwide economic depression was reflected in the decline of financial support to all denominations. Unitarians, too, had to cut corners and reduce their normal denominational activities. A disturbing number of Unitarian churches had closed during the past quarter-century and many others survived only because of endowments or denominational aid. Moreover, the tide was running against liberal ideas in religion. Added to these difficulties, a sharp division over the theist-humanist issue was developing within the Unitarian fellowship. More and more ministers and congregations (outside of New England) were turning to humanism. This brought about a reaction from those who felt it their duty to defend the historic Unitarian position. The result was a good deal of fireworks that made noise, but yielded only faint glimmerings of light. Denominational journals provided a field for theological skirmishes, and denominational gatherings an arena for theological swordplay. In both the Unitarian and the Universalist denominations it was suggested in high places that humanists had no moral right to remain in fellowship, and they were cordially invited to go elsewhere. It was tragic that so much time and energy were drawn away from the other concerns of the denomination. Plainly, something had to be done to unite the factions to boost morale, and make a new start in the Unitarian movement. Under Dr. Eliot, the Commission of Appraisal took on this task.

The Commission took two years to complete its assignment. It held conferences with officials and organizations within the denomination, and employed expert services. The entire structure, aims, and policies of American Unitarian Association and related agencies were given careful study. Unitarian history was reviewed to discover both the errors and the sound policies of the movement in the past. The final report was presented to the American Unitarian Association at the May Meetings in 1936. It was published under the title *Unitarians Face a New Age*, a book of three hundred pages.

The report was an honest work of self-examination, suggesting answers to the questions of why the movement had stopped moving, and why the religion of Unitarianism was not more effective in meeting the needs of the times. Some bold recommendations were aimed at reform in administration, education, and church extension. With few changes the recommendations were approved the following year.

It was well enough to have the study made, to discover weaknesses, and to point out ways for improvement. But unless the recommendations were carried out, and unless Unitarians themselves caught a new vision and were aroused to action, the frontiers would not be occupied. The Association must have a leader, one familiar with the road already travelled and with eyes on far horizons. This person must have the confidence of fellow-workers and the ability to lead them to move together into the new age. Frederick May Eliot was elected President of the American Unitarian Association in 1937. A new, invigorating breeze began blowing through the denomination.

Ernest W. Kuebler had been Director of the Department of Religious Education for two years when the new president came into office. He had battled for a fresh approach to the problems of education and for a program in keeping with modern methods and the aims of liberal religion. Dr. Eliot at once came to his aid, and with his own deep interest in religious education, continued throughout his administration to give strong support to the department. Progressive policies in curriculum-building, publishing of resource material, summer institutes, and field work all helped to raise this area to a level never before reached in the denomination.

Church extension also was soon to be brought to new life. Lon Ray Call, in 1941, as minister-at-large, began gathering groups in communities where there was no liberal church. His efforts led to the creation of the Fellowship Program within the Church Extension Department. Fellowships sprang up across the land, adding a new dimension to the outreach of the denomination and numbers to its membership. In 1944, the Church of the Larger Fellowship was started, to serve by correspondence isolated liberals of all ages, wherever they could be found.

During President Eliot's term of office the Unitarian Service Committee for nondenominational relief work in many parts of the world was established. Beacon Press became known as publisher of books of high quality, the United Unitarian Appeal was brought into being, the American Unitarian Association was re-structured for greater effectiveness, and the Unitarian Development Fund was initiated and sent on its successful mission.

Most important of all was the awakening of the people in the local churches. A new sense of purpose spurred them into action. Congregations formerly proud of their isolation began to feel related to other congregations and to the American Unitarian Association. Local budgets increased along with increased support of the Association. Churches long on relief became self-supporting. The mood of Unitarians changed from looking backward to a more or less glorious past to the possibilities of the future. They began to realize that emphases ought to be made in religion that only liberals would make.

During the twenty years that Dr. Eliot was president, the Unitarian membership increased seventy-five percent, and the enrollment of church schools even more. New churches were established, and the construction of church buildings set a record for the denomination. While credit for this progress was shared, it is nevertheless true that without Dr. Eliot, a strong leader with vision and devotion to the task, the dramatic upsurge of Unitarianism would not have taken place.

The advance was not always free of obstacles. The policies were frequently opposed by some members of the governing board of the American Unitarian Association, and were not always freely accepted by some of the staff at headquarters. By nature Dr. Eliot was overly sensitive to criticism, and inclined to regard disagreement with his plans as a personal attack upon himself. But no one who knew him well ever doubted that any proposals he advanced were meant for the good of the cause. Moreover, when he was overruled, as he sometimes was by the Board of Directors and by delegates to the Annual Meeting of the Association, he did not withhold support of others' policies.

Although deeply rooted in Unitarian traditions, Dr. Eliot showed a generous tolerance and appreciation of other religions. Not a humanist himself, he went far in interpreting humanism to his fellow theists, and in stressing the need of unity in action by people of diverse viewpoints. He was most interested in uniting religious liberal forces. In 1947, at the Universalist General Assembly, he turned aside for a moment from a prepared address on religious education to speak of his dream of a united liberal church, beginning with Unitarians and Universalists, and eventually including other religious liberals of Christian and nonChristian origins. His remarks met with hearty response, and during the following years he gave unswerving support to the efforts that brought the consolidation of the Unitarian and Universalist bodies.

In addition to responsibilities of his office, Dr. Eliot gave freely of time and labor in other areas of the public good. He served on the boards of trustees of Proctor Academy and of the Hackley School. At the time of his death Dr. Eliot was president of the board of trustees of Mount Holyoke College. For ten years he was chaplain to the Massachusetts Senate. He was also a director of the American Civil Liberties Union and a member of the American Academy of Arts and Sciences. He was on the Board of Preachers at Harvard University.

He gave of himself unsparingly in the office of President of the American Unitarian Association. Ever on call for special occasions, he spoke at all sorts of meetings — ordinations and installations of parish ministers, dedications of new churches, and summer institutes, both among his own people and other groups. He was always glad to speak on religious education, which he held to be of prime importance in the local church and in the denomination. At whatever function he spoke, he never failed to reflect honor on the cause of liberal religion.

With the years, Dr. Eliot felt the burdens of the presidency grow heavier. The expanding program called for more money to be raised, more administrative work, more demands upon his time and strength. Those associated with him saw the lines deepen on his brow, his hair turn gray, and his step lose its former lightness. His death came suddenly on February 17, 1958, in New York City at All Souls Church, where he had traveled for a committee meeting.

Dr. Eliot left numerous writings—books, pamphlets, and contributions to periodicals. They reflect the many facets of his thought and the wide range of his interests. Ideals are set forth with a level-headed insistence that in order to count, ideals must be embodied in the practical affairs and institutions of humanity. He wrote, as he spoke, out of the center of his own sober convictions, with no pretense and few illusions.

In grateful memory of his forty-three years of service in the cause of liberal religion one of the administration buildings on Mt. Vernon Place in Boston is named Eliot House. Unity Church in St. Paul, Minnesota, also honored Dr. Eliot by naming its new education building for him. The Fellowship House on the campus of Mount Holyoke College is named for Dr. Eliot in recognition of his devotion to the college and in gratitude for his service as member or president of the institution's board of trustees for seventeen years.

For years, Dr. Eliot had dreamed and labored to bring the liberal forces in America into a closer union. He recognized the Universalists as "standing shoulder to shoulder with the Unitarians as defenders and promoters of the great traditions of liberal religion." He did not live to see the final consolidation of the denominations, but the present bright prospects of the Unitarian Universalist Association are due in no small measure to the broad vision and effective leadership of this clear-minded leader of the church.